Fuzzy Sets, Fuzzy Logic Fuzzy Methods

with Applications

Hans Bandemer
TU Bergakademie Freiberg,
Germany

Siegfried Gottwald
Universität Leipzig,
Germany

JOHN WILEY & SONS
Chichester • New York • Brisbane • Toronto • Singapore

Copyright © 1995 by John Wiley & Sons Ltd,
            Baffins Lane, Chichester,
            West Sussex PO19 1UD, England

            National   01243 779777
            International   (+44) 1243 779777

Originally published in the German language by Akademic Verlag GmbH, Mühlenstr.
33-34, D-13162 Berlin, Federal Republic of Germany under the title Bandemer,
Gottwald: Einfuhrüng in die Fuzzy Methoden. Copyright 1993 by Akademie Verlag
GmbH.

Reprinted November 1995, March 1996, July 1996, November 1996

Other Wiley Editorial Offices

John Wiley & Sons, Inc., 605 Third Avenue,
New York, NY 10158-0012, USA

Jacaranda Wiley Ltd, 33 Park Road, Milton,
Queensland 4064, Australia

John Wiley & Sons (Canada) Ltd, 22 Worcester Road,
Rexdale, Ontario M9W 1L1, Canada

John Wiley & Sons (SEA) Pte Ltd, 37 Jalan Pemimpin #05-04,
Block B, Union Industrial Building, Singapore 2057

British Library Cataloguing in Publication Data

A catalogue record for this book is available from the British Library

ISBN 0 471 95636 8

Produced from camera-ready copy supplied by the authors using LaTeX
Printed and bound in Great Britain by Biddles Ltd, Guildford and King's Lynn

This book is printed on acid-free paper responsibly manufactured from sustainable forestation,
for which at least two trees are planted for each one used for paper production.

Fuzzy Sets, Fuzzy Logic
Fuzzy Methods

with Applications

Contents

Preface

The concept of fuzzy sets and its applications has become a battlefield of conflicting opinions, since its steady development during the sixties. On the one hand, in the engineering camp, we observe a euphoric expectancy that this concept will solve with ease many problems which up to now had resisted any useful mathematical modelling or solution. On the other hand, in the mathematics camp we notice a rejecting scepticism with respect to the scientific validity. With such a background we hesitated for a long time to publicize a detailed presentation of this new field of – pure as well as applied – mathematics. Repeated and increasingly frequent inquiries of potential users have finally initiated this book.

The first German version, issued in 1989, was revised and expanded in 1993 in its fourth edition, and it is this which forms the basis for the present English version. Since the early eighties the manuscript was used again and again in courses for different audiences, mainly for engineers, computer scientists, and mathematicians, and underwent several rewritings, before and after each of its published versions. Of course the present version has also profited from this development. So, compared with the last German version, some subsections have been rewritten completely, others are very much revised, all are, at least, checked to correct mistakes and errors of different type and origin. Nevertheless, we are convinced that some errors may have been overlooked or created newly. Hence, we thank the kind reader in advance for any hint to those errors. We owe especial thanks to Mr. Harald Merk for a long list of errata with respect to the fourth German edition, and to Dr. Heinz Voigt for providing us with the special style-file realising some essential details of the actual layout of this book.

The present book introduces the basic notions of fuzzy sets in a mathematically firm manner. But it also treats them in relation to their essential applications. And the principles of such applications are explained too. Many references are included to open the way to the relevant literature for potential users of fuzzy methods, e.g. engineers, scientists, operational researchers, computer scientists and mathematicians, but – we hope – also for people from management science and the humanities. In some places – indicated by smaller type or by a star with the subsection heading – we have added more mathematical remarks or refer to other types of notation or another terminology. These parts can be omitted for a first reading. We did not intend to write a text aimed at mathematicians. Instead, the standard mathematical courses in engineering or management science at the graduate level should suffice to understand the text.

Our notation is quite standard with some tendency toward set theoretically oriented formulations. But this is caused by the very notion of fuzzy set. Often we have to distinguish between crisp and fuzzy sets. Then upper case italics like $A, B, \ldots, M, N, \ldots$ denote fuzzy sets, and upper case calligraphic letters like $\mathcal{A}, \mathcal{B}, \ldots, \mathcal{M}, \ldots, \mathcal{X}, \mathcal{Y}, \mathcal{Z}$ are used for crisp sets.

Formulas are numbered consecutively inside each chapter: formula $(m.n)$ is the n-th formula of chapter m. References to the literature are given by the name(s) of the author(s) or editor(s) and the year of publication.

Finally we thank both our publishing houses, Akademie-Verlag Berlin as part of the VCH Weinheim group, as well as J. Wiley & Sons Ltd., for all their kind understanding and help, bringing the present book into existence. And, last but not least, we are grateful to our wives who, once again, had some hard months with their husbands completely absorbed by some of their book projects.

The Authors

Freiberg/Leipzig, December 1994

1 Introduction

1.1　Why Fuzzy Sets?

Traditional mathematical modelling as commonly used in the sciences engineering and economics, refers to standard, classical mathematics. Connected with this mathematical modelling there are usually some rationalizations necessary to transform problems from their intuitive basis into a mathematised form. One aspect of such rationalizations is the transformation of notions which are, to some extent, only vaguely fixed, into clear, crisply determined ones. Thus for example, with chemical processes one may have to specify normal values as well as dangerous ones for temperature or pressure, and for manufacturing metal tools with slide-rest lathes one needs normal speeds for the turning-chisel and standard turning frequencies, and also criteria by which to judge if a turning-chisel has to be considered as worn out. Another aspect of such rationalization is often the assumption that precise data or data with precise error bounds are available at all.

There are many diverse applications for which it is impossible to get relevant data. It may not be possible to measure essential parameters of a process such as the temperature inside a molten glass or the homogeneity of a mixture inside some tank or vessel. It may be that a measurement scale does not exist at all, such as the evaluation of offensive smells, or medical diagnoses by touching/fingering, or evaluating the taste of foods.

In all such situations in which traditional mathematical modelling needs exact notions or precise data this means, mathematically, that one needs suitable sets of objects: numerical data, temperatures, frequencies, states of processes, etc., sets in the traditional mathematical sense of that word.

These traditional sets of present day mathematics are named here *crisp sets* to distinguish them from the fuzzy sets which are the central topic of this book. These crisp sets are uniquely characterised by and as the totality of their elements, their numbers.

The members of such a crisp set may be determined by some enumeration or by some characteristic property. Thus one can represent some set $\mathcal{M}$ with elements $a_1, a_2, \ldots, a_{10}$ as

$$\mathcal{M} = \{a_1, a_2, \ldots, a_{10}\} \tag{1.1}$$

or also as

$$\mathcal{M} = \{a_i \mid 1 \leq i \leq 10\}. \tag{1.2}$$

But, if additionally all these elements $a_1, \ldots, a_{10}$ of $\mathcal{M}$ at the same time are objects/members of some more comprehensive class $\mathcal{X}$ of objects then another representation of $\mathcal{M}$ may be preferable: the representation of $\mathcal{M}$ by its characteristic function. This is that one 0-1-valued function $m_{\mathcal{M}} : \mathcal{X} \to \{0, 1\}$ with

$$\forall x \in \mathcal{X} : \quad m_{\mathcal{M}}(x) = \left\{ \begin{array}{ll} 1, & \text{if } x \in \mathcal{M} \\ 0 & \text{otherwise.} \end{array} \right. \tag{1.3}$$

The value 1 of this characteristic function thus *marks* the elements of $\mathcal{M}$ among all the objects of $\mathcal{X}$. (Actually sometimes the value 1 is substituted by some other *mark* but that does not change the main idea behind definition (1.3).)

Thus e.g. in a data base listing the employees of some agency the set $\mathcal{M}$ of all employees with an academic education is realised by adjoining in this list $\mathcal{X}$ of names with each member of $\mathcal{M}$, i.e. each employee with academic education, a mark which characterises just this property, that means which characterises exactly the elements of $\mathcal{M}$.

Mathematically it is completely irrelevant if some crisp set $\mathcal{M}$ is determined as (1.1) or as (1.2) or via its characteristic function (1.3). All these representations can be transformed into one another without any difficulties. For fuzzy sets, yet, we shall prefer their representation via – generalised – characteristic functions.

The main concept behind fuzzy sets is most easily grasped if one has in mind that in everyday life, and thus also in a lot of applicational situations for mathematics, one does not directly meet sets with a crisp "borderline", but quite often it seems that there exists something like a gradual transition between membership and non-membership. And this gradual transition cannot be formalised with crisp sets – on the contrary, quite often just these feelings of gradual transition have to be eliminated by the rationalization we mentioned earlier. But often this eliminates a crucial point of the whole problem. Thus the characteristic function shown in Fig. 1.1 is a description of the set of all real numbers > 18. Here the jump at the point $x = 18$ is completely natural. In the same sense this jump is natural if Fig. 1.1 is read as a characterisation of the set $\mathcal{M}_1$ of all ages of people that have reached their majority. This

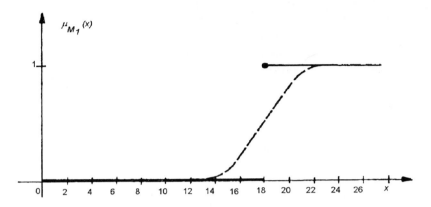

Figure 1.1: Fuzzy vs. crisp set

naturalness of the jump is lost if one intends to understand $\mathcal{M}_1$ as the set of all ages at which a human being is (in the biological sense) full grown, or also if one looks at $\mathcal{M}_1$ as the set of all temperature values of a sufficiently heated room.

The problem with these last two interpretations of course does not consist in the fact that this jump in Fig. 1.1 is not placed in the right point at $x = 18$. Rather, the problem is the jump itself. For, looking at the interpretation of being full-grown, this jump indicates that a person after age 18 is (completely) full-grown, and that at each earlier point in time this is not (entirely) the case. The same type of interpretation applies to the case of a sufficiently heated room. Intuitively, instead, one has the feeling that in reality here properties do not change totally "in the moment" but that there really is some *gentle move* from being not full-grown to being full-grown, or from being not sufficiently heated to being so. (Here it is irrelevant that there are additional variations from one person to another; also in looking at just one fixed person these gentle moves appear.)

It is not hard to find a lot of further examples which realise the same effect that intuitively there does not exist some jump point of a suitable scale which divides membership from non-membership for some suitable set, or which marks the (exact) transition from one property to its opposite one. To have examples consider e.g. (over some suitable scale of real numbers) the properties:

 — that some cars need little petrol;
 — that some computers have sufficient storage capacity;
 — that two cars on a lane have sufficient distance between them;

  – that the lighting of a desk is too bright;
  – that some radiation levels are unhealthy;
  – that some roads are slippery.
Of course, as usual each one of these properties defines a set, the set of all
objects which have this property.

  In each one of these cases intuition tells us that there is a gradual transition from (true, complete) membership in these sets to (true, complete)
non-membership in these sets. But, this intuition is just not grasped by
the usual "crisp" set. Fuzzy sets, instead, are designed to realise just this
specific intuition. Hence they have to realise some gradual transition from
membership to non-membership.

  Mathematically it is not too difficult to realise this idea. One simply has to
adjoin the description of a set by its characteristic function (1.3) to the
membership (coding) degrees 0, 1 with additional membership degrees
"between" 0 and 1. It has become a kind of standard usage to take all the
real numbers between 0 and 1, i.e. the real unit interval

$$\boldsymbol{I} = [0, 1] = \{x \in I\!\!R \mid 0 \le x \le 1\}$$

as the set of all these (additional) "generalised" membership degrees. But,
other choices are possible – and usually only some concrete application can
give any hint whether this choice or another one is the more suitable one.

  In Fig. 1.1 there is additionally shown (lineated) a second graph which may
be understood as indicating such generalised membership degrees and thus
realising such a gradual transition from non-membership 0 to membership 1.

  In the same spirit as we connected the idea of fuzzy sets with vaguely
determined notions (or sets) one can connect fuzzy sets with fuzzy, i.e. vaguely
or imprecisely given data. One way to do this is to look at imprecisely given
data as vaguely given sets of measured values. Sometimes one does not even
need any specific interpretation: vague data may appear in a natural way as
fuzzy sets – e.g. in visual data analysis as grey tone pictures, among others e.g.
as two-dimensional pictures of three-dimensional objects. Similarly, planar
"fuzzy" data may result from hardness measurements, but also in many other
cases (cf. Section 2.2 and Chapter 6).

  Finally it has to be mentioned as an empirical fact that very often quite
difficult chemical, economical, technological etc. processes can be described
relatively briefly, but for practical reasons sufficiently precise in qualitative
terms – without any quantitative analysis. To give some examples one may
think about: instructions for use, recipes, decision criteria etc. And it seems
that there exists a kind of complementarity between the complexity of
processes or systems, on the one hand, and the possibilities of their description and numerical treatment solely by traditional (crisp) methods, on the
other hand. Thus, with the ever growing complexity of the systems which

one intends to use as a model or to control, an ever growing tendency toward an integration of fuzzy notions and methods into the description of such systems has to be expected.

1.2 Development of Theory and Applications

Experiences and reflections of the type we explained in Section 1.1 have been the background ideas which stimulated the American systems engineer L. A. ZADEH since the mid-1960s to initiate and propagate the transition from traditional mathematical modelling in engineering to a new, much more qualitative, "rough" modelling which uses fuzzy sets and fuzzy methods; cf. ZADEH (1965, 1965a, 1969, 1971a, 1973). With these ideas and approaches a door was opened to introduce vague notions in a mathematically sound way, types of notions which had already been discussed in more philosophically-oriented research; cf. GOGUEN (1968/69). A firm mathematical foundation for fuzzy sets can be given within the framework of category theory (cf. GOGUEN (1974) and RODABAUGH/KLEMENT/HÖHLE (1992)) or as a combination of (usual) set theory and many-valued logic; cf. e.g. GILES (1976, 1979), GOTTWALD (1979a, 1981, 1984b, 1993), NOVAK (1986).

These ideas make a lot of non-traditional applications accessible. The best indication is the broad range of successful applications which have been realised since the end of the 1980's. Early, but still interesting surveys of the then actual state of the art have been given e.g. in GAINES (1976), ZIMMERMANN (1979) and GOTTWALD (1981). The book DUBOIS/PRADE (1980) is a standard reference which collects most of the essential results up to about 1978. In fact, many modern introductory, as well as review, texts are available, among them: ZIMMERMANN (1985, 1987), NOVAK (1989), PEDRYCZ (1989).

In the first decade, application-oriented papers in the fuzzy field had been mainly concerned with theoretical studies toward possible applications and sometimes with real applications on the laboratory scale. The most fruitful idea initially was the concept of fuzzy control initiated by the pioneering approach of MAMDANI, cf. Section 4.2 and e.g. MAMDANI/ASSILIAN (1975). The starting point here was just a qualitative "algorithmic" description of control behaviour. The first application realised the automatic control of a steam engine/boiler combination in the laboratory. But soon the control of a cement kiln was realized and sold on the market; cf. HOLMBLAD/ØSTERGAARD (1982). Since then a lot of true applications have been realised, even to partially controlling the behaviour of consumer goods; cf. Section 4.5. But also further topics have successfully been treated, as e.g. problems of classifications, pattern recognition, database management, modelling of chemical processes, operations research etc. Some typical results are presented e.g. in KANDEL (1982), CARLSSON (1984), SCHMUCKER (1984), BOCKLISCH (1987), SMITHSON (1987), D'AMBROSIO (1989), MIYAMOTO (1990), ROMMELFANGER (1994).

Often a more specific problem inside such approaches is the numerical treatment of fuzzy numerical data. But this field of fuzzy arithmetic has its own mathematical interest; cf. KAUFMAN/GUPTA (1985). Another topic more mathematically than applicationally-oriented is the field of equations and system of equations which involve fuzzy relations; cf. PEDRYCZ (1989) DINOLA/SESSA/PEDRYCZ/SANCHEZ (1989).

The highly innovative papers by ZADEH (1973, 1975, 1978, 1978a) opened new applicational areas and initiated the extension of fuzzy methods and ideas toward knowledge representation and artificial intelligence. Also in these fields the main aim is toward an almost direct representation and inferential treatment of vague as well as qualitative information, and thus toward some aspects of natural language modelling. Combined with these ideas one has an interpretation of fuzzy sets as "elastic constraints" for the values of suitable variables and of their membership degrees as indicating a degree of possibility that some possible value of a variable is its actual value. (Here one has to be careful not to read these possibility degrees in probabilistic terms; cf. Sections 3.3 and 5.3.)

These ideas intend to open ways for almost direct storage of and inference with natural language information as well as to quite flexible and user-friendly organised man-machine dialogue systems. The greatest interest of course is in a full integration of these ideas into methodologies of expert system design. The whole field is most often referred to as a *fuzzy logic* or *approximate reasoning*. And it is the central topic of a lot of actual research work; cf. among many other sources: ZEMANKOVA-LEECH/KANDEL (1984), DUBOIS/PRADE (1985), GOODMAN/NGUYEN (1985), O'HIGGINS HALL/KANDEL (1986), PRADE/NEGOITA (1986), DE BESSONET (1991), KRUSE/SCHWECKE/HEINSOHN (1991), SOMBÉ (1991). And ZADEH (1987) is a collection of all the pioneering papers of this highly influential author.

The actual trends in fuzzy sets applications and in the use of all these fuzzy methods center around fuzzy control and the use of fuzzy information in knowledge bases and expert systems. Fuzzy control is almost a highly standard application now, its main problems usually arise out of the intended application. However, for fuzzy logic and approximate reasoning a lot of theoretical problems are still open.

A huge number of research papers on fuzzy topics have appeared in conference proceedings and contributed volumes. The international journal *Fuzzy Sets and Systems* is the oldest journal specially devoted to the fuzzy field. It also is the official publication of the IFSA, the *International Fuzzy Sys-*

tems Association. The main results are often also presented in the *International Journal of Approximate Reasoning*, the *International Journal of Uncertainty, Fuzziness and Knowledge-Based Systems*, the *IEEE Transactions on Fuzzy Systems* as well as in further journals not mainly devoted to fuzzy topics. The recent literature in the fuzzy field is regularly listed in the *Fuzzy Sets and Systems* journal.

V. Slt, Set Ang. , Log, V log

2 Fuzzy Sets

Categorie to fit crisp sets into sets

universe of discourse

membership function of A

2.1 Basic Notions

2.1.1 Membership Functions of Fuzzy Sets

A *fuzzy set* A is characterised by a generalised characteristic function μ_A : $\mathcal{X} \to [0,1]$, called *membership function* of A and defined over a *universe of discourse* $\mathcal{X}$. This universe of discourse in a concrete case has to be chosen according to the specific situation of this case. If one intends to emphasise the universe of discourse $\mathcal{X}$ of a fuzzy set A then one also speaks of A as a *fuzzy set over $\mathcal{X}$* or a *fuzzy subset* of $\mathcal{X}$. In most cases, however, the universe of discourse is determined by the context and not mentioned separately. Further on the calligraphic types $\mathcal{X}, \mathcal{Y}, \ldots$ shall usually denote universes of discourse.

Obviously, for each usual, i.e. *crisp set* $\mathcal{M}$ its usual characteristic function $\mu_\mathcal{M} = \chi_\mathcal{M}$ is such a membership function. Therefore we consider crisp sets as special cases of fuzzy sets, viz. those ones with only 0 and 1 as membership degrees. Fuzzy sets A, B are *equal* if they have the same membership functions:

Check in notes

$$A = B \quad \Leftrightarrow \quad \mu_A(x) = \mu_B(x) \quad \text{for all } x \in \mathcal{X}. \tag{2.1}$$

We use $\mathbb{F}(\mathcal{X})$ to denote the class of all fuzzy subsets of the universe of discourse $\mathcal{X}$. If one intends to describe some fixed fuzzy set A over the universe of discourse $\mathcal{X}$ then one defines its membership function μ_A either by giving some formula to describe μ_A, or by a table of the values, or by a picture of the graph of μ_A. Using a table for this purpose is especially useful for finite universes of discourse $\mathcal{X}$. E.g. for $\mathcal{X}_0 = \{a_1, a_2, \ldots, a_6\}$ the table

$$
C : \quad
\begin{array}{cccccc}
a_1 & a_2 & a_3 & a_4 & a_5 & a_6 \\
0.3 & 0.7 & 0.9 & 0.6 & 0 & 0.2
\end{array}
\tag{2.2}
$$

describes a fuzzy set C with $\mu_C(a_2) = 0.7$ and $\mu_C(a_6) = 0.2$. In the case that one has a natural ordering for the elements of the universe $\mathcal{X}$, as is the case e.g. for $\mathcal{X}_0$ w.r.t. the ordering according to the indices, then instead of using the notation (2.2) one can simply use the vector

$$m_A = (\mu_A(x_1), \ldots, \mu_A(x_n)) \tag{2.3}$$

of membership degrees to represent the fuzzy set A. In actual calculations this is often quite helpful.

Sometimes for C one also uses a representation in form of a "sum":

$$C = 0.3/a_1 + 0.7/a_2 + 0.9/a_3 + 0.6/a_4 + 0/a_5 + 0.2/a_6. \tag{2.4}$$

Here the term $0/a_5$ may also be deleted. But, we will not use this representation of a fuzzy set as a sum in the present book. For finite universes of discourse $\mathcal{X}$ and $A \in I\!\!F(\mathcal{X})$ this representation is also written as

$$A = \sum_{x \in \mathcal{X}} \mu_A(x) \,/\, x \tag{2.5}$$

and for infinite universes $\mathcal{X}$ as

$$A = \int_{x \in \mathcal{X}} \mu_A(x) \,/\, x. \tag{2.6}$$

In all these cases the sign "/" does not mean a slanting fraction line. Also the signs $\sum$ and $\int$ are neither denoting a true sum nor a true integral but have only symbolic meaning.

As simple and truly basic examples of fuzzy sets one immediately gets the *empty fuzzy set* $\emptyset$ with the membership function

$$\forall x \in \mathcal{X} : \mu_\emptyset(x) = 0, \tag{2.7}$$

and has the *universal set* X over $\mathcal{X}$ characterised by the membership function

$$\forall x \in \mathcal{X} : \mu_X(x) = 1. \tag{2.8}$$

Sometimes for any $\alpha \in [0,1]$ one also considers the α-*universal set* $X^{[\alpha]}$, characterised by

$$\forall x \in \mathcal{X} : \mu_{X^{[\alpha]}}(x) = \alpha. \tag{2.9}$$

To take another example, let us look for the fuzzy set A of all reals which are nearly equal to 10. Then, of course, one shall consider the universe $\mathcal{X} = I\!\!R^+$. One possibility for the membership function of A now is to take it as

$$\mu_A(x) = \max\left\{0, 1 - \frac{(10-x)^2}{2}\right\} \tag{2.10}$$

which furthermore shall be written down in a shortened form as

$$\mu_A(x) = \left[1 - \frac{(10-x)^2}{2}\right]^+.$$
(2.11)

Nevertheless, for this fuzzy set A also another membership function could have been chosen, e.g.

$$\mu_A(x) \;=\; [1 - |x - 10|/2]^+$$
$$= \begin{cases} 0, & \text{if } x < 8 \text{ or } x > 12, \\ (x-8)/2, & \text{if } 8 \le x \le 10, \\ (12-x)/2, & \text{if } 10 < x \le 12. \end{cases}$$
(2.12)

This fact represents an effect which one often recognises in applications: the theory of fuzzy sets provides not only the possibility of graduating membership, it also allows the choice of formally different membership functions to represent fuzzy sets which, intuitively, are determined only by some more or less vague idea. How to finally represent such a vaguely determined "fuzzy" set by a concrete membership function, is often therefore determined in practice by additional ideas or assumptions, or even by the desire to have a type of membership function one easily can calculate with, e.g. a piecewise linear function.

2.1.2   Characteristic Values of Fuzzy Sets

For comparison and also for some partial characterisation of fuzzy sets one uses some characteristic values. One of the most important is the *support* of the fuzzy set A:

$$\operatorname{supp}(A) =_{\text{def}} \{x \in \mathcal{X} \mid \mu_A(x) > 0\},$$
(2.13)

i.e. the set of all arguments of the membership function of A which correspond to a nonzero value.

In the case that the support of a fuzzy set is a usual singleton such a fuzzy set is called a *fuzzy singleton*. But, a fuzzy singleton A is not uniquely determined by its support. For, from $\operatorname{supp}(A) = \{a_0\}$ one only has $\mu_A(a_0) > 0$ which for noncrisp A of course does not determine $\mu_A(a_0)$. For a fuzzy singleton A with support $\{a_0\}$ and membership degree $\mu_A(a_0) = \tau$ one therefore writes $\langle\!\langle a_0 \rangle\!\rangle_\tau$ and calls this the τ-*singleton of* a_0.

Another characteristic value is the supremum of the membership degrees, the *height* of a fuzzy set A:

$$\operatorname{hgt}(A) =_{\text{def}} \sup_{x \in \mathcal{X}} \mu_A(x).$$
(2.14)

The fuzzy sets with height equal to one are the *normal* (or *normalised*) ones. The other fuzzy sets different from $\emptyset$ are the *subnormal* ones. Thus, e.g. the fuzzy set C from (2.2) is subnormal; normal fuzzy sets on the other hand are those ones with membership functions (2.11) and (2.12). Hence subnormal fuzzy sets A are characterised by

$$A \text{ subnormal} \iff 0 < \operatorname{hgt}(A) < 1. \tag{2.15}$$

Obviously one also has

$$\operatorname{hgt}(A) = 0 \iff A = \emptyset \iff \operatorname{supp}(A) = \emptyset. \tag{2.16}$$

By a simple transformation of the membership degrees a subnormal fuzzy set can be transformed into a normal fuzzy set: one only has to transform the subnormal fuzzy set A into the fuzzy set A^* with membership function

$$\mu_{A^*}(x) = \mu_A(x)/\operatorname{hgt}(A). \tag{2.17}$$

A^* is a normal fuzzy set with, additionally, $\operatorname{supp}(A) = \operatorname{supp}(A^*)$. If A is already normal then (2.17) gives $A^* = A$.

If the supremum $\operatorname{hgt}(A)$ of (2.14) really is one of the values of the membership function $\mu_A(x)$ for $x \in \mathcal{X}$, and if additionally it is the membership degree of only one point $\mathcal{X}$, in this case A is called a *unimodal* fuzzy set. The graph of the membership function μ_A of a unimodal fuzzy set thus has a unique global maximum point.

A finite crisp set has as a further characteristic value its cardinality, i.e. its number of elements. Formally this number can be found by adding up all values of the characteristic function. Quite analogously one can – for fuzzy sets with finite support – consider the sum of the membership degrees

$$\operatorname{card}(A) =_{\text{def}} \sum_{x \in \mathcal{X}} \mu_A(x) \tag{2.18}$$

as *cardinality* of the fuzzy set $A \in \mathbb{F}(\mathcal{X})$. For infinite $\mathcal{X}$ this sum of course is to be restricted to the support $\operatorname{supp}(A)$ because of $\mu_A = 0$ for all $x \in \mathcal{X}$ with $x \notin \operatorname{supp}(A)$. In the case of countably infinite universes of discourse, e.g. for discrete universes of the form $\mathcal{X} = \{a_i \mid i \geq 1\}$, fuzzy sets with infinite support can have finite, but also infinite cardinality in the sense of (2.18).

Otherwise, if $\mathcal{X}$ is the real line $\mathbb{R}$, one of the n-dimensional spaces $\mathbb{R}^n$, some interval of such a space, or in general some "continuous" set with a measure function P, then instead of (2.18) one considers a generalised "content" as the cardinality of a fuzzy set and uses

$$\operatorname{card}(A) =_{\text{def}} \int_{\mathcal{X}} \mu_A(x)\, dP. \tag{2.19}$$

For IR, IR^n and subspaces thereof, one normally chooses P as the usual content (area, volume, etc.) and the integral in (2.19) as the normal (Riemann or Lebesgue) one with $dP = dx$. Of course, in such a case one discusses only such fuzzy sets which have integrable membership functions.

Often it is of interest to consider a kind of relative cardinality of a fuzzy set with respect to another set, e.g. relative to the universe of discourse. In the case that both these cardinalities are finite, such a *relative cardinality* (w.r.t. the universe of discourse) is given by

$$\mathrm{card}\,_{\mathcal{X}}(A) =_{\mathrm{def}} \sum_{x \in \mathcal{X}} \mu_A(x) \Big/ \sum_{x \in \mathcal{X}} 1 \tag{2.20}$$

or shortened to

$$\mathrm{card}\,_{\mathcal{X}}(A) = \mathrm{card}\,(A)\,/N, \tag{2.21}$$

with N the number of elements of the universe of discourse $\mathcal{X}$. Even in cases with infinite universe of discourse $\mathcal{X}$ the relative cardinality (2.20) can make sense, assuming simultaneous summation in numerator and denominator, because of a possibly finite sum – and sometimes also an intuitive interpretation. For "continuous" universes of discourse $\mathcal{X}$ with a finite P-measure, for the relative cardinality (w.r.t. the universe of discourse) the definition

$$\mathrm{card}\,_{\mathcal{X}}(A) =_{\mathrm{def}} \int_{\mathcal{X}} \mu_A(x)\,dP \Big/ \int_{\mathcal{X}} dP, \tag{2.22}$$

is a preferable approach. And this can also be written in form (2.21), now with N being the P-measure of $\mathcal{X}$. Again, as in the case of summation, also for this fraction of integrals more general interpretations are possible if both integrals diverge.

These cardinalities, however, do not constitute kinds of cardinal numbers in the stronger sense of traditional set theory. The core idea there is that crisp sets $\mathcal{A}, \mathcal{B}$ have the same cardinal number iff there exists a bijection of $\mathcal{A}$ onto $\mathcal{B}$. To be able to adapt this type of approach for fuzzy sets, of course, one first needs a suitable notion of bijection between fuzzy sets or of "equipotency" of fuzzy sets. We shall not enter into this matter in more detail here but only refer e.g. to GOTTWALD (1971, 1980) and WYGRALAK (1986, 1993).

Besides the support defined in (2.13) one considers further crisp sets connected with a fuzzy set A. Of considerable importance for many discussions are the α-*cuts* $A^{>\alpha}$, defined for each $\alpha \in I = [0, 1]$ as:

$$A^{>\alpha} =_{\mathrm{def}} \{x \in \mathcal{X} \mid \mu_A(x) > \alpha\}, \tag{2.23}$$

as well as the *strong α-cuts* $A^{\geq \alpha}$:

$$A^{\geq \alpha} =_{\text{def}} \{x \in \mathcal{X} \mid \mu_A(x) \geq \alpha\}. \tag{2.24}$$

The support supp (A) obviously is an α-cut:

$$\text{supp}(A) = A^{>0}.$$

Furthermore, the strong 1-cut $A^{\geq 1} = \{x \in \mathcal{X} \mid \mu_A(x) = 1\}$ is called the *kernel* of A. Hence the fuzzy sets with a nonempty kernel $A^{\geq 1} \neq \emptyset$ are normal. And the unimodal fuzzy sets A are characterised by the fact that their strong hgt (A)-cut $A^{\geq \text{hgt}(A)}$ is a crisp singleton.

Each fuzzy set uniquely determines all its α-cuts and strong α-cuts. It is remarkable and useful that conversely all the α-cuts as well as all the strong α-cuts uniquely determine the fuzzy set. This is the case because for each $x \in \mathcal{X}$ it holds true:

$$\mu_A(x) = \sup_{\alpha \in [0,1)} \alpha \cdot \mu_{A^{>\alpha}}(x) = \sup_{\alpha \in (0,1]} \alpha \cdot \mu_{A^{\geq \alpha}}(x). \tag{2.25}$$

This possibility, to "split" a fuzzy set into a family of crisp sets, is often used to "reduce" relations and operations between fuzzy sets to relations and operations between crisp sets.

2.1.3   Inclusion for Fuzzy Sets

We will demonstrate this "reduction" for the *inclusion* relation for fuzzy sets. Given two fuzzy subsets A, B of $\mathcal{X}$ we call A a *subset of* B, denoted $A \subseteq B$, iff the membership degree $\mu_A(x)$ is never greater than the membership degree $\mu_B(x)$:

$$A \subseteq B \iff_{def} \mu_A(x) \leq \mu_B(x) \text{ for all } x \in \mathcal{X}. \tag{2.26}$$

It is obvious that for fuzzy sets $A, B \in \mathbb{F}(\mathcal{X})$ one has that

$$\emptyset \subseteq A \subseteq X, \tag{2.27}$$

$$A \subseteq B, \ B \subseteq A \Rightarrow A = B \tag{2.28}$$

hold true. Furthermore, $\emptyset, X$ are the smallest and the biggest member of $\mathbb{F}(\mathcal{X})$ relative to $\subseteq$. And because of (2.28), for fuzzy sets A, B as for crisp sets one can give the proof of the equality of A, B by simply proving $A \subseteq B$ as well as $B \subseteq A$.

One also immediately verifies that

$$A \subseteq A \quad \text{and} \quad A \subseteq B, \ B \subseteq C \Rightarrow A \subseteq C \tag{2.29}$$

holds true for any $A, B, C \in \mathbb{F}(\mathcal{X})$. Thus $\subseteqq$ is a partial ordering in the class $\mathbb{F}(\mathcal{X})$ of all fuzzy subsets of $\mathcal{X}$. For α-cuts and strong α-cuts one has

$$A \subseteqq B \ \Rightarrow \ A^{>\alpha} \subseteq B^{>\alpha} \text{ and } A^{\geq\alpha} \subseteq B^{\geq\alpha} \qquad (2.30)$$

for all $\alpha \in [0, 1]$ and therefore also

$$A \subseteqq B \ \Rightarrow \ \operatorname{supp}(A) \subseteq \operatorname{supp}(B). \qquad (2.31)$$

Additionally one has

$$A \subseteqq B \ \Rightarrow \ \operatorname{hgt}(A) \leq \operatorname{hgt}(B). \qquad (2.32)$$

But it is especially important that one can reverse (2.30) and has that

$$
\begin{aligned}
A \subseteqq B \ &\Leftrightarrow \ A^{>\alpha} \subseteq B^{>\alpha} && \text{for all } \alpha \in [0, 1) \\
&\Leftrightarrow \ A^{\geq\alpha} \subseteq B^{\geq\alpha} && \text{for all } \alpha \in (0, 1]
\end{aligned}
\qquad (2.33)
$$

holds true. That means that the inclusion relation for fuzzy sets A, B can completely be characterised using the usual subset relation for all the α-cuts of A, B. Via (2.28) one also has a characterisation of equality for fuzzy sets:

$$
\begin{aligned}
A = B \ &\Leftrightarrow \ A^{>\alpha} = B^{>\alpha} && \text{for all } \alpha \in [0, 1) \\
&\Leftrightarrow \ A^{\geq\alpha} = B^{\geq\alpha} && \text{for all } \alpha \in (0, 1].
\end{aligned}
\qquad (2.34)
$$

Especially for crisp sets A, B as special fuzzy sets one gets that $A \subseteqq B$ holds true iff A in the usual sense is a subset of B. Therefore definition (2.26) is a straightforward generalisation of inclusion for crisp sets.

2.1.4 Fuzzy Sets and Many-Valued Logic*

Up to now we have not discussed which kind of mathematical object a fuzzy set is. From the mathematical point of view the most simple approach is to identify a fuzzy set with its membership function, i.e. to consider for a given universe of discourse $\mathcal{X}$ the class $\mathbb{F}(\mathcal{X}) = [0, 1]^{\mathcal{X}}$ as the class of all fuzzy subsets of $\mathcal{X}$. The background idea here is that, mathematically, the structure of the class of fuzzy subsets is much more important then some "true nature" of its objects. Also not of crucial importance, regarding the basic idea of degrees of membership, is the choice of the real unit interval $I = [0, 1]$ as set of membership degrees: any other set L – e.g. the set of elements of some lattice – with two distinguished elements 0 and 1 could do this job and then did produce the set $F_{\mathsf{L}}(\mathcal{X}) = \mathsf{L}^{\mathcal{X}}$ of all L-*fuzzy sets*. Regarding the actual treatment of fuzzy sets, which is often combined with the case of a finite universe of discourse $\mathcal{X}$, it sometimes proves preferable to restrict the membership degrees to a set

$$\mathsf{L}_m = \{k/(m-1) \mid 0 \leq k \leq m-1\} \subseteq I \qquad (2.35)$$

of finitely many equidistant points of $[0, 1]$.

After all, a universe of discourse $\mathcal{X}$ itself may contain as elements – solely or among others – fuzzy sets. One can have e.g. $\mathcal{X} = I\!\!F(\mathcal{Y})$ and thus $I\!\!F(\mathcal{X}) = I\!\!F(I\!\!F(\mathcal{Y}))$. In this sense the construction of the class of fuzzy subsets of some universe can be iterated. Such fuzzy sets *of higher level* become interesting inside classes of fuzzy sets which one likes to be closed w.r.t. the construction of fuzzy subsets. And this is the case if one intends to study fuzzy sets in the style of traditional cumulative set theory (cf. CHAPIN (1974/75), GOTTWALD (1979a), DUBOIS/PRADE (1980), ZHANG (1980), WEIDNER (1981)).

On the other hand the idea of fuzzification, i.e. the graduation of membership, can be iterated in a second way and used for determining membership degrees only vaguely or "to some degree" – or to suppose them to be determined only in such a manner. More detailed studies of such *fuzzy sets of higher type* are often restricted to the special case of fuzzy sets of *type 2*, i.e. to the case that membership degrees are (usual) fuzzy sets, e.g. fuzzy subsets of the unit interval $I\!\!F([0,1])$, or even to the case that one considers only intervals from $[0, 1]$ as membership degrees (e.g. SAMBUC (1975), JAHN (1975)). A variant of these "interval valued" fuzzy sets, from a mathematical point of view isomorphic with them, was introduced by ATANASSOV (1986) and termed *intuitionistic fuzzy sets*: the core idea is to adjoin with each point $x \in \mathcal{X}$ of the universe of discourse two values $\mu_A^+(x)$, $\mu_A^-(x)$, the interval end points, and to look at them as "degree of membership" and "degree of non-membership" in A, respectively.

The finite sets L_m of (2.35) are natural candidates for the set of all membership degrees. Taking into consideration other, more general sets as sets of membership degrees first seems to look a bit artificial. But it very much depends on the application one has in mind whether it is natural to consider some kind of L-fuzzy sets. In the case of image analysis, e.g., it may be natural to have (at any pixel) degrees of intensity, chosen from $[0, 1]$, for each (basic) colour – but to discuss different colours in parallel. For n colours then $\mathsf{L} = [0, 1]^n$ looks like a good choice of a set of membership degrees. Nevertheless, even in such a situation it is not necessary to have $\mathsf{L} = [0, 1]^n$ as a set of membership degrees: one also has the possibility to normalise the maximal intensity to 1 and to use these normalised intensities as membership degrees over a universe of discourse of wavelengths (and maybe of other relevant aspects); cf. Fig. 2.4.

In any case one can interpret the membership degrees which graduate the property of being a member of some set as degrees of truth of a sentence expressing this property of being a member. Of course, these truth degrees then vary between the degree 0 (for "false") and the degree 1 (for "true"). Accepting this point of view makes it natural to try to develop the theory of fuzzy sets within the framework of a suitable many-valued logic which has as its set of truth degrees just the set of membership degrees of the fuzzy sets. The formalised language of this many-valued logic then, besides variables $x, y, z, \ldots$ and constants $a, b, c, \ldots$ for elements of the universe of discourse, uses symbols (usually some upper case letters – the details do not matter here) to denote fuzzy sets and a binary many-valued membership predicate ε such that

$$\mu_A(x) = [\![\, x \,\varepsilon\, A \,]\!] \tag{2.36}$$

holds true, with $[\![H]\!]$ the truth degree of some well-formed formula H of that language. (For the case that H has free variables besides x one has to refer to an additional valuation of all these free variables. We always assume that this is fixed by the context.) From this point of view fuzzy sets become the sets of a generalised set theory based on a suitable many-valued logic. This type of interpretation proves quite useful: it opens the doors to clarify far reaching analogies between notions and results related to fuzzy sets and those ones related to usual sets. To demonstrate this, let us assume that $[0, 1]$ or one of the sets L_m is the set of membership degrees. Then there exist systems of many-valued logic with just these sets of truth degrees, discussed e.g. in LUKASIEWICZ/TARSKI (1930), with a function $\mathrm{seq}_L : [0, 1]^2 \to [0, 1]$, defined as

$$\mathrm{seq}_L(u, v) = \min\{1, 1 - u + v\}, \tag{2.37}$$

which is acting as truth function of an implication connective $\to$. Using this implication together with a generalisation quantifier $\forall$ interpreted as taking the infimum of truth degrees, definition (2.26) of inclusion for fuzzy sets reads

$$A \subseteqq B \;\;\Leftrightarrow\;\; [\![\forall x\,(x\,\varepsilon\,A \to x\,\varepsilon\,B)]\!] = 1. \tag{2.38}$$

It is obviously much more natural, from a logical point of view, to define more generally

$$A \subseteqq B \;\;=_{\mathrm{def}}\;\; \forall x\,(x\,\varepsilon\,A \to x\,\varepsilon\,B). \tag{2.39}$$

In this last way inclusion for fuzzy sets itself becomes a many-valued, i.e. graded property of fuzzy sets – which is very much in accordance with the basic idea of fuzziness. And indeed, (2.39) proves to be quite useful for discussions related e.g. to applications of fuzzy sets (cf. GOTTWALD/PEDRYCZ (1986a) as well as Proposition 4.3, the remarks which follow it, and GOTTWALD (1993)). Another example concerns the notation used to denote fuzzy sets. For usual, i.e. crisp sets $\mathcal{M}$ their *class term notation* as $\mathcal{M} = \{x \mid H(x)\}$ is flexible and elegant. It is in the same way flexible and very useful to accept a corresponding notation for fuzzy sets fixed by

$$A = \{x \in \mathcal{X} \,\|\, H(x)\} \;\Leftrightarrow\; \mu_A(x) = [\![H(x)]\!] \quad \text{for all } x \in \mathcal{X}, \tag{2.40}$$

with again H a well-formed formula of the language of many-valued logic we already mentioned above.

The characterisations (2.25) and (2.34) of fuzzy sets by their families of (strong) α-cuts are, by the way, just representation theorems. And these characterisations can be completed in an obvious way by an additional one using the α-*components* $A^{=\alpha}$:

$$A^{=\alpha} =_{\text{def}} \{x \in \mathcal{X} \mid \mu_A(x) = \alpha\} \qquad (2.41)$$

of a fuzzy set A. Again, the membership function μ_A can be reconstructed out of all those α-components just as in (2.25).

2.2   Examples for Fuzzy Sets and Their Specification

After having introduced basic notions for fuzzy sets we will now consider a series of examples of quite different kinds of such fuzzy sets, and of possibilities and ways to assess membership functions. If the universe $\mathcal{X}$ contains only *finitely* many elements, e.g. is consisting of natural subjects or objects, variants, and the like, then there is, as a rule, only the possibility of specifying a fuzzy set A over $\mathcal{X}$ by assigning a membership value $\mu_A(x)$ to each element $x \in \mathcal{X}$ separately. This assignment can sometimes be obtained from available information on the behaviour of an x with respect to A in the past, however, an expert with his knowledge of the background of the problem in question, or even a table of experts, must help authoritatively. The aggregating of differing statments can then be performed by (possibly weighted) averaging or via some complicated procedure for arriving at a group consent (cf. CIVANLAR/TRUSSELL(1986); MIRKIN (1979); CHOLEWA (1985); KHURGIN/POLYAKOV (1986)). A further possibility, assigning *fuzzy* membership values, in such a way going over to fuzzy sets of a higher type, would complicate the treatment of a common practical problem essentially.

2.2.1   Specifying Membership Function Types

If the number n of elements of $\mathcal{X}$ is very large or if the assumption is reasonable that $\mathcal{X}$ is a *continuum* (e.g. temperature, mass, funds), then the performance as in the finite case is no longer practicable. As a basis of specification for fuzzy sets then, as a rule, *mathematical objects* are used.

For the following examples let $\mathcal{X}$ be a suitable Euclidean space.

The most simple mathematical object is a number, $x_0 \in \mathbb{R}^1$. A *fuzzy number* A, e.g. the fuzzy number $A = $ "approximately 10", is obtained by taking a crisp number (here $x_0 = 10$) as the kernel of A, and then choosing

μ_A as a function, to the right and to the left, monotonically decreasing to 0. As already mentioned with the settings (2.10), (2.12) above, the choice of the type of a membership function is open to some arbitrariness. Hence it seems reasonable to specify μ_A by a parametric set-up, the parameters of which can be fitted to the practical problem, e.g.

$$\mu(x;c_1) = [1 - c_1|x - x_0|]^+; \qquad c_1 > 0, \qquad (2.42)$$
$$\mu(x;c_2) = [1 - c_2(x - x_0)^2]^+; \qquad c_2 > 0, \qquad (2.43)$$
$$\mu(x;c_3) = [1 + c_3|x - x_0|]^{-1}; \qquad c_3 > 0, \qquad (2.44)$$
$$\mu(x;c_4,p) = [1 + c_4|x - x_0|^p]^{-1}; \qquad c_4 > 0;\ p > 1, \qquad (2.45)$$
$$\mu(x;c_5,p) = \exp\{-c_5|x - x_0|^p\}; \qquad c_5 > 0;\ p > 1 \qquad (2.46)$$

with the abbreviation already used $[v]^+ = \max\{0, v\}$. Instead of the absolute value of the difference we can insert also other distances between x and x_0. When the functions should be asymmetric, then we can, e.g., couple, at $x = x_0$, branches with different parameters or even different types of functions. The fuzzy set $A =$ "approximately 10" could also have the following asymmetric membership function, defined for every $x \in \mathbb{R}$ as:

$$\mu_A(x) = \begin{cases} [1 - |10 - x|]^+ & \text{for } x \le 10 \\ [1 - (x - 10)^2/10]^+ & \text{for } x > 10. \end{cases} \qquad (2.47)$$

An interesting parametric membership function, considered by ZADEH (1976), is provided also by the following S-shaped function f_1 over $[0, 100]$ with the parameters α, β, γ, and the definition

$$f_1(x;\alpha,\beta,\gamma) = \begin{cases} 0 & \text{for } x \le \alpha, \\ 2\left(\dfrac{x - \alpha}{\gamma - \alpha}\right)^2 & \text{for } \alpha < x < \beta, \\ 1 - 2\left(\dfrac{x - \gamma}{\gamma - \alpha}\right)^2 & \text{for } \beta \le x < \gamma, \\ 1 & \text{for } \gamma \le x, \end{cases} \qquad (2.48)$$

in which the restriction $\beta = \frac{1}{2}(\alpha + \gamma)$ is assumed. Hence these three parameters can vary only with two degrees of freedom. Deduced from this set-up also the following bell-shaped function f_2 over $[0, 100]$ is used, which has only 2 parameters α, β and is defined by

$$f_2(x;\alpha,\beta) = \begin{cases} f_1(x;\beta - \alpha, \beta - \frac{1}{2}\alpha, \beta) & \text{for } x \le \beta, \\ 1 - f_1(x;\beta, \beta + \frac{1}{2}\alpha, \beta + \alpha) & \text{for } x > \beta. \end{cases} \qquad (2.49)$$

When we want to drop the condition $\beta = \frac{1}{2}(\alpha + \gamma)$, then we can, instead of (2.48), choose the following set-up

$$
f_1^*(x; \alpha, \beta, \gamma) = \begin{cases} 0 & \text{for } x \leq \alpha, \\ \frac{1}{2}\left(\dfrac{x - \alpha}{\beta - \alpha}\right)^2 & \text{for } \alpha < x < \beta, \\ 1 - \frac{1}{2}\left(\dfrac{\gamma - x}{\gamma - \beta}\right)^2 & \text{for } \beta \leq x < \gamma, \\ 1 & \text{for } \gamma \leq x, \end{cases} \tag{2.50}
$$

which always yields a continuous membership function f_1^*, however, a differentiable one only if $\beta = \frac{1}{2}(\alpha + \gamma)$ – but then we have even $f_1^*(x; \alpha, \beta, \gamma) = f_1(x; \alpha, \beta, \gamma)$.

Parametric set-ups like (2.42) to (2.46) form the starting point also for the so-called L/R-representation for fuzzy numbers, which simplifies the performance of arithmetic calculations with such numbers essentially (cf. Section 2.5).

When considering membership function types of the form (2.44) to (2.46) we have to take care that the support of a so specified fuzzy number is always the whole real axis $\mathbb{R}$. Hence, when using computers approximations will become necessary.

After having chosen a set-up for μ_A, corresponding to the idea of the form of fuzziness of the set A, the parameter values can still be fitted to the actual conditions. Frequently it will be easy to agree on numbers x_1, x_2, x_3, x_4, for which it holds, given a certain (small) $d > 0$,

$$
\begin{aligned}
x_1 &= \sup\{x \in \mathcal{X} \mid \mu_A(x) = 0,\ \mu_A(x + d) > 0\} \\
x_2 &= \sup\{x \in \mathcal{X} \mid \mu_A(x) = 1/2,\ \mu_A(x + d) > 1/2\}, \\
x_3 &= \inf\{x \in \mathcal{X} \mid \mu_A(x) = 1/2,\ \mu_A(x - d) > 1/2\}, \\
x_4 &= \inf\{x \in \mathcal{X} \mid \mu_A(x) = 0,\ \mu_A(x - d) > 0\}
\end{aligned}
$$

or for which one has, instead, for some given (small) $\epsilon > 0$

$$
\begin{aligned}
x_1 &= \sup\{x \in \mathcal{X} \mid \mu_A(x) = \epsilon,\ \mu_A(x + d) > \epsilon\}), \\
x_4 &= \inf\{x \in \mathcal{X} \mid \mu_A(x) = \epsilon,\ \mu_A(x - d) > \epsilon\}).
\end{aligned}
$$

The parameters of this set-up are then fitted, in a suitable manner, to get the relations $\mu_A(x_1) = \mu_A(x_4) = 0$; $\mu_A(x_2) = \mu_A(x_3) = 1/2$; $\mu_A(x_0) = 1$.

Sometimes it is suggested that μ_A is fitted to available smoothed histograms. In this context we have to notice that a relative frequency need not reflect the degree of membership (cf. Section 5.3 and CIVANLAR/TRUSSELL (1986)).

2.2.2 Fuzzy Points and Fuzzy Regions

When specifying a fuzzy number we can act in accordance with its performance when specifying a *fuzzy point*, e.g. in $\mathbb{R}^k$. A crisp point $x_0 \in \mathbb{R}^k$ provides the kernel, from which the membership function decreases in all directions monotonically. The difference $(x - x_0)$ in (2.42) to (2.46) is to be replaced by some distance $d(x, x_0)$ of the two points in each of the corresponding set-ups. In the set-up we can introduce a monotonically decreasing function h containing some parameters to be chosen

$$\mu(x; c) = h(d(x, x_0); c) \quad \text{with } c \in \mathcal{C} \subseteq \mathbb{R}^r. \tag{2.51}$$

But quite different types can also be useful, when considered from the practical problem.

As frequently used special cases of (2.51) we mention: the *hyperpyramid* (see Figure 2.1)

$$\mu(x; c_1, ..., c_k) = [1 - \sum_{j=1}^{k} c_j |x_j - x_{j0}|]^+ \tag{2.52}$$

with $x = (x_1, \ldots, x_k)^\top$ and $x_0 = (x_{10}, \ldots, x_{k0})^\top$ and $c_j > 0$ for $j = 1, \ldots, k$, over a hyperrectangle

$$\mathcal{K} := \{x \in \mathbb{R}^k \mid |x_j - x_{j0}| < c_{j0} < c_j; \, j = 1, \ldots, k\};$$

and the elliptical *hyperparaboloid* (see Figure 2.2)

$$\mu(x; B) = [1 - (x - x_0)^\top B(x - x_0)]^+ \tag{2.53}$$

with a positive definite $k \times k$-matrix B over the hyperellipsoid

$$\mathcal{E} := \{x \in \mathbb{R}^k \mid (x - x_0)^\top B(x - x_0) < 1\}.$$

Naturally, other types in analogy with (2.44) to (2.46) can also be constructed and are used. Additionally, there is the possibility of building fuzzy points out of fuzzy numbers in the components, e.g. by taking a fuzzy cartesian product of these components (cf. Sections 2.3 and 2.4). A practical example is contained in BANDEMER/KRAUT/VOGT (1988).

Fuzzy points are specified, e.g., when (pseudo-exact) point-shaped recorded observations should be endowed with an expression of their impreciseness. In (2.52) this expression consists in (symmetric) intervals for the components, reflecting this impreciseness; in (2.53) impreciseness is included with respect to all directions of the space by the matrix B, which plays, in such way, an analogous role as the covariance matrix in mathematical statistics, although now only for the special observed point x_0. From a formal mathematical

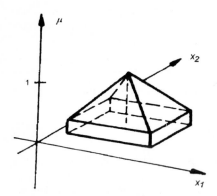

Figure 2.1: Fuzzy point with a tetraeder-shaped membership function according to (2.53)

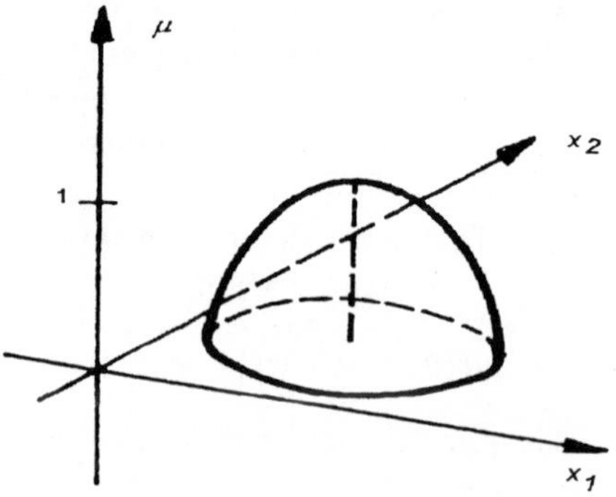

Figure 2.2: Fuzzy point with an elliptical paraboloid as shape of the membership function according to (2.54); casually called a "bean"

standpoint (2.53) is a quadratic approximation of a normal distribution density, but we connect no idea of a probability theory based model with this fact.

When it seems to be impossible to specify fuzziness for each of the point-shaped recorded observations separately, then, sometimes, we can infer a local fuzziness of the "total observation" from the totality of the pseudo-exact observations. Then we can move a morphological structure element (SERRA (1982)), e.g. a hyperball

$$(\boldsymbol{x} - \boldsymbol{x}_s)^\top (\boldsymbol{x} - \boldsymbol{x}_s) = \delta^2,$$

with a given radius δ, within $I\!\!R^k$, in every position assigning to the momentary centre of the structure element $\boldsymbol{x}_s$ the relative number of those point-shaped observations, which are covered by the hyperball, as its membership value $\mu_A(\boldsymbol{x}_s)$. So we obtain a *fuzzy total observation*, which is no fuzzy point, but can be used very well for an investigation of relationships among the components of the observations. (With respect to an example cf. BANDEMER/ROTH (1987).)

Fuzzy intervals can be specified either by choosing a crisp interval to form the kernel, from which the membership function decreases to zero, or by choosing two fuzzy numbers as the ends of the interval. In general we can construct a *fuzzy region* in some $I\!\!R^k$ by choosing a crisp region, which is surrounded by a fuzzy transition zone, in which the membership function decreases monotonically, in a given fixed sense, to zero. Alternatively, we can characterise a fuzzy region by specifying a *fuzzy hypersurface* forming its boundary. This fuzzy hypersurface has a crisp hypersurface as its kernel, from which the membership values will decrease "in all directions" monotonically. Though, we must still say precisely, how the membership values for the fuzzy region should be determined by that of the fuzzy hypersurface. (Such a representation of a fuzzy region via a fuzzy hypersurface was used, e.g., by BANDEMER/KRAUT (1988) for a problem of shape description, cf. Section 6.2.)

If we interpret the values of the membership function for $\mathcal{X} \subseteq I\!\!R^2$ as greytones (e.g. 1 as the darkest black and 0 as the brightest white), then fuzzy sets correspond to *grey-tone pictures*, not necessarily to fuzzy regions in the sense just given. However, such grey-tone pictures can occur as (generalised) fuzzy observations, e.g., when investigating transparent sections of finite thickness from some material or cellular tissue. In evaluating such pictures, their interpretation as fuzzy sets can be frequently useful (cf. e.g. BANDEMER/KRAUT (1988); BANDEMER/KRAUT/VOGT (1988) and Section 6.3).

2.2.3 Fuzzy Relations

A further important problem for application is the specifying of *fuzzy relations*: e.g. "approximately equal", "more or less smaller than", or the like. Such binary relations are usually understood as sets of ordered pairs, in the case of real numbers as subsets of $I\!\!R^2$, hence, e.g., equality "=" is interpreted as the set

$$\mathcal{D} = \{(x,y) \in I\!\!R^2 \mid x = y\}. \tag{2.54}$$

This set represents the graph of the straight line $y = x$ in $I\!\!R^2$. When turning to the fuzzy relation R_0 : "approximately equal" points in the neighbourhood of this straight line are also considered, again assigning to them graded membership values. For specifying the membership function μ_{R_0} for this fuzzy relation R_0 we can start with considering such points, for which the deviation from the crisp equality is just tolerable. From this consideration an order of decreasing can be determined for this membership function, reflecting the ideas and essentials of the practical problem. A result of such a performance could be

$$\mu_{R_0}(x,y) = [1 - a|x - y|]^+; \qquad a > 0 \tag{2.55}$$

reflecting a linear order of decreasing with a factor a. However, it is also possible to consider the difference in proportion to the absolute value, when specifying the membership function, e.g. by

$$\mu_{R_0}(x,y) = \frac{1 - b\,(x-y)^2}{(1 + x^2 + y^2)}\,; \qquad b \in (0,1) \tag{2.56}$$

or

$$\mu_{R_0}(x,y) = \exp\{-c\,(x-y)^2 / (1 + x^2 + y^2)\}; \qquad c > 0. \tag{2.57}$$

For the relation R_1 : "more or less smaller than" we will start at the crisp relation "$\leq$" and its corresponding set representation

$$\{(x,y) \in I\!\!R^2 \mid x \leq y\}. \tag{2.58}$$

This set is the halfplane over the straight line $y = x$. The wording "more or less" will be interpreted here in the sense that a slight surplus is tolerable, hence the halfplane will be endowed with a "fuzziness band" downwards. So, the performance is analogous to that used when specifying fuzzy equality R_0. E.g., we can write:

$$\mu_{R_1}(x,y) = \begin{cases} [\,1 - a|x-y|\,]^+ & \text{for } x > y, \\ 1 & \text{for } x \leq y. \end{cases} \tag{2.59}$$

We can obtain another interpretation of the relation R_1 (as of any other relation R), if we understand the coordinate axes as domains of two real variables u, v, connected by the considered relation. This interpretation will play an essential role within Chapter 3.

When fixing one of the variables u or v, being in relation R_1, to some value, e.g. $v = y_0$, then the relation R_1 acts as a *fuzzy bound* S_u for the other variable, for instance

$$\mu_{S_u}(x) := \mu_{R_1}(x, y_0) = \begin{cases} [\,1 - a|x-y_0|\,]^+ & \text{for } x < y_0 \\ 1 & \text{for } y_0 \leq x. \end{cases} \tag{2.60}$$

When the other variable is fixed, $u = x_0$ say, then we find accordingly, a fuzzy bound S_v for the values of v for the values of v from the fuzzy relation R_1.

$$\mu_{S_v}(y) := \mu_{R_1}(x_0, y) = \begin{cases} 1 & \text{for } y \leq x_0, \\ [\,1 - a|x_0-y|\,]^+ & \text{for } x_0 < y. \end{cases} \tag{2.61}$$

Such fuzzy analoga of mathematical objects will be used, among others, in fuzzy versions of mathematical programming (cf. Section 3.5).

2.2.4 Fuzzy Mappings and Fuzzy Functions

Functions, which have variables in common with each other, are special relations, as is well known. For distinguishing the general case from the following particular specifications, we shall call fuzzy analoga to functions in general *fuzzy mappings*.

Let a (crisp) function $f : I\!R \to I\!R$ be given, then we shall choose its graph

$$\{(x, y) \in I\!R^2 \mid y = f(x)\} \qquad (2.62)$$

as the kernel of a fuzzy set F, the membership values of which may, e.g., decrease monotonically with increasing distance from this graph. This fuzzy set F represents a *fuzzy function*. For *explicit* functions f we can interpret F as a family (with family parameter x) of fuzzy numbers $Y(x)$, each possessing $\{f(x)\}$ as its kernel and

$$\mu_{Y(x)}(y) = \mu_F(x, y) \qquad (2.63)$$

as its membership function. The membership function μ_{R_0}, already considered in (2.55), provides an example of such a fuzzy function: it is a fuzzy straight line with the kernel $\mathcal{D}$ (cf. (2.54)).

When specifying a fuzzy function from a given set of observed graphs we can, alternatively to a specification of fuzzy numbers for every $x \in I\!R$, sometimes proceed in analogy with the morphological construction of a total observation from point-shaped original data. For every $x \in I\!R$ now the structure element is a straight line segment of fixed length moving on the straight line erected in x and parallel to the y-axis. The momentary midpoint of the segment is assigned as its membership value the relative number of graphs (curves) cut by the segment. The staircase function so obtained can, if necessary, be fitted to a type of curve, which is convenient for mathematical handling in the given context. With respect to an application of this proposal as a practical problem see BANDEMER/OTTO (1986). Figure 2.3 shows the result of such a performance. A bunch of sample absorbance spectra for dissolved pain relieving tablets was handled in this way and the staircase function obtained was fitted pointwise by a quadratic function.

For the case of an *implicit* function f with the graph

$$\{(x, y) \in I\!R^2 \mid f(x, y) = 0\} \qquad (2.64)$$

we may use the frequently possible clear interpretation as a (crisp) boundary of a region, when going to fuzzy implicit functions. This boundary is then, so to speak, endowed with a grey-tone band.

As an example we consider the circle

$$\mathcal{K} = \{(x, y) \in I\!R^2 \mid x^2 + y^2 = r^2\}. \qquad (2.65)$$

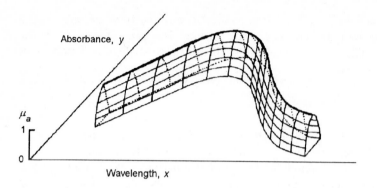

Figure 2.3: Example of a UV-spectrum considered as a fuzzified sample spectrum

A possible fuzzy version K is provided by the membership function

$$\mu_K(x, y) = \exp\{-|x^2 + y^2 - r^2|\}. \tag{2.66}$$

The restriction to the two-dimensional case, for relations and functions is not essential and has served up to now only for simplification of presentation, generalisation to spaces of higher dimension, e.g. to $\mathbb{R}^k$, is obvious.

In many problems of application, so with approximation and differential equations, the solution function $f : \mathbb{R}^k \to \mathbb{R}$ is determined only up to a vector of parameters $\boldsymbol{a} = (a_1, \ldots, a_r)^{\top}$, hence it belongs to a family of functions

$$(f(.\,;\boldsymbol{a}))_{\boldsymbol{a} \in \mathcal{A}}; \qquad \mathcal{A} \subseteq \mathbb{R}^r. \tag{2.67}$$

If these parameters can be specified only *fuzzily* by a membership function μ_A, then the family of functions from (2.67) becomes a *fuzzy family of functions* on $\mathbb{R}^k \times \mathbb{R}$ with the fuzzy set $A \in \mathbb{F}(\mathbb{R}^r)$ of family parameters. (Note the analogy to problems with distributed parameters, in which over $\mathcal{A}$ a random variable is introduced.)

The *contrast* to a fuzzy function on $\mathbb{R}^k \times \mathbb{R}$ is that every parameter vector $\boldsymbol{a} \in \operatorname{supp}(A)$ corresponds to a *crisp* function on $\mathbb{R}^k \times \mathbb{R}$, which has the membership value $\mu_A(\boldsymbol{a})$ to the *family*. When such a fuzzy family $(f(.\,;\boldsymbol{a}))$ of functions on $\mathbb{R}^k \times \mathbb{R}$ with the fuzzy parameter set A is given, then we can assign to it uniquely a fuzzy mapping F on $\mathbb{R}^k$ in putting

$$\mu_F(\boldsymbol{x}, y) = \sup_{\substack{\boldsymbol{a} \in \operatorname{supp}(A) \\ y = f(x;\boldsymbol{a})}} \mu_A(\boldsymbol{a}). \tag{2.68}$$

However, from this fuzzy mapping F the original fuzzy family of functions cannot be regained uniquely.

The specification of a fuzzy set over the parameter space $\mathcal{A}$ is, formally, very similar to the determination of a prior distribution, when modelling a problem by the BAYESian approach to mathematical statistics. However, the essentially less specific conditions necessary for a membership function, in contrast with those for a probability distribution, can simplify the problem of specification essentially with regard to notion as well as form.

When considering fuzzy families of functions it takes only one step to arrive at fuzzy sets in function spaces (HILBERT-space, BANACH-space, or the like) and hence at further analoga of fuzzy notions and methods, practicability of which is to be checked in every special case of application.

2.2.5 The Determination of Membership Functions

In the examples, explained up to now, continuity of the Euclidean space was only used implicitly for specifying fuzzy sets. If we succeed in interpreting a finite universe as a subset of some Euclidean (or, more general, of a measurable linear) space, e.g. as a lattice, then all those settings will remain useful, possibly with suitable modifications.

As examples from practical applications we present two figures (Figure 2.4 and Figure 2.5) from OTTO/BANDEMER (1988a), showing membership functions for different colours and for different degrees of solubility of a compound in water.

Sometimes the question is raised whether there is a method of specifying membership functions uniquely from the practical problem, like a differential equation from a mechanical problem. When this question is answered in the negative, this fact is used by opponents of fuzzy theory for blaming the theory for this supposed drawback. From the standpoint of an engineer the numerical assessment of a membership function is a modelling of second or even third order to take into account effects of uncertainty. Demanding precise specifications would contradict the whole concept of fuzzy thinking. In other fields of mathematics and its applications people are much less specific. Nobody would seriously ask an engineer how he has specified the coefficient and boundary values of the differential equation, which he assumes is appropriate to the problem he is considering. Usually not even the structure of the differential equation is questioned. Essentially the same holds true in (usual) control theory with the design of linear controllers. We will touch on the problem of specifying fuzzy probability distributions in Chapter 5.

Moreover, as varied applications of fuzzy set theory have shown, the choice of the type and the precise values for the parameters have, in general, only

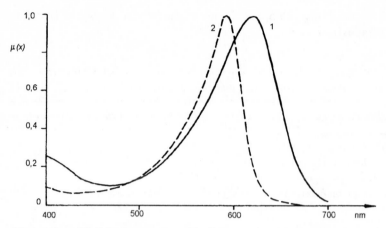

Figure 2.4: Visible spectrum of indicators in the wavelength range between 400 and 700 nm renormed to the interval [0,1] and used as membership functions for the feature "colour": 1 – Bromocresol green, 2 – Bromophenol blue

little influence on the results, decisions, and conclusions obtained, as long as a local monotonicity is preserved. Let μ_1 and μ_2 be two *different* specifications, then local monotonicity means that

$$\forall x_1, x_2 \in \mathcal{X} : \ \mu_1(x_2) \leqq \mu_1(x_1) \Leftrightarrow \mu_2(x_2) \leqq \mu_2(x_1). \tag{2.69}$$

Hence, after all, only the *qualitative* order of the elements of the universe matters, and this can be obtained from the practical facts much more easily. The analytical representation follows, very frequently, the rules of mathematical convenience.

Finally, we shall mention here (cf. Section 4.1 for details) that even linguistic formulations can be represented by fuzzy sets. So, e.g., "high temperature" (say, in the context with fever) can be specified as a fuzzy set over the temperature scale.

2.3 Operations with Fuzzy Sets

2.3.1 Basic Set Algebraic Operations

The most elementary operations for usual sets are the union as well as the intersection of any two sets and the complement of any set w.r.t. some superset of it. Furthermore, for applications involving some correspondences or functions one has the operation of a cartesian product. Sometimes one is also forced to extend an operation defined for the members of some class to the

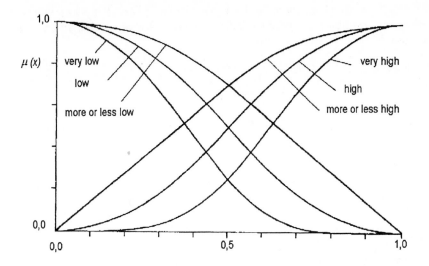

Figure 2.5: Membership functions for characterising "solubility in water"

subsets of that class. All those compositions shall here become extended to
fuzzy sets.

For the basic set algebraic operations ZADEH (1965) has already given
such extensions. For the *union* $A \cup B$ of fuzzy sets A, B he considered the
definition

$$C := A \cup B :$$
$$\mu_C(x) =_{\text{def}} \max\{\mu_A(x), \mu_B(x)\} \quad \text{for all } x \in \mathcal{X}, \tag{2.70}$$

for the *intersection* $A \cap B$ of fuzzy sets A, B the definition

$$D := A \cap B :$$
$$\mu_D(x) =_{\text{def}} \min\{\mu_A(x), \mu_B(x)\} \quad \text{for all } x \in \mathcal{X}, \tag{2.71}$$

and for the *complement* A^c of a fuzzy set A (relative to the universe of discourse $\mathcal{X}$) the definition

$$K := A^c : \quad \mu_K(x) =_{\text{def}} 1 - \mu_A(x) \quad \text{for all } x \in \mathcal{X}. \tag{2.72}$$

All these operations on fuzzy sets are straightforward generalisations of the
corresponding operations on usual sets. If one e.g. in (2.71) has A, B as crisp
sets, i.e. if always $\mu_A(x)$, $\mu_B(x) \in \{0, 1\}$, then $A \cap B$ is also a crisp set and
exactly the (usual) intersection of these crisp sets A, B. The same holds true

for definition (2.70) of a union and for definition (2.72) of a complement. Regarding the α-cuts, one finds as quite simple relations to the union and intersection of crisp sets the results.

$$(A \cup B)^{>\alpha} = A^{>\alpha} \cup B^{>\alpha}, \quad (A \cap B)^{>\alpha} = A^{>\alpha} \cap B^{>\alpha}. \tag{2.73}$$

For the complement on the other hand one has

$$(A^c)^{>\alpha} = A^{<1-\alpha} = \{x \in \mathcal{X} \mid \mu_A(x) < 1 - \alpha\}. \tag{2.74}$$

These results hold true also for strong α-cuts, respectively.

These results on cuts make it possible to reduce these set algebraic operations on fuzzy sets to the corresponding operations on crisp sets. But, one should bear in mind that the definitions (2.70), (2.71) are essential in order to get (2.73). Later on in (2.98) to (2.100) and (2.102) to (2.104) we shall define further versions of intersections and unions of fuzzy sets, but simple reductions like (2.73) do not exist for these operations.

Without any difficulties one finds as corollaries of definitions (2.70) to (2.72) a series of simple laws. Thus for union one gets for any fuzzy sets A, B, C

$$A \cup B = B \cup A, \qquad \text{(commutativity)} \tag{2.75}$$
$$A \cup (B \cup C) = (A \cup B) \cup C, \qquad \text{(associativity)} \tag{2.76}$$
$$A \cup A = A, \qquad \text{(idempotency)} \tag{2.77}$$
$$A \subseteqq B \Rightarrow A \cup C \subseteqq B \cup C, \qquad \text{(monotonicity)} \tag{2.78}$$

as well as

$$A \cup \emptyset = A, \qquad A \cup X = X. \tag{2.79}$$

Rules (2.75) to (2.78) hold true in the same way also for the intersection of fuzzy sets. Instead of (2.79) of course one then has

$$A \cap \emptyset = \emptyset, \qquad A \cap X = A. \tag{2.80}$$

In fuzzy sets, just as in traditional set algebra, two kinds of distributivity hold true for the operations (2.70), (2.71):

$$\begin{aligned} A \cup (B \cap C) &= (A \cup B) \cap (A \cup C), \\ A \cap (B \cup C) &= (A \cap B) \cup (A \cap C). \end{aligned} \tag{2.81}$$

Complementation is idempotent: $A = A^{cc}$, for fuzzy sets as for crisp sets, and it reverses inclusion:

$$A \subseteqq B \iff B^c \subseteqq A^c. \tag{2.82}$$

It is also very important for fuzzy sets that one has a simple possibility to calculate the complement of an intersection and a union. For this one has the deMorgan laws:

$$(A \cap B)^c = A^c \cup B^c, \tag{2.83}$$
$$(A \cup B)^c = A^c \cap B^c. \tag{2.84}$$

Despite the fact that we were calling A^c the complement of A, this complementation lacks some of the basic properties of complementation in the crisp case: $A \cup A^c \neq X$ as well as $A \cap A^c \neq \emptyset$ are possible for fuzzy sets A! Definitely, one has $0 \neq \mu_D(a)$ for $D = A \cap A^c$ if and only if $0 \neq \mu_A(a) \neq 1$ holds true. Hence, not all the laws from an algebra set of traditional set theory generalise for fuzzy sets.

Sometimes one has to consider the union or the intersection for a whole family of fuzzy sets. For this one defines for families $(A_j \mid j \in \mathcal{J})$ of fuzzy sets (with a usual, crisp set $\mathcal{J}$ as set of indices) the *generalised union* $\bigcup_{j \in \mathcal{J}} A_j$ and the *generalised intersection* $\bigcap_{j \in \mathcal{J}} A_j$ of this family by

$$C := \bigcup_{j \in \mathcal{J}} A_j : \quad \mu_C(x) =_{\text{def}} \sup_{j \in \mathcal{J}} \mu_{A_j}(x) \quad \text{for all } x \in \mathcal{X}, \tag{2.85}$$

$$D := \bigcap_{j \in \mathcal{J}} A_j : \quad \mu_D(x) =_{\text{def}} \inf_{j \in \mathcal{J}} \mu_{A_j}(x) \quad \text{for all } x \in \mathcal{X}. \tag{2.86}$$

Both formulas immediately generalise (2.70) and (2.71).

As important laws we mention the distributivities

$$B \cap \bigcup_{j \in \mathcal{J}} A_j = \bigcup_{j \in \mathcal{J}} (B \cap A_j), \quad B \cup \bigcap_{j \in \mathcal{J}} A_j = \bigcap_{j \in \mathcal{J}} (B \cup A_j), \tag{2.87}$$

and the monotonicity properties

$$\bigcap_{j \in \mathcal{J}} A_j \subseteqq A_k \subseteqq \bigcup_{j \in \mathcal{J}} A_j \quad \text{for each } k \in \mathcal{J}, \tag{2.88}$$

$$B \subseteqq A_k \quad \text{for all } k \in \mathcal{J} \;\Rightarrow\; B \subseteqq \bigcap_{j \in \mathcal{J}} A_j, \tag{2.89}$$

$$A_k \subseteqq B \quad \text{for all } k \in \mathcal{J} \;\Rightarrow\; \bigcup_{j \in \mathcal{J}} A_j \subseteqq B. \tag{2.90}$$

All the operations on fuzzy sets we have discussed up to now are operations in $\mathbb{F}(\mathcal{X})$, i.e. the result of applying such an operation to fuzzy sets from $\mathbb{F}(\mathcal{X})$ is again a fuzzy set from $\mathbb{F}(\mathcal{X})$.

Another basic operation for sets is the cartesian product. The corresponding notion for fuzzy sets is that of a *fuzzy cartesian product* which for fuzzy sets $A, B \in \mathbb{F}(\mathcal{X})$ is the fuzzy set $A \otimes B \in \mathbb{F}(\mathcal{X} \times \mathcal{X})$ with membership function defined for all $a, b \in \mathcal{X}$ by

$$C := A \otimes B :$$

$$\mu_C((a, b)) =_{\text{def}} \min\{\mu_A(a), \mu_B(b)\}. \tag{2.91}$$

Here (a, b) is the – usual – ordered pair of a, b. By the way, for definition (2.91) it is completely unimportant to take A, B as fuzzy subsets of the same universe of discourse: for $A \in \mathbb{F}(\mathcal{X})$ and $B \in \mathbb{F}(\mathcal{Y})$ one can use the same definition for $A \otimes B$ as in (2.91) and simply gets $A \otimes B \in \mathbb{F}(\mathcal{X} \times \mathcal{Y})$.

Immediately a series of laws results. For any fuzzy sets A, B, C one e.g. has

$$
\begin{array}{rcll}
A \otimes (B \cup C) & = & (A \otimes B) \cup (A \otimes C), & \tag{2.92} \\
A \otimes (B \cap C) & = & (A \otimes B) \cap (A \otimes C), & \tag{2.93} \\
A \otimes (B \otimes C) & = & (A \otimes B) \otimes C, & \tag{2.94} \\
A \otimes \emptyset & = & \emptyset \otimes A = \emptyset & \tag{2.95}
\end{array}
$$

and also the condition

$$A \otimes B = \emptyset \quad \Leftrightarrow \quad A = \emptyset \quad \text{or} \quad B = \emptyset. \tag{2.96}$$

The distributive laws (2.92), (2.93) extend to the case of generalised union and generalised intersection and hold true also in the case that one interchanges the "factors" of these cartesian products. Also of importance are the monotonicity properties

$$A \subseteqq B \implies A \otimes C \subseteqq B \otimes C \quad \text{and} \quad C \otimes A \subseteqq C \otimes B. \tag{2.97}$$

2.3.2   Further Variants of Intersections and Unions

Despite the simplicity and naturalness of the set algebraic operations defined in (2.70), (2.71) as generalisations of the usual union and intersection to fuzzy sets – one is not forced to choose these definitions. Already ZADEH (1965) mentioned other variants, but did not however consider them as variants of union and intersection. Among a wealth of possibilities, preferred candidates for intersections of fuzzy sets, differing from (2.71), are often the *algebraic product* $A \bullet B$ defined by

$$D := A \bullet B : \quad \mu_D(x) =_{\text{def}} \mu_A(x) \cdot \mu_B(x) \quad \text{for all } x \in \mathcal{X}, \tag{2.98}$$

the *bounded product* $A \odot B$ with the definition

$$D := A \odot B :$$

$$\mu_D(x) =_{\text{def}} [\mu_A(x) + \mu_B(x) - 1]^+ \quad \text{for all } x \in \mathcal{X}, \tag{2.99}$$

and the *drastic product* $A \star B$ defined by

$$D := A \star B : \tag{2.100}$$

$$\mu_D(x) =_{\text{def}} \begin{cases} \min\{\mu_A(x), \mu_B(x)\}, & \text{if } \mu_A(x) = 1 \\ & \text{or } \mu_B(x) = 1 \\ 0 & \text{otherwise.} \end{cases}$$

Denoting by $\star$ any one of these additional intersection operations, one connects with it a related union using the definition schema

$$A \# B =_{\text{def}} (A^c \star B^c)^c, \tag{2.101}$$

i.e. using a relationship in form of a deMorgan law to connect intersection and union, respectively. In this way one finds as connected with the algebraic product the *algebraic sum* $A + B$ characterised for all $x \in \mathcal{X}$ by

$$C := A + B : \tag{2.102}$$

$$\mu_C(x) =_{\text{def}} \mu_A(x) + \mu_B(x) - \mu_A(x) \cdot \mu_B(x),$$

as connected with the bounded product the *bounded sum* $A \oplus B$ characterised by

$$C := A \oplus B :$$

$$\mu_C(x) =_{\text{def}} \min\{1, \mu_A(x) + \mu_B(x)\} \quad \text{for all } x \in \mathcal{X}, \tag{2.103}$$

and as connected with the drastic product the *drastic sum* $A \diamond B$ with definition

$$C := A \diamond B : \tag{2.104}$$

$$\mu_C(x) =_{\text{def}} \begin{cases} \max\{\mu_A(x), \mu_B(x)\}, & \text{if } \mu_A(x) = 0 \\ & \text{or } \mu_B(x) = 0 \\ 1 & \text{otherwise.} \end{cases}$$

All these additional unions and intersections for fuzzy sets are suitable generalisations of the traditional union and intersection of usual, i.e. crisp sets, in the sense that they coincide with these traditional operations for crisp sets. The essential difference between these new operations and the earlier ones $\cap, \cup$ defined in (2.71), (2.70) lies in the fact that in case of $\bullet, \odot$ and $\star$ as well as of $+, \oplus$ and $\diamond$ the membership degrees $\mu_A(x)$, $\mu_B(x)$ *interact* in the sense that in general neither $\mu_A(x)$ nor $\mu_B(x)$ is the membership degree of x in the resulting fuzzy set. Therefore these additional union and intersection operations are called *interactive* in contrast to the *non-interactive* operations $\cup, \cap$, with the property that always $\mu_{A \cup B}(x)$, $\mu_{A \cap B}(x) \in \{\mu_A(x), \mu_B(x)\}$ holds true. All these interactive operations lack e.g. the idempotency property (2.77).

This very idea of interactivity is often responsible for a change from the – usually preferred – non-interactive operations $\sqcup, \sqcap$ to the interactive ones. But this heavily depends on the actual application one has in mind, cf. e.g. (4.62) and (4.63), (5.54) and (5.58), but also (3.41) and (3.42) as well as Section 2.4. In the majority of applications, however, up to now one prefers $\sqcup, \sqcap$, also because of the very simple definitions of these two operations.

Our approach toward additional operations which are variants of $\sqcup, \sqcap$ up to now was to present such variants. The problem now is whether there are – besides our remark that the choice of such variants may be directed by applicational ideas – theoretical motives to prefer some of these variants over others. A partial answer to this problem is given by a result of BELLMAN/GIERTZ (1973).

Theorem: *Suppose that $\sqcup, \sqcap$ are a union and an intersection operation for fuzzy sets defined in analogy with (2.70), but with reference to two binary operations $\sqcup, \sqcap$ in $[0, 1]$ instead of* max, min. *Under the conditions that*

(1) $\sqcup$ and $\sqcap$ are operations in $[0, 1]$ which are commutative, associative and mutually distributive,

(2) $\sqcup$ and $\sqcap$ are continuous functions in $[0, 1]$ which also are nondecreasing in both arguments,

(3) it holds true $1 \sqcap 1 = 1$ and $0 \sqcup 0 = 0$ as well as $a \sqcup b \geq \max\{a, b\}$ and $a \sqcap b \leq \min\{a, b\}$ for all $a, b \in [0, 1]$,

(4) the unary functions $a \mapsto a \sqcup a$ and $a \mapsto a \sqcap a$ are strictly increasing in $[0, 1]$

then one has $\sqcup = $ max and $\sqcap = $ min, i.e. the fuzzy set operations $\sqcup, \sqcap$ are exactly the union and intersection defined by (2.70), (2.71).

Thus it may seem that the operations $\sqcup, \sqcap$ are in some sense distinguished ones. But, it is not at all clear whether all these assumptions (1), ... , (4) really are natural ones to be imposed. In particular, assumptions (2) and (4) look quite strong, as does the mutual distributivity in (1). Therefore it is more appropriate not to ask for conditions which allow exclusion of some of the variants for union or intersection. Instead we will consider in Section 2.4 a whole class of such operations.

Contrary to this situation, for complementation there are only very few variants which differ from (2.72), and essentially no one of them was considered as of special importance. Nevertheless, there are possible variants which have been considered from a theoretical perspective e.g. in LOWEN (1978), DUBOIS/PRADE (1980), WEBER (1983) and also in GOTTWALD (1989). In the last case this is done from the logical point of view which relates them to negations in many-valued logic which themselves can be defined via implication operators.

2.3.3 Extending Point Operations to Fuzzy Sets

Up to now we were concerned with generalising such set algebraic operations for fuzzy sets which are of central importance in classical set theory. Now we move to another point of view and look at the problem of how to generalise an operation, which is defined in the universe of discourse $\mathcal{X}$, from an operation acting on the points of this universe to an operation acting on its fuzzy subsets. Hence now $g : \mathcal{X}^n \to \mathcal{X}$ shall be an n-ary operation which associates with any values $a_1, \ldots, a_n$ of variables $u_1, \ldots, u_n$ a value b of a variable v.

Our intuitive understanding of this situation is that the values of the variables $u_1, \ldots, u_n$ are given only imprecisely. How then to connect with values $A_1, \ldots, A_n \in \mathbb{F}(\mathcal{X})$ of these variables $u_1, \ldots, u_n$ a value $B \in \mathbb{F}(\mathcal{X})$ of the variable v?

Of course, the possible true value of v, i.e. some one of the points of $\text{supp}\,(B)$, shall result according to the function g out of the possible true values of the variables u_i, i.e. out of members of the sets $\text{supp}\,(A_i)$. Furthermore, one expects that the membership degrees $\mu_{A_i}(a_i)$, $i = 1, \ldots, n$, completely determine the membership degree $\mu_B(g(a_1, \ldots, a_n))$. Therefore the function $g : \mathcal{X}^n \to \mathcal{X}$ has to be extended to a function $\hat{g} : \mathbb{F}(\mathcal{X})^n \to \mathbb{F}(\mathcal{X})$. For this extension of g to $\hat{g}$ we refer to a method proposed by ZADEH (1975) and called *extension principle*.[1]

Extension Principle: *A function $g : \mathcal{X}^n \to \mathcal{Y}$ shall become extended to a function $\hat{g} : \mathbb{F}(\mathcal{X})^n \to \mathbb{F}(\mathcal{Y})$ by defining for all fuzzy sets $A_1, \ldots, A_n \in \mathbb{F}(\mathcal{X})$*

$$B := \hat{g}(A_1, \ldots, A_n) :$$

$$\mu_B(y) =_{\text{def}} \sup_{\substack{x_1, \ldots, x_n \in \mathcal{X} \\ y = g(x_1, \ldots, x_n)}} \min\{\mu_{A_1}(x_1), \ldots, \mu_{A_n}(x_n)\}$$

$$\text{for all } y \in \mathcal{Y}. \tag{2.105}$$

Looking at the result which definition (2.105) has for α-cuts, one finds for each $\alpha \in [0, 1]$:

$$B^{>\alpha} = g(A_1^{>\alpha}, \ldots, A_n^{>\alpha}). \tag{2.106}$$

In the special case that for each $y \in \mathcal{Y}$ the supremum in formula (2.105) is one of the values it has taken over, then formula (2.106) holds true also for strong α-cuts. In (2.106) in any case we use the extension of g to crisp sets: but this is according to the canonical understanding of this situation and to be read

---

[1] Here as in all other cases zero is the supremum of the empty set.

as the set of all $g(a_1, \ldots, a_n)$ for always $a_i \in A_i^{\geq \alpha}$.

Using the class term notation introduced in (2.40) allows for a much simpler notation. Formula (2.105) then can be written as

$$\hat{g}(A_1, \ldots, A_n) = \{g(a_1, \ldots, a_n) \parallel a_1 \varepsilon A_1 \wedge \ldots \wedge a_n \varepsilon A_n\}, \qquad (2.107)$$

which is obviously shorthand for

$$\hat{g}(A_1, \ldots, A_n) = \{y \in \mathcal{Y} \parallel \exists a_1 \ldots \exists a_n (a_1 \varepsilon A_1 \wedge \ldots \wedge a_n \varepsilon A_n$$
$$\wedge \, y \doteq g(a_1, \ldots, a_n))\}. \qquad (2.108)$$

In these formulas $\wedge$ is to be taken as that conjunction of many-valued logic which is characterised by the function min as its truth function. Furthermore, $\exists$ is the particularisation quantifier which semantically means to take the supremum of truth degrees, and $\doteq$ is a many-valued identity relation characterised by

$$[\![a \doteq b]\!] =_{\text{def}} \begin{cases} 1, & \text{if } a = b, \\ 0 & \text{otherwise.} \end{cases} \qquad (2.109)$$

In this reformulation it becomes completely obvious that the extension principle (2.105) is a straightforward generalisation of the HAUSDORFFian approach to define operations for sets assuming that corresponding operations for their members are given.

2.4   Generalised, t-Norm-Based Operations

2.4.1   A General Class of Set Algebraic Operations

In the preceding Section 2.3 we discussed the basic non-interactive set algebraic operations $\cap, \cup$ on fuzzy sets, which are based on taking the minimum or maximum of membership degrees, and interactive set algebraic operations like $\bullet, \odot, \star$, etc. Their choice however was not governed by any principle. Furthermore, an extreme reading of the result of BELLMAN/GIERTZ (1973) could suggest that these interactive operations are of some exotic nature. Even admitting that such an impression was not completely untrue e.g. in the time of the first paper by ZADEH (1965) on fuzzy sets, actually the situation is completely different. The essential point is that not only the interactive intersections $\bullet, \odot, \star$, but also the non-interactive one $\cap$ are realisations of a common concept: general intersection operations for fuzzy sets which are based on so called t-norms in a uniform way.

By a *t-norm* we mean a binary operation t in $[0, 1]$, i.e. a binary function t from $[0, 1]$ into $[0, 1]$, which is commutative, associative, as well as monotonically nondecreasing, and which has 1 as a neutral and 0 as a zero element. At all thus for any $x, y, z, u, v \in [0, 1]$ the following conditions have to be satisfied for a t-norm t:

(T1) $x\,t\,y = y\,t\,x$;

(T2) $x\,t\,(y\,t\,z) = (x\,t\,y)\,t\,z$;

(T3)   if $x \leq u$ and $y \leq v$, then $x\,t\,y \leq u\,t\,v$;

(T4) $x\,t\,1 = x$ and $x\,t\,0 = 0$.

Connected with each t-norm t one gets an *intersection operation* $\cap_t$ on fuzzy sets by defining the fuzzy set $A \cap_t B$ as

$$D := A \cap_t B :$$
$$\mu_D(x) =_{\text{def}} \mu_A(x)\,t\,\mu_B(x) \quad \text{for all } x \in \mathcal{X}. \tag{2.110}$$

All the intersection operations of Section 2.3 are generated in this form from suitable t-norms. For $A \cap B$ according to (2.71) the corresponding t-norm is the operation t_0 with:

$$u\,t_0\,v = \min\{u, v\} \quad \text{for } u, v \in [0, 1]; \tag{2.111}$$

the algebraic product (2.98) is generated by the following t-norm t_1:

$$u\,t_1\,v = u \cdot v \quad \text{for } u, v \in [0, 1]; \tag{2.112}$$

the bounded product (2.99) has the generating t-norm t_2 characterised by:

$$u\,t_2\,v = [u + v - 1]^+ \quad \text{for } u, v \in [0, 1]; \tag{2.113}$$

and the drastic product (2.100) is generated by the t-norm t_3 with definition:

$$u\,t_3\,v = \begin{cases} \min\{u, v\}, & \text{if } u = 1 \text{ or } v = 1 \\ 0 & \text{otherwise} \end{cases} \quad \text{for } u, v \in [0, 1]. \tag{2.114}$$

As a consequence of the commutativity and associativity of any t-norm, and of (T4), for each intersection operation $\cap_t$ defined via (2.110) one immediately finds for all fuzzy sets $A, B, C \in \mathbb{F}(\mathcal{X})$:

$$A \cap_t B = B \cap_t A, \tag{2.115}$$
$$A \cap_t (B \cap_t C) = (A \cap_t B) \cap_t C, \tag{2.116}$$
$$A \cap_t \emptyset = \emptyset, \qquad A \cap_t X = A. \tag{2.117}$$

The monotonicity condition (T3) together with (T4) yields for any t-norm the result that one always has $u\,t\,v \leq u\,t\,1 = u$ as well as $u\,t\,v \leq v$. Hence one always has $u\,t\,v \le \min\{u, v\}$ and thus for all $A, B \in \mathbb{F}(\mathcal{X})$ the inclusion relation

$$A \cap_t B \subseteqq A \cap B, \tag{2.118}$$

and therefore moreover also

$$A \cap_t B \subseteqq A, \qquad A \cap_t B \subseteqq B. \tag{2.119}$$

On the other hand, in general the fuzzy set $A \cap_t A$ does not coincide with A, but is only a subset of it. This is caused by the fact that together with $u\,t\,u \le u$ for each $u \in [0, 1]$ one sometimes has $u_0\,t\,u_0 < u_0$, e.g. for the t-norms t_1, t_2 which define the algebraic product $A \bullet B$ or the bounded product $A \odot B$: one simply has to choose $u_0 = \frac{1}{2}$ in these cases. To assume for a t-norm $\hat{t}$, that the equality $u\,\hat{t}\,u = u$ holds true for all $u \in [0, 1]$, means to have for all $u, v \in [0, 1]$ with additionally $u \le v$ also

$$u = u\,\hat{t}\,u \le u\,\hat{t}\,v \le u\,\hat{t}\,1 = u = \min\{u, v\}$$

and thus at all $\hat{t} = \min$. Therefore one has

$$A \cap_t A = A \quad \text{for all } A \in \mathbb{F}(\mathcal{X}) \Leftrightarrow t = \min, \tag{2.120}$$

which means that only for the intersection (2.71) always $A \cap A = A$ holds true.

Furthermore, the definition (2.71) of the intersection operation $A \cap B$ is the only one of all these t-norm based intersection operations (2.110) which is non-interactive. For, having non-interactivity of $\cap_t$ means to have $u\,t\,v \in \{u, v\}$ in any case and hence also $u\,t\,u = u$ for each $u \in [0, 1]$. But already this forces $t = \min$.

As already done in (2.101), via reference to the complementation (2.72) one connects with any intersection operation $\cap_t$ a dual t-norm based *union operation* $\cup_t$ by defining

$$A \cup_t B =_{\text{def}} (A^c \cap_t B^c)^c. \tag{2.121}$$

In essentially the same manner with each t-norm t one connects a t-*conorm* s_t dual to t using the definition

$$u\,s_t\,v =_{\text{def}} 1 - (1 - u)\,t\,(1 - v) \quad \text{for } u, v \in [0, 1]. \tag{2.122}$$

Writing in the case of the t-norms $t_0, \ldots, t_3$, which we defined earlier, only s_i instead of s_{t_i}, these dual t-conorms become the functions with for all $u, v \in$

$[0, 1]$:

$$
\begin{aligned}
u \, s_0 \, v &= \max\{u, v\}, \\
u \, s_1 \, v &= u + v - uv, \\
u \, s_2 \, v &= \min\{1, u + v\}, \\
u \, s_3 \, v &= \begin{cases} \max\{u, v\}, & \text{if } u = 0 \text{ or } v = 0 \\ 1 & \text{otherwise.} \end{cases}
\end{aligned}
$$

Because of (2.121) and (2.122) now the membership degrees of $A \cup_t B$ are always determined by

$$
C := A \cup_t B : \quad \mu_C(x) = \mu_A(x) \, s_t \, \mu_B(x) \text{ for all } x \in \mathcal{X}. \tag{2.123}
$$

The conditions (T1), $\ldots$, (T4) which characterise t-norms, together with definition (2.122) of the corresponding t-conorm have as a consequence that the t-conorms s_t are also binary operations in $[0, 1]$ which are commutative, associative, as well as monotonously nondecreasing, and for which $u \, s_t \, 0 = u$ and $u \, s_t \, 1 = 1$ hold true for all $u \in [0, 1]$.

Therefore, for each one of these t-norm based unions $\cup_t$ for all fuzzy sets $A, B, C \in \mathbb{F}(\mathcal{X})$ one has the properties

$$
\begin{aligned}
A \cup_t B &= B \cup_t A, & (2.124) \\
A \cup_t (B \cup_t C) &= (A \cup_t B) \cup_t C, & (2.125) \\
A \cup_t \emptyset &= A, \qquad A \cup_t X = X, & (2.126)
\end{aligned}
$$

as well as the inclusion relation

$$
A \cup B \subseteqq A \cup_t B, \tag{2.127}
$$

and hence also

$$
A \subseteqq A \cup_t B, \qquad B \subseteqq A \cup_t B. \tag{2.128}
$$

As in the case of the generalised, t-norm based intersections $A \cap_t B$ also for the t-norm based unions one generally has that $A \cup_t A$ is different from A and that it holds true

$$
A \cup_t A = A \quad \text{for all } A \in \mathbb{F}(\mathcal{X})
$$
$$
\Leftrightarrow \quad t = \min \quad \Leftrightarrow \quad s_t = \max. \tag{2.129}
$$

Hence, again the only non-interactive operation among the ones defined in (2.123), (2.121) is the old union $A \cup B$ of (2.70).

Definition (2.121) for each t-norm t yields the deMorgan laws

$$
\begin{aligned}
(A \cap_t B)^c &= A^c \cup_t B^c, & (2.130) \\
(A \cup_t B)^c &= A^c \cap_t B^c & (2.131)
\end{aligned}
$$

for any $A, B \in F(\mathcal{X})$, generalising (2.84), (2.83). On the other hand, the distributivity laws (2.81) do not generalise for all t-norm based operations – even more: these distributivities (2.81) hold true *only* for the operations $\cap, \cup$ according to (2.71), (2.70).

To see this let us suppose we have $A \cap_t (B \cup_t C) = (A \cap_t B) \cup_t (A \cap_t C)$ true for all $A, B, C \in F(\mathcal{X})$. In the special case $B = C = X$ this results in the condition that one has to have $A = A \cup_t A$ for each $A \in F(\mathcal{X})$. But this was already proven to hold true only in the case $t = \min$. In the same way the assumption that the dual distributivity law $A \cup_t (B \cap_t C) = (A \cup_t B) \cap_t (A \cup_t C)$ holds true for all $A, B, C \in F(\mathcal{X})$ forces also $t = \min$.

A consequence of the monotonicity condition (T3) for t-norms is that the equations

$$u \, t \, \max\{v, w\} \;\;=\;\; \max\{u \, t \, v, u \, t \, w\}, \tag{2.132}$$
$$u \, t \, \min\{v, w\} \;\;=\;\; \min\{u \, t \, v, u \, t \, w\} \tag{2.133}$$

hold true for all $u, v, w \in [0, 1]$. For all $A, B, C \in F(\mathcal{X})$ and any t-norm t therefore one has the additional distributivities

$$A \cap_t (B \cup C) \;\;=\;\; (A \cap_t B) \cup (A \cap_t C), \tag{2.134}$$
$$A \cap_t (B \cap C) \;\;=\;\; (A \cap_t B) \cap (A \cap_t C), \tag{2.135}$$

and because of the deMorgan laws (2.130), (2.131) also the distributivities

$$A \cup_t (B \cap C) \;\;=\;\; (A \cup_t B) \cap (A \cup_t C), \tag{2.136}$$
$$A \cup_t (B \cup C) \;\;=\;\; (A \cup_t B) \cup (A \cup_t C). \tag{2.137}$$

Unfortunately, on the left hand sides of these distributive laws it is not allowed to exchange the roles of the general t-norm based set algebraic operations with their counterparts based on the t-norm $t_0 = \min$. The background is that for these cases one has only the inequalities

$$\max\{u, v\} \, t \, \max\{u, w\} \;\;\leq\;\; \max\{u, v \, t \, w\}, \tag{2.138}$$
$$\min\{u, v\} \, t \, \min\{u, w\} \;\;\leq\;\; \min\{u, v \, t \, w\} \tag{2.139}$$

instead of the equalities (2.132), (2.133). Therefore one has for this situation only the subdistributivities

$$(A \cup B) \cap_t (A \cup C) \;\;\subseteq\;\; A \cup (B \cap_t C), \tag{2.140}$$
$$(A \cap B) \cap_t (A \cap C) \;\;\subseteq\;\; A \cap (B \cap_t C), \tag{2.141}$$

and therefore, via the deMorgan laws (2.130), (2.83) (2.84) and the relation (2.82) also the subdistributivities

$$(A \cap B) \cup_t (A \cap C) \;\;\subseteq\;\; A \cap (B \cup_t C), \tag{2.142}$$
$$(A \cup B) \cup_t (A \cup C) \;\;\subseteq\;\; A \cup (B \cup_t C). \tag{2.143}$$

The essential idea which led us from intersection (2.110) to the t-norm based intersections – and via (2.121) or (2.122) also to the t-norm based unions – was the exchange of the minimum operator with a t-norm. This idea, of course, can also be applied in other cases, e.g. in the definition (2.91) of the fuzzy cartesian product. In this way instead of $A \otimes B$ one gets a new *t-norm based fuzzy cartesian product* $A \otimes_t B$ characterised by

$$C := A \otimes_t B :$$
$$\mu_C((a,b)) =_{\text{def}} \mu_A(a) \, t \, \mu_B(b) \quad \text{for all } a,b \in \mathcal{X}. \tag{2.144}$$

Usually one is assuming that $A, B \in \mathbb{F}(\mathcal{X})$ are fuzzy subsets of the same universe of discourse and then has $A \otimes_t B \in \mathbb{F}(\mathcal{X} \times \mathcal{X})$. But again, as already mentioned after definition (2.91), $A \in \mathbb{IF}(\mathcal{X})$ and $B \in \mathbb{IF}(\mathcal{Y})$ are also possible and yield $A \otimes_t B \in \mathbb{F}(\mathcal{X} \times \mathcal{Y})$.

Some of the basic properties (2.92) to (2.97) of the fuzzy cartesian product (2.91) hold true also for the t-norm based version of this product. The defining conditions (T1), ..., (T4) of t-norms yield the associativity

$$A \otimes_t (B \otimes_t C) = (A \otimes_t B) \otimes_t C \tag{2.145}$$

as well as the monotonicity

$$A \subseteq B \;\Rightarrow\; A \otimes_t C \subseteq B \otimes_t C \text{ and } C \otimes_t A \subseteq C \otimes_t B. \tag{2.146}$$

Furthermore one has

$$A \otimes_t \emptyset = \emptyset \otimes_t A = \emptyset, \tag{2.147}$$

but it may happen that $A \otimes_t B = \emptyset$ holds true also in the case that $A \neq \emptyset$ and $B \neq \emptyset$ hold true. A very simple example for such a situation provides the t-norm t_2 with the fuzzy sets A_0, B_0 e.g. both chosen as the $\frac{1}{2}$-universal set $X^{[\frac{1}{2}]}$: in this case one has $A_0 \otimes_{t_2} B_0 = \emptyset$ because of the fact that $\mu_A(x) \, t_2 \, \mu_B(x) = t_2(\frac{1}{2}, \frac{1}{2}) = 0$ holds true for all $x \in \mathcal{X}$.

As earlier for intersection and union operations, the relations (2.132) and (2.133) are basic results which yield distributivity results for the fuzzy cartesian product w.r.t. to the operations $\cap, \cup$ in $\mathbb{F}(\mathcal{X})$:

$$A \otimes_t (B \cap C) \;=\; (A \otimes_t B) \cap (A \otimes_t C), \tag{2.148}$$
$$A \otimes_t (B \cup C) \;=\; (A \otimes_t B) \cup (A \otimes_t C). \tag{2.149}$$

But these distributivity laws cannot be generalised to the t-norm based intersections $\cap_t$ and unions $\cup_t$. Because otherwise, supposing e.g. that for $\cap_t$ instead of $\cap$ equation (2.148) would hold true, then for $B = C = X$, this equation would reduce to $A = A \cap_t A$: but this condition $A = A \cap_t A$, if true for any $A \in \mathbb{F}(\mathcal{X})$, implies $t = \min$. Thus one has

$$A \otimes_t (B \cap_t C) = (A \otimes_t B) \cap_t (A \otimes_t C) \quad \text{for all } A, B, C$$
$$\Leftrightarrow \quad t = \min. \tag{2.150}$$

Exactly the same type of argument shows that in case one writes $\cup_t$ for $\cup$ in equation (2.149), the additional assumption $B = C = X$ reduces this equation to the condition $A = A \cup_t A$ for all $A \in \mathbb{F}(\mathcal{X})$. Thus one has again:

$$A \otimes_t (B \cup_t C) = (A \otimes_t B) \cup_t (A \otimes_t C) \quad \text{for all } A, B, C$$
$$\Leftrightarrow \quad t = \min. \tag{2.151}$$

2.4.2   Special Classes of t-Norms

The properties (T1), ..., (T4) which characterise the class of t-norms at all are quite general. Therefore this class is a large one which contains a lot of operations in $[0, 1]$. Among them are also discontinuous ones like the t-norm t_3 which defines the drastic product $A \star B$. Actually it seems impossible to have a more uniform characterisation of all the members of the class of t-norms as given in the definition. Therefore one is often interested in subclasses which cover some of the most interesting candidates of t-norms like our t_i for $i = 0, \ldots, 3$. Different such subclasses have been proposed and are usually presented as parametrized families of functions.

HAMACHER (1978) e.g. considers the one-parametric family of t-norms $t_{H,\gamma}$ with parameter $\gamma \geq 0$ defined as

$$u \, t_{H,\gamma} \, v \quad =_{\text{def}} \quad \frac{uv}{\gamma + (1 - \gamma)(u + v - uv)} \tag{2.152}$$
$$= \quad \frac{uv}{1 + (\gamma - 1)(1 - u)(1 - v)}.$$

According to (2.122) then the dual t-conorms $s_{H,\gamma}$ are characterised by

$$u \, s_{H,\gamma} \, v =_{\text{def}} \frac{u + v - uv - (1 - \gamma)uv}{1 - (1 - \gamma)uv} = 1 - \frac{(1 - u)(1 - v)}{1 + (\gamma - 1)uv}. \tag{2.153}$$

The intersections and unions based via (2.110) and (2.123) on these t-norms, themselves denoted by $\cap_{H,\gamma}$ and $\cup_{H,\gamma}$, contain for $\gamma = 1$ the algebraic product and the algebraic sum. And for $\gamma \to \infty$ the intersections $\cap_{H,\gamma}$ obviously converge toward the drastic product $\star$ and the unions $\cup_{H,\gamma}$ toward the drastic sum $\diamond$.

YAGER (1980) introduced another family of t-norms $t_{Y,p}$ with parameter $p > 0$ by

$$u \, t_{Y,p} \, v =_{\text{def}} 1 - \min\{1, ((1 - u)^p + (1 - v)^p)^{1/p}\}; \tag{2.154}$$

which has as its family of corresponding t-conorms $s_{Y,p}$ the family of functions

$$u \, s_{Y,p} \, v =_{\text{def}} \min\{1, (u^p + v^p)^{1/p}\}. \tag{2.155}$$

The t-norm based intersections which one gets via (2.110) from these t-norms are denoted by $\cap_{Y,p}$. For $p \to 0$ these intersection operations converge toward the drastic product $\star$, and for $p \to \infty$ they converge toward the non-interactive intersection $\cap$. Additionally, for $p = 1$ one has the bounded product $\odot$. Accordingly, via (2.123) one gets the t-norm based unions $\cup_{Y,p}$. For $p \to 0$ they converge toward the drastic sum $\diamond$, and for $p \to \infty$ toward the union $\cup$. Again, $p = 1$ gives the bounded sum $\oplus$.

To prove these convergence properties it is enough to look at the conorms (2.155) and to discuss the limits of $(u^p + v^p)^{1/p}$ for $p \to 0$ as well as for $p \to \infty$. But one has for $u \neq 0 \neq v$ and additionally $u \leq v$ that

$$
\begin{aligned}
\lim_{p \to +0} (u^p + v^p)^{1/p} &= \lim_{p \to +0} \exp(\frac{1}{p} \log(u^p + v^p)) \\
&= \exp(\lim_{p \to +0} \frac{1}{p} \log(u^p + v^p)) \\
&\geq \exp(\lim_{p \to +0} \frac{1}{p} \log(2 \cdot u^p)) \\
&= \exp(\lim_{p \to +0} (\frac{\log 2}{p} + \log u) \quad = \quad \infty
\end{aligned}
$$

holds true and thus also

$$\lim_{p \to +0} u \, s_{Y,p} \, v = 1.$$

For $u = 0$ one also has

$$\lim_{p \to +0} u \, s_{Y,p} \, v = \lim_{p \to +0} (v^p)^{1/p} = v$$

and a corresponding result for $v = 0$. Therefore the limit $p \to 0$ gives the drastic sum.

For the other limit $p \to \infty$ one has in the case that $u = v$

$$
\begin{aligned}
\lim_{p \to \infty} (u^p + v^p)^{1/p} &= \lim_{p \to \infty} (u^p \cdot 2)^{1/p} \\
&= \lim_{p \to \infty} (u \cdot 2^{1/p}) \\
&= u \cdot \exp(\lim_{p \to \infty} \frac{1}{p} \cdot \log 2) \\
&= u \quad = \quad \max\{u, v\}.
\end{aligned}
$$

In the case $u \neq v$ one may additionally assume that $u > v$ with $u = v + w$ for some $w > 0$. Using $a = \frac{u-w}{u}$ and thus having $0 \leq a < 1$ one then finds

$$\lim_{p \to \infty} (u^p + v^p)^{1/p} = \lim_{p \to \infty} (u^p \times (1 + a^p))^{1/p}$$

$$= \quad u \cdot \exp \lim_{p \to \infty} (\frac{1}{p} \cdot \log(1 + a^p))$$
$$= \quad u \cdot \exp 0 \quad = u$$
$$= \quad \max\{u, v\}.$$

Hence also the limit $p \to \infty$ gives the result which was mentioned.

A third family $t_{W,\lambda}$ with parameter $\lambda > -1$ was introduced by WEBER (1983). He defined

$$u \, t_{W,\lambda} \, v =_{\text{def}} \left[\frac{u + v - 1 + \lambda uv}{1 + \lambda} \right]^+ \tag{2.156}$$

and has as the dual t-conorms $s_{W,\lambda}$ hence

$$u \, s_{W,\lambda} \, v =_{\text{def}} \min \left\{ 1, u + v - \frac{\lambda uv}{1 + \lambda} \right\}. \tag{2.157}$$

In parallel he also introduces a separate family of t-conorms $\bar{s}_{W,\lambda}$ with definition

$$u \, \bar{s}_{W,\lambda} \, v =_{\text{def}} \min\{1, u + v + \lambda uv\}, \tag{2.158}$$

and has for them as dual t-norms the parametrized family of functions with definition

$$u \, \bar{t}_{W,\lambda} \, v =_{\text{def}} \left[(1 + \lambda)(u + v - 1 - \frac{\lambda uv}{1 + \lambda}) \right]^+. \tag{2.159}$$

Parameter $\lambda = 0$ here in both cases gives the bounded product and the bounded sum as corresponding t-norm based operations. For $\lambda \to -1$ the t-norms $t_{W,\lambda}$ converge toward the drastic product and the t-norms $\bar{t}_{W,\lambda}$ converge toward the algebraic product. And for $\lambda \to \infty$, finally, the t-norms $t_{W,\lambda}$ converge toward the algebraic product and the t-norms $\bar{t}_{W,\lambda}$ converge toward the drastic product.[2]

To define parametrized families of t-norms via real parameters is one approach toward subclasses of the class of t-norms. Another way is to refer to some method of generation of t-norms out of simpler, e.g. unary, functions. This idea turns out especially well for the class of archimedean t-norms. A t-norm t is called *archimedean* iff t is continuous (as a binary function) and $u \, t \, u < u$ holds true for each $u \in (0, 1)$.

---

[2]At first it looks astonishing that WEBER (1983) introduces even two families of t-norms (2.156) and (2.159). But he really mentions only the families (2.156) and (2.158), i.e. one family of t-norms and one family of t-conorms. And this is connected with his further discussions which concern also other, more general types of many-valued negation operations. In this context the t-norms $t_{W,\lambda}$ and the t-conorms $\bar{s}_{W,\lambda}$ become dual w.r.t. some suitable negation function.

The essential result is that to each archimedean t-norm t there exists a continuous and monotonically decreasing function $f : [0,1] \to [0,\infty]$ with $f(1) = 0$ and for all $u, v \in [0,1]$

$$u\,t\,v = f^{(-1)}\big(f(u) + f(v)\big).$$

Here the *pseudoinverse* $f^{(-1)}$ of f is defined for each $z \in [0,\infty]$ by

$$f^{(-1)}(z) = \begin{cases} f^{-1}(z), & \text{if } z \in [0, f(0)] \\ 0, & \text{if } z \in (f(0), \infty]. \end{cases}$$

And this generating function f is uniquely determined up to a positive factor by the archimedean t-norm t.

Dually a t-conorm s is called *archimedean* iff it is a continuous binary function with always $u\,s\,u > u$. The archimedean t-conorms are exactly the duals of archimedean t-norms. An archimedean t-conorm can be represented as

$$u\,s\,v = g^{[-1]}\big(g(u) + g(v)\big)$$

using a continuous and monotonically increasing function $g : [0,1] \to [0,\infty]$ with $g(0) = 0$. Here one uses another *pseudoinverse*

$$g^{[-1]}(z) = \begin{cases} g^{-1}(z), & \text{if } z \in [0, g(1)] \\ 1, & \text{if } z \in (g(1), \infty]. \end{cases}$$

2.4.3 A Model Theoretic View on General Set Algebraic Operations*

The t-norms we are considering have been introduced by SCHWEIZER/SKLAR (1960, 1961) in studies on statistical metric spaces under the name *triangular norms*. There they appear e.g. in connection with the triangle inequality. But, their essential importance for considerations on fuzzy sets has other sources. One of them is the distinction of interactive and non-interactive set algebraic compositions of fuzzy set. But even more important is another, more theoretical point of view: t-norms are very good candidates for conjunction operations in many-valued logic. The main reason for this is that conditions (T1), . . . , (T4) formulate the kind of minimal constraints one likes to have satisfied by such a conjunction operation. Additionally, one should have in mind that in a canonical manner a conjunction in (many-valued) logic corresponds to an intersection operation for (fuzzy) sets.

It is in this role that generalised, many-valued conjunction operations are responsible for the broad use of t-norms in today's fuzzy set theory. As a kind of "rule" one even has: usually a t-norm can be taken at all places where initially only the min-operation was used. Besides the intersection ∩ the most simple example here is the cartesian product.

But also in the case of the extension principle one uses a (generalised, viz. many-valued) conjunction ∧ which appeared also formally in formulas (2.107) and (2.108) – and whose traditional reading as min-operator can be transformed into reading it as any t-norm. Thus it becomes clear that even in the very first formulation (2.105) of that extension principle for min one can take any other t-norm, i.e. even an interactive combination of the membership degrees $\mu_{A_1}(x_1)$, ..., $\mu_{A_n}(x_n)$.

Another aspect of this reduction of intersection operators for fuzzy sets to some suitable conjunction operation of the logic behind the theory of fuzzy sets now becomes clear: operations for truth degrees determine in a canonical way set algebraic operations on fuzzy sets. Thus, as the set of (truth and membership) degrees $I = [0, 1]$ could become exchanged into another set L, one is also able to change the operations quite widely which one considers given in L. The canonical way from operations in the set of (truth and membership) degrees to their corresponding set algebraic operations for fuzzy sets proceeds "pointwise" for each $a \in \mathcal{X}$, i.e. one defines the membership degree $\mu_C(a)$ for a fuzzy set C which shall be the result of a set algebraic operation applied to fuzzy sets $A_1, \ldots, A_n$ only using the membership degrees $\mu_{A_i}(a)$ for all $i = 1, \ldots, n$.

Mathematically this procedure is meant to consider the class $\mathbb{F}_L(\mathcal{X})$ of all L-fuzzy subsets of X as the direct product

$$\mathbb{F}_L(\mathcal{X}) = \prod_{x \in \mathcal{X}} L.$$

Assuming then that one has given in L an n-ary operation $O^n : L^n \to L$, in the direct product $\mathbb{F}_L(\mathcal{X})$ there is a corresponding operation $\hat{O}^n : \mathbb{F}_L(\mathcal{X})^n \to \mathbb{F}_L(\mathcal{X})$ defined by

$$C = \hat{O}^n(A_1, \ldots, A_n) \quad \Leftrightarrow_{def} \tag{2.160}$$
$$\mu_C(a) = O^n(\mu_{A_1}(a), \ldots, \mu_{A_n}(a)) \quad \text{for each } a \in \mathcal{X}.$$

Using the class term notation of (2.40), this can be written down much more simply as

$$\hat{O}^n(A_1, \ldots, A_n) = \{x \in \mathcal{X} \,||\, O^n(x \,\varepsilon\, A_1, \ldots, x \,\varepsilon\, A_n)\}. \tag{2.161}$$

Here we additionally read the operation O^n in L as defining (via being its truth degree function) a connective $\mathcal{O}^n$ of a system of many-valued logic with L as set of truth degrees. Now it is obvious that all the set algebraic operations we considered earlier are generated this way for $I = [0, 1]$: ∩ by the min-operation, ∪ by the max-operation, • by the product, etc. Therefore, a standard algebraic construction corresponds to the canonical connection between operations on membership degrees and set algebraic operations for fuzzy sets.

This idea produces even more results. To see this, one should have in mind that universal algebra also yields laws for operations in $I\!F_L(\mathcal{X})$, defined via (2.160), (2.161). The reason is that for whole classes of formulas their validity for L is transferred to their validity for suitable direct products. For simplicity a more detailed formulation shall now be given only for binary operations in the truth/membership degree structure L.

Let $*_1, \ldots, *_m$ be (symbols for) binary operations in L. With lower case letters $a, b, c, \ldots$ we denote variables for members of L. In a standard way this vocabulary allows the building of terms to denote the results of the applications of these operations, hence members of L. Such terms are e.g.: $a *_1 b$, $c *_2 c$, b, $(a *_1 c) *_2 a, \ldots$. With terms T_1, T_2 one forms *term equations* $T_1 = T_2$ and *term inequalities* $T_1 \neq T_2$. The disjunctions of one term equation and finitely many term inequalities are the *elementary* HORN-*formulas* for L. These elementary HORN-formulas together with all the formulas which can be built out of them using the conjunction connective and the quantifiers for "there exist" and "for all" relative to L, form the HORN-*formulas* for L. Such HORN-formulas for L express arithmetic laws for L and its operations. By HORN-formulas one can express e.g.: the commutativity of $*_1$, the associativity of $*_3$, the distributivity of $*_1$ over $*_2$, etc. If in a HORN-formula H for L one exchanges the (symbols for the) operations $*_1, \ldots, *_m$ with (the symbols for) those operations $\hat{*}_1, \ldots, \hat{*}_m$ in $I\!F_L(\mathcal{X})$ which are defined via (2.160), (2.161), and at the same time exchanges the variables for members of L by – corresponding – variables for members of $I\!F_L(\mathcal{X})$, then there results a HORN-formula $\hat{H}$ for $I\!F_L(\mathcal{X})$. Using this notation, the following principle holds true.

Transfer Principle: *If a* HORN-*formula H for* L *is true in the structure* L *of membership degrees, then the corresponding* HORN-*formula $\hat{H}$ for* $I\!F_L(\mathcal{X})$ *is true in the structure* $I\!F_L(\mathcal{X})$ *of the L-fuzzy subsets of $\mathcal{X}$.*

By the way, all the laws we discussed in (2.75) to (2.84) in this manner result from arithmetic properties of the real interval $[0, 1]$.

A further, general question concerns the structure of the set L of membership degrees. It may be formulated as the problem whether L should have some (minimal) algebraic structure. Unfortunately, no general results are available for this problem. Nevertheless, one often assumes that L has the structure of a distributive lattice with zero and unit element. Usually one also assumes completeness and finite distributivity of this lattice – at least if one considers set algebraic operations defined á la (2.85), (2.86). Essentially

it seems to be preferable to have, besides the idempotent lattice, another
non idempotent "product" $\bowtie$, sometimes also called "context" operation.
This additional operation is usually supposed to be commutative and
associative, to have the unit element of the lattice as a neutral element, and
to be monotonously nondecreasing w.r.t. the lattice ordering $\preceq$. For $\mathsf{L} = [0,1]$
these "products" are just the t-norms characterised by (T1),..., (T4).

Additionally, it is often quite useful to have also a *relative pseudocom-
plementation* for $\bowtie$, a so-called *residuation* $\rhd$, which is monotonically nondecreasing in its second argument relative to the lattice ordering $\preceq$, which is
monotonically nonincreasing in its first argument, and for which the characteristic relation

$$(a \bowtie b) \preceq c \quad \text{iff} \quad a \preceq (b \rhd c). \tag{2.162}$$

holds true. Thus L often is supposed to be a *residuated lattice*.

But, depending on actual applications, these structural assumptions for L
can be modified almost indefinitely.

2.5 Fuzzy Numbers and Their Arithmetic

2.5.1 Fuzzy Numbers and Fuzzy Intervals

In Section 2.2 we introduced fuzzy (real) numbers intuitively as imprecisely
given or imprecisely determined reals. Here we will define fuzzy numbers in
a mathematically strict manner and discuss properties of them.

A very basic idea connected with the intuition that a fuzzy number should
represent some imprecisely determined numerical value is that the membership function of a fuzzy number should not have distinct local maximal points.
Hence fuzzy numbers should be "convex" in some suitable sense.

Generally, a fuzzy set $A \in I\!F(I\!R)$ is called *convex*, iff all (strong) α-cuts
of A are intervals, i.e. themselves convex sets in the usual sense. Equivalently,
a fuzzy subset A of the real line is convex iff for all $a, b, c \in I\!R$ there holds
true

$$a \leq c \leq b \Rightarrow \mu_A(c) \geq \min\{\mu_A(a), \mu_A(b)\}. \tag{2.163}$$

The characteristic difference between a convex and a nonconvex fuzzy subset
of $I\!R$ is shown in Fig. 2.6 where the fuzzy set A is a convex one, but B is not.

This notion of convexity which is characterised by (2.163) for fuzzy subsets
of $I\!R$, in exactly the same way can be defined for fuzzy subsets $A \in I\!F(\mathcal{X})$
of other universes of discourse. The only essential point is that in $\mathcal{X}$ one has
to have a notion which corresponds to the usual "betweenness" relation for

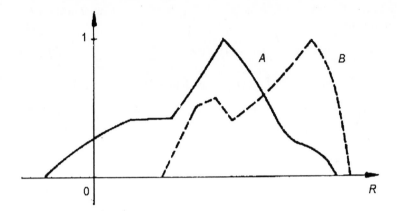

Figure 2.6: Convex vs. non-convex fuzzy sets

real numbers, i.e. one has to have a notion of interval $[a, b]$ with endpoints a, b because then (2.163) can be understood as

$$c \in [a, b] \;\Rightarrow\; \mu_A(c) \geq \min\{\mu_A(a), \mu_A(b)\}$$

which itself could have been taken as a definition for the convexity of A.

A fuzzy set $A \in I\!\!F(I\!\!R)$ is called a *fuzzy (real) number*, iff A is convex and if there exists exactly one real number a with $\mu_A(a) = 1$. In the case that A is only convex and normal, then A is called a *fuzzy interval*. Thus each fuzzy number is also a unimodal fuzzy set. And the unimodal fuzzy intervals are just the fuzzy numbers.

The kernel of a fuzzy interval is a crisp interval. Hence fuzzy numbers and fuzzy intervals generalise the principal idea of *interval arithmetic*. This field of numerical mathematics arose out of the usual calculus of errors and is based on the idea of working directly with intervals instead of doing this with real numbers and their error bounds. The core of the further generalisation from crisp to fuzzy intervals is the observation that crisp intervals have to have precisely fixed endpoints – but that for fuzzy sets and intervals one has a certain vagueness concerning their "true" endpoints. (The reader who likes to read more about traditional interval arithmetic or interval mathematics is referred to MOORE (1966, 1979), ALEFELD/HEREZBERGER (1974) and NEUMAIER (1990).)

2.5.2 Arithmetic Operations

Calculating with fuzzy numbers and fuzzy intervals first needs the definition of the basic arithmetic operations for them. For this one applies the extension principle (2.105). Therefore the *sum* $S := A \oplus B$ of two fuzzy numbers or intervals is determined as

$$\mu_S(a) = \sup_{x \in \mathbb{R}} \min\{\mu_A(x), \mu_B(a - x)\} \quad \text{for all } a \in \mathbb{R}. \tag{2.164}$$

In the same way the *difference* $D := A \ominus B$ is defined as

$$\mu_D(a) = \sup_{x \in \mathbb{R}} \min\{\mu_A(x), \mu_B(x - a)\} \quad \text{for all } a \in \mathbb{R}, \tag{2.165}$$

and the *product* $P := A \odot B$ as

$$\mu_P(a) = \sup_{\substack{x, y \in \mathbb{R} \\ a = xy}} \min\{\mu_A(x), \mu_B(y)\} \quad \text{for all } a \in \mathbb{R}. \tag{2.166}$$

The fuzzy sets resulting from these definitions are always fuzzy intervals if A, B are intervals, and they are fuzzy numbers for fuzzy numbers A, B. Also the *negative* $N = {}^-A$ of a fuzzy interval is defined in this way by

$$\mu_N(a) = \mu_A(-a) \quad \text{for each } a \in \mathbb{R}. \tag{2.167}$$

But one has to be cautious in defining a quotient of fuzzy intervals. One first defines under the additional assumption $0 \notin \text{supp}\,(B)$ the *reciprocal* $K := B^{-1}$ of a fuzzy interval B by

$$\mu_K(a) = \begin{cases} \mu_B(1/a) & \text{for all } a \text{ with } 1/a \in \text{supp}\,(B), \\ 0 & \text{otherwise.} \end{cases} \tag{2.168}$$

Using this and again assuming $0 \notin \text{supp}\,(B)$, one defines the *quotient* $Q := A \odot B$ as $A \odot B =_{\text{def}} A \odot B^{-1}$ which yields for the membership function the characterisation

$$\mu_Q(a) = \sup_{\substack{x, y \in \mathbb{R} \\ a = x/y}} \min\{\mu_A(x), \mu_B(y)\} \quad \text{for all } a \in \mathbb{R}. \tag{2.169}$$

Without the assumption $0 \notin \text{supp}\,(B)$ neither the fuzzy set B^{-1} nor the fuzzy set $A \odot B$ need to be a fuzzy interval, even in the case that A, B are fuzzy intervals.

These arithmetical operations for fuzzy numbers and fuzzy intervals generalise the usual arithmetical operations for the real numbers as well as the arithmetical operations of interval arithmetic. With them together one can define further arithmetical operations also based upon the extension principle and related to these basic operations in the same way as the t-norm based set algebraic operations are related to the most elementary ones $\cap, \cup$. To do this one simply has to apply a generalised version of the extension principle which refers to some t-norm instead of the use

of the min-operator in (2.105). But, in distinction to the situation with the set algebraic operations, up to now those generalisations have not found specific interest.

Many laws which hold true for the arithmetic of the real numbers also
generalise to these operations (2.164) to (2.169) for fuzzy intervals. But not
all of them do. For addition and multiplication of fuzzy intervals one has
commutativity as well as *associativity*. But *distributivity* does not hold true
unrestrictedly. Nevertheless, in the case that $0 \notin \operatorname{supp}(A)$ and $0 < \operatorname{supp}(B \odot C)$, i.e. $0 < x$ for all $x \in \operatorname{supp}(B \odot C)$, or in the case that A is a (crisp)
singleton one has for such fuzzy intervals $A, B, C \in I\!F(I\!R)$

$$A \odot (B \oplus C) = (A \odot B) \oplus (A \odot C). \tag{2.170}$$

Moreover, in any case one has instead of the distributive law the subdistributivity

$$A \odot (B \oplus C) \subseteqq (A \odot B) \oplus (A \odot C). \tag{2.171}$$

Furthermore one has to have in mind that ^-A is not necessarily the additive
inverse of A, because in general one has $A \oplus {}^-A \neq \mathbf{o}$ for the fuzzy number
"zero" $\mathbf{o}$ with $\mu_{\mathbf{o}}(x) = 1$ for $x = 0$, $\mu_{\mathbf{o}}(x) = 0$ for $x \neq 0$. Nevertheless this
fuzzy number $\mathbf{o}$ yet is the only fuzzy number G with $A \oplus G = A$ for each fuzzy
number A. For an example which illustrates these arithmetic operations for

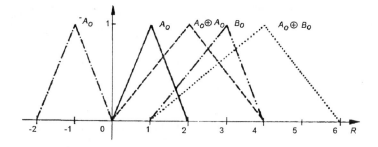

Figure 2.7: Sums and a negative of fuzzy numbers

fuzzy numbers look at Fig. 2.7 with the fuzzy numbers A_0, B_0 shown there.
Then one has $A_0 \oplus B_0, A_0 \oplus A_0$ and $^-A_0$ as shown in Fig. 2.7. Additionally
Fig. 2.8 shows $A_0 \oplus {}^-A_0$ as well as $(A_0 \oplus B_0) \ominus A_0$. Thus one has $A_0 \oplus {}^-A_0 \neq \mathbf{o}$
and also e.g. $(A_0 \oplus B_0) \ominus A_0 \neq B_0$. If furthermore, one tries to solve the
equations

$$A_0 \oplus X = B_0 \quad \text{and} \quad B_0 \oplus Y = A_0 \tag{2.172}$$

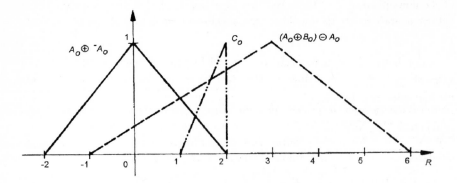

Figure 2.8: Results of arithmetic operations

with A_0, B_0 as presented in Fig. 2.7, then one immediately recognises that the fuzzy number C_0 as shown in Fig. 2.8 is a solution of equation $A_0 \oplus X = B_0$. But the equation $B_0 \oplus Y = A_0$ does not have any solution: in the case that Y would be a solution one would have to have $\mu_Y(-2) = 1$ and hence $\mu_{B_0} \oplus_Y (0) \geq 1/2$ contradicting $\mu_{A_0}(0) = 0$.

By the way, the unsolvability of the equation $B_0 \oplus Y = A_0$ also can be seen as a corollary of the fact that the equation

$$(1, 4) + x = (0, 2)$$

as an equation of usual interval arithmetic does not have any solution. But this equation for our example is the equation

$$\mathrm{supp}\,(B_0) + x = \mathrm{supp}\,(A_0).$$

This type of reduction of problems of fuzzy arithmetic to problems of interval arithmetic coresponds to the fact that for w.r.t. definitions (2.164) to (2.169) one has for all the α-cuts

$$
\begin{aligned}
(^-A)^{>\alpha} &= \{-a \mid a \in A^{>\alpha}\}, & (2.173)\\
(A \circledast B)^{>\alpha} &= \{a * b \mid a \in A^{>\alpha} \text{ and } b \in B^{>\alpha}\} & (2.174)
\end{aligned}
$$

with $\circledast$ any one of the operations $\oplus, \ominus, \odot, \oslash$. In particular, each α-cut $(^-A)^{>\alpha}$, $(A \circledast B)^{>\alpha}$ is an interval for convex fuzzy sets A, B.

Generally, such a treatment "cut by cut" enables a reduction of problems of fuzzy arithmetic to (families of) corresponding problems of interval arithmetic. In all those cases in which an arithmetic rule holds true in interval arithmetic, then the very same rule holds true in fuzzy arithmetic, simply because of (2.174). In all those cases in which an arithmetic rule holds true in interval arithmetic only under some additional assumption, the "transfer" of this rule to fuzzy arithmetic holds true for all those fuzzy intervals from $I\!F(I\!R)$ for which all their α-cuts satisfy these additional assumptions. In this way e.g. (2.170), (2.171) result from corresponding rules of interval arithmetic.[3] It is, however, essential for this type of "transfer" of results from interval arithmetic to fuzzy arithmetic to have the basic operations of fuzzy arithmetic as in (2.164) to (2.169) based on the use of the min-operator, i.e. to have them based on the extension principle in its basic form (2.105). If instead, one uses some other t-norm for the min-operator in (2.105) or in (2.164) to (2.169) respectively, then one in general loses this possibility of reduction "cut by cut".

As another example of the use of the extension principle (2.105) in the realm of fuzzy arithmetic we consider the fuzzy maximum. For any fuzzy numbers or fuzzy intervals $A, B \in I\!F(I\!R)$ their *fuzzy maximum* $\widetilde{\max}(A, B)$ is defined as

$$C := \widetilde{\max}(A, B):$$
$$\mu_C(z) = \sup_{\substack{x,y \in R \\ z=\max\{x,y\}}} \min\{\mu_A(x), \mu_B(y)\}. \qquad (2.175)$$

Fig. 2.9 explains that, geometrically, it is very simple to determine the membership function of $\widetilde{\max}(A, B)$ out of the membership functions μ_A, μ_B. Having in mind that $z = \max\{x, y\}$ holds true for $z = x \geq y$ or $z = y \geq x$, one gets from (2.175)

$$\mu_C(z)$$
$$= \max\left\{ \sup_{y \leq z} \min\{\mu_A(z), \mu_B(y)\}, \sup_{x \leq z} \min\{\mu_A(x), \mu_B(z)\}\right\}$$
$$= \max\left\{ \min\left\{\mu_A(z), \sup_{y \leq z} \mu_B(y)\right\},\right.$$
$$\left. \min\left\{\sup_{x \leq z} \mu_A(x), \mu_B(z)\right\}\right\}. \qquad (2.176)$$

This immediately shows that $\widetilde{\max}(A, B)$ is determined correctly in Fig. 2.9. Even arithmetically (2.176) is preferable over (2.175) for determining the fuzzy maximum $\widetilde{\max}(A, B)$.

---

[3] The distributive law (2.170) holds true iff it holds true in usual interval arithmetic for all the α-cuts. A more detailed characterisation of all the cases in which this corresponding distributive law holds true in the usual interval arithmetic is given e.g. in RATSCHEK (1971).

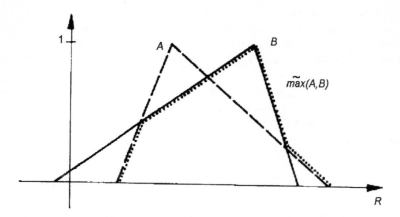

Figure 2.9: Fuzzy maximum of fuzzy numbers

The very same approach can be used to define a *fuzzy minimum* $\widetilde{\min}\,(A,B)$ for fuzzy numbers or intervals A, B. And these fuzzy maxima and fuzzy minima can immediately also be defined for more than two fuzzy intervals.

2.5.3 Fuzzy Numbers of Restricted Shape and Their Representation

For the numerical treatment another aspect is of main importance too. Up to now in our examples we have considered only the "linear" arithmetic operations $\oplus$ and $\ominus$, and we also have chosen only fuzzy numbers A_0, B_0 with "triangular shaped" membership functions. Therefore also $A_0 \oplus B_0$ and of $A_0 \ominus B_0$ did have such "triangular shaped" membership functions. Thus, knowledge of the kernel and of the support of $A_0 \oplus B_0$ and $A_0 \ominus B_0$ did suffice to completely determine the corresponding membership functions. For the fuzzy maximum $\widetilde{\max}\,(A_0, B_0)$, and moreover also for the product $A_0 \odot B_0$ and for $A_0 \oslash B_0$ the situation is not so simple. Figs. 2.10 and 2.11 represent the membership functions for this product and for two quotients. Their form is not of a "triangular shape".

Therefore, especially for the numerical treatment of fuzzy numbers and fuzzy intervals it seems to be an interesting possibility to discuss some restrictions to be imposed on the form of the membership functions of the fuzzy intervals to be considered. Arithmetically this means restricting the membership functions to some prespecified types of functions. An elementary approach toward this idea is to split, for any fuzzy number $A \in I\!\!F(I\!\!R)$ with $\mu_A(a_0) = 1$, the membership function μ_A into two functions: the monotonously nonde-

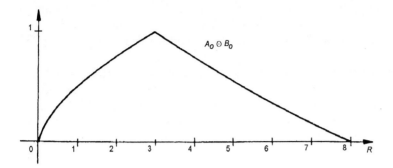

Figure 2.10: A product of fuzzy numbers

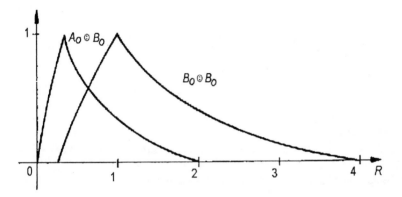

Figure 2.11: Quotients of fuzzy numbers

creasing part defined on the interval $(-\infty, a_0)$ and the monotonously non-increasing part defined on the interval (a_0, ∞). And the types of these two "partial membership functions" may become restricted, e.g. to (piecewise) linear functions as for A_0, B_0 and as in (2.42). If, additionally, the support of A is the interval (a_1, a_2), then de facto only the restrictions of the membership function $\mu_A : \mathbb{R} \to [0,1]$ to the intervals (a_1, a_0) and (a_0, a_2) are of interest. These restrictions shall be denoted by μ_A^L, μ_A^R, respectively.

An L/R-*representation* of a fuzzy number A is given iff A is characterised just by the restrictions μ_A^L, μ_A^R of its membership function. As fuzzy numbers with *linear* L/R-representation we shall denote those fuzzy numbers A for which the restrictions μ_A^L, μ_A^R are linear functions. Often such fuzzy numbers with linear L/R-representations are also called *triangular* fuzzy num-

bers. Accordingly fuzzy intervals A, with kernel $A^{\geq 1} = (a_0, a_0')$ and support
$\text{supp}(A) = (a_1, a_2)$, usually are called *trapezoidal* fuzzy numbers iff the restrictions of the membership function μ_A to the intervals (a_1, a_0) and (a_0', a_2)
are linear functions.

Computing with triangular fuzzy numbers becomes especially simple because only the "characteristic" numbers a_0, a_1, a_2, which are determined by
$\mu_A(a_0) = 1$ and $\text{supp}(A) = (a_1, a_2)$, uniquely determine such a fuzzy number
A. Moreover, only these "characteristic" numbers are needed to compute sum,
difference, and the negative of triangular fuzzy numbers. Let us introduce the
notation

$$A = < a_0; a_1, a_2 > \quad \text{iff} \tag{2.177}$$
$$\mu_A(a_0) = 1 \quad \text{and} \quad \text{supp}(A) = (a_1, a_2).$$

For triangular fuzzy numbers $A = < a_0; a_1, a_2 >, B = < b_0; b_1, b_2 >$ one then
immediately has

$$A \oplus B \quad = \quad < a_0 + b_0; a_1 + b_1, a_2 + b_2 >, \tag{2.178}$$
$$A \ominus B \quad = \quad < a_0 - b_0; a_1 - b_2, a_2 - b_1 >, \tag{2.179}$$
$$^-A \quad = \quad < -a_0; -a_2, -a_1 > . \tag{2.180}$$

Unfortunately, product and quotient of triangular fuzzy numbers need not
themselves be triangular fuzzy numbers.

For simple and fast computations with fuzzy numbers, nevertheless, a
global restriction to triangular fuzzy numbers is often preferable. Therefore
approximations of the product and the quotient of triangular fuzzy numbers
by triangular fuzzy numbers become of interest. Possible approximations in
the case of $a_1, b_1 \geq 0$ are

$$A \odot B \quad \approx \quad < a_0 \cdot b_0; a_1 \cdot b_1, a_2 \cdot b_2 > \quad \text{if} \quad a_1, b_1 \geq 0, \tag{2.181}$$
$$A \oslash B \quad \approx \quad < a_0/b_0; a_1/b_2, a_2/b_1 > \quad \text{if} \quad a_1 \geq 0, b_1 > 0, \tag{2.182}$$

which allow approximation of products and quotients of all triangular fuzzy
numbers A, B with $0 \notin \text{supp}(A)$ and $0 \notin \text{supp}(B)$. For $0 \notin \text{supp}(B)$ an
approximation of the reciprocal is provided by

$$B^{-1} \approx < 1/b_0; 1/b_2, 1/b_1 > . \tag{2.183}$$

Without any restriction concerning the supports $\text{supp}(A), \text{supp}(B)$ one
has for $\text{supp}(A \odot B) = (c_l, c_r)$ even

$$c_l \quad = \quad \min\{a_1 \cdot b_1, a_1 \cdot b_2, a_2 \cdot b_1, a_2 \cdot b_2\}, \tag{2.184}$$
$$c_r \quad = \quad \max\{a_1 \cdot b_1, a_1 \cdot b_2, a_2 \cdot b_1, a_2 \cdot b_2\} \tag{2.185}$$

which yields the further approximation

$$A \odot B \approx\; < a_0 \cdot b_0; c_l, c_r > . \tag{2.186}$$

Of course, instead of discussing only triangular fuzzy numbers A with their linear L/R-representations, as done up to now, one can use also other types of functions for $\mu_A{}^L, \mu_A{}^R$, even quite different types for $\mu_A{}^L$ and $\mu_A{}^R$, e.g. $\mu_A{}^L$ may be a linear function and $\mu_A{}^R$ an exponential function. DUBOIS/PRADE (1978) have approached this problem quite generally. They assume of the restrictions $\mu_A{}^L, \mu_A{}^R$ that they are determined via some reference functions $L, R : I\!R \rightarrow [0, 1]$. These reference functions are supposed to satisfy that:

(1) $L(0) = R(0) = 1$,

(2) L, R are monotonically nonincreasing for positive arguments.

On this basis and with additional parameters $a_0 \in I\!R$ and $q, p > 0$ one introduces the "partial membership functions" $\mu_A{}^L, \mu_A{}^R$ as

$$\mu_A{}^L(x) = L((a_0 - x)/q) \quad \text{for all } x \leq a_0, \tag{2.187}$$
$$\mu_A{}^R(x) = R((x - a_0)/p) \quad \text{for all } x \geq a_0. \tag{2.188}$$

The notational convention of (2.177) for triangular fuzzy numbers can easily be transferred to this more general situation. But, instead of the reference in (2.177) to the "central point" a_0 and the support (a_1, a_2) as characterising data, now for given reference functions L, R one has to refer to the parameters q, p together with the "central point" a_0. Therefore one writes

$$A =\; < a_0; q, p >_{L/R} \qquad \text{iff} \tag{2.189}$$
$$\mu_A{}^L(x) = L\left((a_0 - x)/q\right) \quad \text{and} \quad \mu_A{}^R(x) = R\left((x - a_0)/p\right).$$

The main new point here is that one cannot use the borderline points a_1, a_2 of the support interval as parameters. And this is an immediate consequence of the fact that the choice $L(x) = R(x) = \exp(-x)$ satisfies (1), (2), and that in this case the support $\text{supp}(A)$ is not bounded. Of course, choosing L, R as linear functions $L(x) = 1 - bx$ and $R(x) = 1 - cx$ results in simple relationships between the parameters a_1, a_2 and q, p :

$$q = b(a_0 - a_1), \qquad p = c(a_2 - a_0). \tag{2.190}$$

Hence in this case it is easy to transform the representations (2.177) and (2.189) into one another.

An advantage of the representation (2.189) again is that one gets simple representations for sums, differences, products, and quotients like the ones in (2.178) to (2.182). Starting from

$$A =\; < a; q, p >_{L/R}, \qquad B =\; < b; q', p' >_{L/R} \tag{2.191}$$

one immediately has

$$A \oplus B \;=\; < a + b; q + q', p + p' >_{L/R}, \tag{2.192}$$

$$^{-}A \;=\; < -a; p, q >_{R/L}, \tag{2.193}$$

which by $A \ominus B = A \oplus {}^{-}B$ also gives the difference. But one has to be careful here and to have in mind that in (2.193) the left and right reference functions L, R change their roles! Hence one obtains only for $L = R$ a really simple L/R-representation of the difference $A \ominus B$ as a result of (2.192), (2.193).

Other useful and easily computable approximations of the product of fuzzy numbers in L/R-representation, again as a fuzzy number in L/R-form, are given by DUBOIS/PRADE (1978, 1980). Assuming $0 \notin \mathrm{supp}\,(A)$ and $0 \notin \mathrm{supp}\,(B)$ they offer the approximation

$$A \odot B \;\approx\; < ab; aq' + bq, ap' + bp >_{L/R} \quad \text{for } a, b > 0 \tag{2.194}$$

for the case that additionally p and p' are small relative to a or b, respectively. And for the case that p and p' are not small relative to a or b, respectively, they propose

$$A \odot B \;\approx\; < ab; aq' + bq - qq', ap' + bp - pp' >_{L/R} \quad \text{for } a, b > 0. \tag{2.195}$$

This last formula reduces to (2.181) for linear reference functions L, R.

Via $(^{-}A \odot B) = {}^{-}(A \odot B) = A \odot {}^{-}B$ one can extend (2.194), (2.195) to larger classes of fuzzy numbers in L/R-form. Again this makes it easy to handle approximations in L/R-form only for $L = R$ (or if one has $L = R$ after a parameter transformation).

The same approach works for the quotient as well. The starting point is the following approximation which parallels (2.193):

$$B^{-1} \;\approx\; < 1/b; p'/b^2, q'/b^2 >_{R/L} . \tag{2.196}$$

Of course, one has to assume $0 \notin \mathrm{supp}\,(B)$. This then yields a good approximation at least in the neighbourhood of $1/b$. Again, by (2.196) together with (2.194), (2.195) one computes L/R-representations of the quotients $A \oslash B$. All together, thus, L/R-representations and these approximations give easily computable algorithms for the arithmetic operations on fuzzy numbers in L/R-form.

There are numerous applications of fuzzy arithmetic to computations involving fuzzy numerical data or incompletely specified parameters. For further information we refer the interested reader to DUBOIS/PRADE (1980), KAUFMANN/GUPTA (1985) and Section 3.4.

2.5.4   Integrating Fuzzy Functions

A completely different aspect of fuzzy numerical data becomes possible if one discusses the problems of integrating a fuzzy function or of integrating a crisp function over a fuzzy domain. The last situation is what happens if one wishes to determine the area of a domain with a fuzzy borderline. In these cases it is natural to treat the value of such an integral as a fuzzy number. Different approaches toward this problem are possible. Some of them will be considered now.

Suppose that $\tilde{f}(x)$ is a fuzzy function as defined in Section 2.2. This means according to (2.63) considering a family $\{\tilde{f}(x) \mid x \in [a, b] \subset I\!\!R\}$ of fuzzy numbers. The range of $\tilde{f}$ shall be $\mathcal{Y} \subseteq I\!\!R$. Moreover we assume that for each $c \in (0, 1)$ equation

$$\mu_{\tilde{f}}(y; x) = c, \tag{2.197}$$

which is characteristic for the membership function, having exactly two continuous solutions.

$$y = f_c^+(x); \qquad y = f_c^-(x). \tag{2.198}$$

And for $c = 1$ equation (2.197) shall have a unique continuous solution

$$y = f(x). \tag{2.199}$$

We additionally assume that f^+ and f^- are determined such that one has for all $c_2 \leq c_1$:

$$f_{c_2}^-(x) \leq f_{c_1}^-(x) \leq f_{c_1}^+(x) \leq f_{c_2}^+(x). \tag{2.200}$$

Intuitively it is very natural now, cf. DUBOIS/PRADE (1980), to refer to the c-level lines and the integration over these lines to define the fuzzy integral value I as the fuzzy number with membership function given by

$$\mu_I\left(\int_a^b f_c^-(x)\,\mathrm{d}x\right) = \mu_I\left(\int_a^b f_c^+(x)\,\mathrm{d}x\right) = c \tag{2.201}$$

and

$$\mu_I\left(\int_a^b f(x)\,\mathrm{d}x\right) = 1. \tag{2.202}$$

By the above mentioned continuity assumptions these integrals do exist.

Reference to the extension principle (2.105) in this case would give exactly the same result. Obviously this also is a natural generalisation of the well-known RIEMANN integral for the case of a fuzzy integrand.

This approach proves especially useful in the case that the integrand itself is given in L/R-form

$$\tilde{f}(x) = \ < f(x); s(x), t(x) >_{L/R}; \quad x \in [a, b] \tag{2.203}$$

in such a way that the (usual) functions f, s, t are integrable on $[a, b]$. Computation according to (2.201) and (2.202) yields

$$I = \left\langle \int_a^b f(x)\,dx; \ \int_a^b s(x)\,dx; \ \int_a^b t(x)\,dx \right\rangle_{L/R}. \tag{2.204}$$

As a second approach toward fuzzy integrals now, contrary to the previous case, suppose that f is a crisp real function and that the integration interval has the *fuzzy* sets A, B as its boundary points. In this situation the extension principle gives for the membership function of the fuzzy integral I the relation

$$\mu_I(z) = \sup_{(u,v) \in \mathcal{J}} \min\{\mu_A(u), \mu_B(v)\}, \tag{2.205}$$

with $\mathcal{J} = \{(u, v) \mid z = \int_u^v f(w)\,dw\}$ (cf. DUBOIS/PRADE (1980)).

There is a nice simplification of formula (2.205). In the case that F is an antiderivative of f one has

$$\mu_I(z) = \sup_{x \in \mathbb{R}} \min \left\{ \mu_A(x), \sup_{\substack{v \\ z = F(v) - F(x)}} \mu_B(v) \right\}. \tag{2.206}$$

Of course, in essentially the same manner one can – via the extension principle – also discuss fuzzy integrals over fuzzy functions and fuzzy intervals. But the results hardly look promising.

For some linearity properties and for results concerning the set algebraic union of fuzzy components we refer to DUBOIS/PRADE (1980).

And as a concluding remark we mention that yet another approach toward integration of a crisp function over a fuzzy interval starts from the idea that the fuzzy interval is determined by its membership function $\mu_C(x)$ instead of having its fuzzy boundary points A and B. Then a *crisp* integral value is provided by

$$J = \int_{\mathbb{R}} \mu_C(x) f(x)\,dx. \tag{2.207}$$

3 Fuzzified Relationships

3.1 Fuzzy Relations

3.1.1 Basic Notions and Operations

Our examples given in Section 2.2 show that fuzzy relations, i.e. more or less vague relationships between some fixed number of objects, can formally become treated like fuzzy sets. For simplicity further on we shall restrict our considerations mainly to binary relations.

We now suppose to have a class whose members are ordered pairs as the universe of discourse $\mathcal{Y}$. Usually one additionally assumes that $\mathcal{Y}$ is of the form

$$\mathcal{Y} = \mathcal{X}_1 \times \mathcal{X}_2 = \{(x, y) \mid x \in \mathcal{X}_1 \text{ and } y \in \mathcal{X}_2\}.$$

A *fuzzy (binary) relation* R in $\mathcal{Y}$ then is nothing other than a fuzzy subset of $\mathcal{Y}$, which means $R \in IF(\mathcal{Y})$. The membership degree $\mu_R(a, b)$ in this case is interpreted as the degree to which the fuzzy relation R holds true for the objects (a, b). As usual also for fuzzy sets, we read $\mu_R(a, b) = 1$ as the fact that the fuzzy relation R for (a, b) completely, certainly, really, ... holds true, and we read $\mu_R(a, b) = 0$ as the fact that the fuzzy relation R for (a, b) does not hold true at all.

In Section 2.2 as examples of fuzzy relations we have already considered the fuzzy equality R_0: "nearly equal" with the variants (2.55) to (2.57) for its membership function, as well as the fuzzy ordering relation R_1: "more or less smaller than" with membership function (2.59). Both are examples of binary fuzzy relations.

In the case that the universe of discourse $\mathcal{Y}$, within which a fuzzy relation R is considered, is a finite set of ordered pairs and at the same time a (usual, i.e. nonfuzzy) cartesian product $\mathcal{Y} = \mathcal{X}_1 \times \mathcal{X}_2$ of finite sets, then R can be represented by a matrix with elements from $[0, 1]$. For $\mathcal{X}_1 = \{a_1, a_2, a_3\}$ and

$\mathcal{X}_2 = \{b_1, b_2, b_3, b_4\}$, e.g., by

$$
R_3 \; : \quad
\begin{array}{c}
\\
a_1 \\
a_2 \\
a_3
\end{array}
\begin{array}{cccc}
b_1 & b_2 & b_3 & b_4 \\
\left(0.8 \right. & 0.3 & 0 & 0 \\
1 & 0.7 & 1 & 0.2 \\
\left. 0.6 \right. & 0.9 & 1 & 0.5
\end{array}
\qquad (3.1)
$$

a fuzzy relation R_3 in $\mathcal{X}_1 \times \mathcal{X}_2$ is described for which one has e.g. $\mu_R(a_1, b_2) = 0.3$ and $\mu_R(a_3, b_4) = 0.5$.

Obviously a fuzzy relation $R \in \mathbb{F}(\mathcal{X}_1 \times \mathcal{X}_2)$ results if one starts from fuzzy sets $A \in \mathbb{F}(\mathcal{X}_1)$, $B \in \mathbb{F}(\mathcal{X}_2)$, constructs their fuzzy cartesian product $A \otimes B \in \mathbb{F}(\mathcal{X}_1 \times \mathcal{X}_2)$, and takes $R = A \otimes B$. But not every fuzzy relation $R \in \mathbb{F}(\mathcal{X}_1 \times \mathcal{X}_2)$ is a fuzzy cartesian product, nevertheless for each $R \in \mathbb{F}(\mathcal{X}_1 \times \mathcal{X}_2)$ there exist fuzzy sets $A \in \mathbb{F}(\mathcal{X}_1)$, $B \in \mathbb{F}(\mathcal{X}_2)$ such that $R \subseteq A \otimes B$.

For each fuzzy relation $R \in \mathbb{F}(\mathcal{Y})$ its support is a crisp, i.e. usual relation in $\mathcal{Y}$, and the same holds true for each α-cut $R^{>\alpha}$ and each strong α-cut $R^{\geq\alpha}$. Caused by the fact that fuzzy relations are only special fuzzy sets, every proposition which holds true for fuzzy sets in general also holds true for fuzzy relations. And each operation which is defined for fuzzy sets, in general is also applicable to fuzzy relations, and its result is again a fuzzy relation – with the exception of some projection operations which may produce fuzzy sets which are not fuzzy relations.

Additionally there are other operations defined only for (fuzzy) relations. The most essential ones of such operations are: taking the inverse relation and taking the composition, i.e. the relational product of two fuzzy relations.

For a fuzzy relation $R \in \mathbb{F}(\mathcal{Y})$ the *inverse relation* for R, denoted R^{-1}, is defined by:

$$
S := R^{-1}: \quad \mu_S(x, y) =_{\text{def}} \mu_R(y, x) \quad \text{for all } (x, y) \in \mathcal{Y}. \qquad (3.2)
$$

Thus the degree to which an inverse fuzzy relation R^{-1} holds true for objects (a, b) is the same degree to which the original relation R holds true for the objects (b, a).

For fuzzy relations $R \in \mathbb{F}(\mathcal{X}_1 \times \mathcal{X}_2)$ and $S \in \mathbb{F}(\mathcal{X}_2 \times \mathcal{X}_3)$ as well as, more restricted, for fuzzy relations $R, S \in \mathbb{F}(\mathcal{Y})$ with $\mathcal{Y} \subseteq \mathcal{X} \times \mathcal{X}$, one defines their *composition* or *relational product* $R \circ S$ by the membership function:

$$
T := R \circ S \; :
$$
$$
\mu_T(x, y) =_{\text{def}} \sup_{z \in \mathcal{X}_2} \min\{\mu_R(x, z), \mu_S(z, y)\}
$$
$$
\text{for all } (x, y) \in \mathcal{X}_1 \times \mathcal{X}_3. \qquad (3.3)
$$

Each α-cut, and hence also the support as the 0-cut, as well as each strong α-cut of an inverse fuzzy relation R^{-1} is, in the standard sense, the inverse relation of the crisp relation $R^{>\alpha}$ or $R^{\geq\alpha}$. For the α-cuts of the relational product one has an analogous reduction to the crisp case:

$$(R \circ S)^{>\alpha} = (R^{>\alpha}) \circ (S^{>\alpha}). \tag{3.4}$$

Here the sign $\circ$ means the fuzzy relational product on the left hand side and the standard relational product on the right hand side. A corresponding equation holds true for all the strong α-cuts.

It is an easy exercise to prove for fuzzy relations R, S, T the associativity of the relational product

$$(R \circ S) \circ T = R \circ (S \circ T) \tag{3.5}$$

as well as its distributivity over union

$$R \circ (S \cup T) = (R \circ S) \cup (R \circ T). \tag{3.6}$$

A corresponding result for the case that one of the relations in the relational product is an intersection, i.e. that one considers $R \circ (S \cap T)$, holds true only as a subdistributivity:

$$R \circ (S \cap T) \subseteq (R \circ S) \cap (R \circ T). \tag{3.7}$$

For the operation of taking the inverse fuzzy relation one furthermore has

$$(R \circ S)^{-1} = S^{-1} \circ R^{-1}, \tag{3.8}$$

$$(R \cup S)^{-1} = R^{-1} \cup S^{-1}, \qquad (R \cap S)^{-1} = R^{-1} \cap S^{-1}, \tag{3.9}$$

as well as for taking complements and inverse relations

$$(R^{-1})^{-1} = R, \qquad (R^c)^{-1} = (R^{-1})^c. \tag{3.10}$$

Interesting properties for quite a lot of applications moreover are the monotonicity rules

$$R \subseteq S \quad \Rightarrow \quad R \circ T \subseteq S \circ T \text{ and } T \circ R \subseteq T \circ S. \tag{3.11}$$

Looking back to the examples of fuzzy relations we considered in Section 2.2, then e.g. the inverse relation R_1^{-1} expresses the intuitive relationship of "being essentially greater than", and the union $R_0 \cup R_1^{-1}$ can be understood as formalising "being essentially greater than or nearly equal to". As another example we define for the real numbers a fuzzy relation R_2 by

$$\mu_{R_2}(x, y) =_{\text{def}} [1 - (x - y^2)^2]^+. \tag{3.12}$$

This fuzzy relation formalises the intuitive idea of "... being nearly equal to the square of ..." or of "... being indistinguishable from the square of ...".

Then the relational product $R_1 \circ R_2$ codifies the idea of "... being more or less smaller than the square of ...", and the relational product $R_2{}^{-1} \circ R_1{}^{-1}$ formalises the intuition behind "... has a square which is essentially greater than ...".

If in the case of a finite universe of discourse one uses the matrix representation (3.1) then it is easy to represent R^{-1} and $R \circ S$ by matrices too. Let be $\mathcal{U} = \{u_1, \ldots, u_n\}$, $\mathcal{V} = \{v_1, \ldots, v_m\}$, $\mathcal{W} = \{w_1, \ldots, w_l\}$ universes of discourse, $R \in \mathbb{F}(\mathcal{U} \times \mathcal{V})$ and $S \in \mathbb{F}(\mathcal{V} \times \mathcal{W})$ fuzzy relations, and denote the matrix representations of R, S by $R \hat{=} ((r_{ij}))$ and $S \hat{=} ((s_{jk}))$ with $i = 1, \ldots, n$, $j = 1, \ldots, m$, $k = 1, \ldots, l$ such that

$$r_{ij} = \mu_R(u_i, v_j), \qquad s_{jk} = \mu_S(v_j, w_k). \tag{3.13}$$

Denoting for $T = R \circ S$ the matrix representation by $T \hat{=} ((t_{ik}))$ then yields the equations

$$t_{ik} = \sup_j \min\{r_{ij}, s_{jk}\}. \tag{3.14}$$

Formally, this is the well known method of computing the usual product of two matrices, but with the sup-operation instead of the sum, and with the min-operator instead of the product. For the inverse relation R^{-1} one gets as representing matrix simply the conjugate matrix of $((r_{ij}))$: $R^{-1} \hat{=} ((r_{ij}))^{\mathsf{T}}$. This is an immediate consequence of (3.13) and (3.2).

3.1.2   t-Norm Based Operations

Definition (3.3) of the relational product $R \circ S$ can become t-norm based in the same way as was done for the definitions of union and intersection $\cap, \cup$, which simply means the exchange in this definition (3.3) of the min-operator by some, here usually left continuous, t-norm t. Thus for each t-norm t one has a corresponding relational product $R \circ_t S$ defined by

$$T = R \circ_t S :$$
$$\mu_T(x, y) =_{\text{def}} \sup_{z \in \mathcal{X}_2} \mu_R(x, z) \, t \, \mu_S(z, y) \tag{3.15}$$
$$\text{for all } (x, y) \in \mathcal{X}_1 \times \mathcal{X}_3$$

By the commutativity of each t-norm t one immediately has

$$(R \circ_t S)^{-1} = S^{-1} \circ_t R^{-1}. \tag{3.16}$$

And the monotonicity condition for t-norms yields

$$R \subseteqq S \quad \Rightarrow \quad R \circ_t T \subseteqq S \circ_t T \text{ and } T \circ_t R \subseteqq T \circ_t S \tag{3.17}$$

which means that $\circ_t$ is monotonously nondecreasing w.r.t. $\subseteq$. Associativity condition (T2) together with (2.132) furthermore leads to

$$R \circ_t (S \circ_t T) = (R \circ_t S) \circ_t T, \tag{3.18}$$
$$R \circ_t (S \cup T) = (R \circ_t S) \cup (R \circ_t T) \tag{3.19}$$

which hold true for all fuzzy relations R, S, T. Finally also the subdistributivity rule

$$R \circ_t (S \cap T) \subseteq (R \circ_t S) \cap (R \circ_t T) \tag{3.20}$$

holds true for each t-norm t.

The same argument which was used together with (2.151) applies here too. So therefore (3.19) cannot be extended from $\cup$ to $\cup_t$ and one has again

$$R \circ_t (S \cup_t T) = (R \circ_t S) \cup_t (R \circ_t T) \quad \text{for all } R, S, T$$
$$\Leftrightarrow \quad t = \min. \tag{3.21}$$

Moreover, even the subdistributivity rule (3.20) does not generalise; and as in (2.150) one again has

$$R \circ_t (S \cap_t T) \subseteq (R \circ_t S) \cap_t (R \circ_t T) \quad \text{for all } R, S, T$$
$$\Leftrightarrow \quad t = \min. \tag{3.22}$$

Using the class term notation of (2.40) gives to the definition (3.3) the form

$$R \circ S = \{(x,y) \| \exists z((x,z) \varepsilon R \wedge (z,y) \varepsilon S)\}. \tag{3.23}$$

Thus this definition formally has exactly the same structure as the traditional definition of the relational product of crisp relations. Furthermore one realises that the conjunction operation $\wedge$ in (3.23) can be read as min-operation as in (3.3), but it also can be understood as some t-norm (cf. Section 2.4). In this last mentioned case then one has to suppose that this t-norm is left continuous, i.e. lower semicontinuous. And this assumption of left continuity of a t-norm t is equivalent with the assumption that the generalised distributivity

$$B \cap_t \bigcup_{j \in \mathcal{J}} A_j = \bigcup_{j \in \mathcal{J}} (B \cap_t A_j), \tag{3.24}$$

holds true generally in the case that the intersection $\cap_t$ is based on just this t-norm t and defined as $A \cap_t B = \{x \| (x \varepsilon A)\, t\, (x \varepsilon B)\}$; additionally $\bigcup$ is supposed to be defined by (2.85).

In the same way as presented by (3.23) also all the other operations on fuzzy relations which have been discussed in this section are exact formal analogues to well known operations on crisp relations.

3.1.3 Projections and Cylindrifications

There are other basic operations on fuzzy relations which change the number of objects which are related by such a fuzzy relation, i.e. which change the arity of the fuzzy relations. Reductions as well as enlargements of the arities happen.

Reductions of these numbers of related objects, i.e. of the arities are realised by *projections*. For each binary fuzzy relation $R \in I\!F(\mathcal{X}_1 \times \mathcal{X}_2)$ there are exactly two projections $\mathsf{pr}_1(R)$, $\mathsf{pr}_2(R)$ with membership functions

$$C := \mathsf{pr}_1(R): \qquad \mu_C(a) = \sup_{y \in \mathcal{X}_2} \mu_R(a, y) \quad \text{for all } a \in \mathcal{X}_1, \tag{3.25}$$

$$D := \mathsf{pr}_2(R): \qquad \mu_D(b) = \sup_{x \in \mathcal{X}_1} \mu_R(x, b) \quad \text{for all } b \in \mathcal{X}_2. \tag{3.26}$$

For each ternary fuzzy relation $R \in I\!F(\mathcal{X}_1 \times \mathcal{X}_2 \times \mathcal{X}_3)$ over the universe of discourse $\mathcal{Y} = \mathcal{X}_1 \times \mathcal{X}_2 \times \mathcal{X}_3$, there are on the one hand the "one-dimensional" projections $\mathsf{pr}_j(R)$, $j = 1, \ldots, 3$, defined by the membership functions

$$C := \mathsf{pr}_j(R):$$

$$\mu_C(a) = \sup_{\substack{(x_1, x_2, x_3) \in \mathcal{Y} \\ x_j = a}} \mu_R(x_1, x_2, x_3) \quad \text{for all } a \in \mathcal{X}_j. \tag{3.27}$$

On the other hand now there are "two-dimensional" projections $\mathsf{pr}_{j,k}(R)$, $1 \leq j, k \leq 3$, defined by the membership functions

$$D := \mathsf{pr}_{j,k}(R):$$

$$\mu_D(a, b) = \sup_{\substack{(x_1, x_2, x_3) \in \mathcal{Y} \\ x_j = a, \, x_k = b}} \mu_R(x_1, x_2, x_3) \tag{3.28}$$

$$\text{for all } a \in \mathcal{X}_j \text{ and } b \in \mathcal{X}_k.$$

In general, for each n-ary fuzzy relation R in the universe of discourse $\mathcal{Y} = \mathcal{X}_1 \times \cdots \times \mathcal{X}_n$, for each index k with $1 \leq k < n$, and each increasing sequence $j_1 < j_2 < \ldots < j_k$ of indices from $\{1, \ldots, n\}$, there is a projection of R into the universe $\mathcal{Z} = \mathcal{X}_{j_1} \times \cdots \times \mathcal{X}_{j_k}$, resulting in a fuzzy relation over this universe of discourse with membership function

$$D := \mathsf{pr}_{j_1, \ldots, j_k}(R): \tag{3.29}$$

$$\mu_D(a) =_{\text{def}} \sup_{\substack{x \in \mathcal{Y} \\ x_{j_i} = a_{j_i} \text{ for } i=1,\ldots,k}} \mu_R(x) \quad \text{for all } a = (a_{j_1}, \ldots, a_{j_k}) \in \mathcal{Z}.$$

To get an intuitive idea of what happens if one builds up the projection of a fuzzy relation it is preferable to try to have some sort of geometric visualisation. Thus let us consider the fuzzy relation K in $I\!R^2$ with membership function

$$\mu_K(x, y) = [\, 1 - c\,((x^2 + y^2)^{1/2} - 1)^2\,]^+. \tag{3.30}$$

Geometrically, for pairs (a, b) of real numbers this fuzzy relation indicates to which degree the point (a, b) of $I\!R^2$ has a distance approximately $= 1$ from the origin $(0, 0)$. Hence the fuzzy relation K describes the fuzzy boundary of the unit circle. Its projection

$$A := \mathsf{pr}_1(K) :$$
$$\mu_A(x) = \sup_{y \in I\!R} [\, 1 - c\,((x^2 + y^2)^{1/2} - 1)^2 \,]^+ \qquad (3.31)$$
$$= \begin{cases} 1, & \text{if } -1 \le x \le 1, \\ [\, 1 - c\,(1 - |x|)^2 \,]^+ & \text{otherwise} \end{cases}$$

obviously is a fuzzy interval which reaches from "about -1" to "about 1".

A standard way to extend a k-ary (fuzzy) relation R to a n-ary one (with $k \le n$, of course) is to construct a *cylindrical extension* of R. Let a universe of discourse $\mathcal{Y} = \mathcal{X}_1 \times \cdots \times \mathcal{X}_n$ be given together with an increasing sequence $1 \le j_1 < \ldots < j_k \le n$ and a fuzzy relation $R \in I\!\!F(\mathcal{X}_{j_1} \times \cdots \times \mathcal{X}_{j_k})$. The cylindrical extension of this fuzzy relation R, denoted by $\mathsf{c}_{(j_1, \ldots, j_k)}(R)$ and a fuzzy relation in $\mathcal{Y}$, one defines as

$$C := \mathsf{c}_{(j_1, \ldots, j_k)}(R) :$$
$$\mu_C(\boldsymbol{x}) = \mu_R(x_{j_1}, \ldots, x_{j_k}) \qquad \text{for all } \boldsymbol{x} = (x_1, \ldots, x_n) \in \mathcal{Y}. \quad (3.32)$$

To have an example consider again the fuzzy relation K as defined in (3.30). To extend K to a fuzzy relation in $I\!R^3$ one can build up the cylindrical extension

$$C := \mathsf{c}_{(1,2)}(K) : \quad \mu_C(a, b, c) = \mu_K(a, b) \quad \text{for all } a, b, c. \qquad (3.33)$$

Geometrically this cylindrical extension, which itself is a fuzzy set $C \in I\!\!F(I\!R^3)$, describes the fuzzy lateral surface of a (fuzzy) cylinder. (Just this geometric visualisation was the reason to call this type of extension "cylindrical".)

As can be seen from (3.27) and (3.29), each n-ary fuzzy relation $R \in I\!\!F(\mathcal{X}_1 \times \cdots \times \mathcal{X}_n)$ determines exactly n "one-dimensional" projections $\mathsf{pr}_j(R) \in I\!\!F(\mathcal{X}_j)$ for $j = 1, \ldots, n$. Conversely, now the problem arises whether all these projections $\mathsf{pr}_j(R)$ suffice to determine the fuzzy relation R. This usually, however, is not the case. To see this, let us look at the fuzzy relation $K \in IF(I\!R^2)$ as defined in (3.30). We can consider instead the fuzzy relation $Q \in IF(I\!R^2)$, defined by

$$Q = \mathsf{c}_1(\mathsf{pr}_1(K)) \cap \mathsf{c}_2(\mathsf{pr}_2(K)) \qquad (3.34)$$

which geometrically represents a fuzzy unit square. Then one has

$$\mathsf{pr}_i(K) = \mathsf{pr}_i(Q) \qquad \text{for } i = 1, 2,$$

but $K \neq Q$. In the special case that a fuzzy relation $R \in I\!\!F(\mathcal{X}_1 \times \cdots \times \mathcal{X}_n)$ can be reconstructed from all its one-dimensional projections $\mathsf{pr}_j(R)$, $j = 1, \ldots, n$, as the fuzzy cartesian product

$$R = \mathsf{pr}_1(R) \otimes \cdots \otimes \mathsf{pr}_n(R), \tag{3.35}$$

such a fuzzy relation R is called *separable*. Such separable fuzzy relations are of special interest in the case that one looks at fuzzy relations as fuzzy relationships between variables (cf. Section 3.3).

3.2   Properties of Fuzzy Relations

3.2.1   Basic Relational Properties

For applications some types of crisp relations are of special importance. Equivalence relations constitute one of these important types. As is well known, each equivalence relation generates within its universe $\mathcal{X}$ disjoint classes of pairwise equivalent elements. Hence an equivalence relation provides a classification of the elements of its universe. On the other hand, any (complete) classification within some universe can be realised by an equivalence relation.

For applications, yet, such a crisp classification often seems to be a bit artificial: in a lot of cases it seems to be preferable to "classify" some elements into different classes to different degrees – diagnostic problems in medicine or technology provide a lot of suitable examples. For a serious discussion of such *fuzzy classifications* it seems reasonable to guess that fuzzy analoga of crisp equivalence relations may constitute a key notion. Usual, i.e. crisp equivalence relations are defined to be reflexive, symmetric, and transitive relations. Therefore as a basis for introducing fuzzy equivalence relations we first look for suitable definitions of these properties for fuzzy relations.

At the same time, this transfer of special properties from crisp to fuzzy relations will also provide a paradigm for suitably transferring further properties.

Immediately at hand is the idea of calling a fuzzy relation $R \in I\!\!F(\mathcal{X} \times \mathcal{X})$ *reflexive* iff

$$\mu_R(x, x) = 1 \quad \text{for all } x \in \mathcal{X} \tag{3.36}$$

holds true, and calling it *symmetric* iff

$$\mu_R(x, y) = \mu_R(y, x) \quad \text{for all } x, y \in \mathcal{X} \tag{3.37}$$

holds true. The symmetric fuzzy relations can easily be characterised using their inverse relations:

$$R \text{ symmetric} \quad \Leftrightarrow \quad R = R^{-1}. \tag{3.38}$$

Another approach toward reflexivity, also not counterintuitive, is to call a fuzzy relation $R \in I\!\!F(\mathcal{X} \times \mathcal{X})$ *weakly reflexive* iff $\mu_R(x, x) > 0$ for all $x \in \mathcal{X}$. But, we shall not consider this notion of weak reflexivity further on.

A fuzzy relation which is reflexive as well as symmetric is called a fuzzy *proximity relation*. These proximity relations formalise the property of being "near" to one another: each element is really near to itself, and if x, y are near to one another to some degree then also y, x are near to the same degree. Another view toward proximity relations is that they formalise some weak sort of "similarity". An example of such a fuzzy proximity relation was already given by the fuzzy relation R_0 of (2.55). Of course, with R, R^{-1} is always a fuzzy proximity relation. And for each reflexive fuzzy relation R the fuzzy relation $R \cup R^{-1}$ is a fuzzy proximity relation too. Thus also $R_2 \cup R_2^{-1}$, with R_2 as defined in (3.12), is a fuzzy proximity.

For getting fuzzy versions of equivalence relations we finally need to determine what we understand by the transitivity of a fuzzy relation. Having in mind that $R \circ R \subseteqq R$ characterises the transitivity of crisp relations, one immediately has as a natural generalisation to define a fuzzy relation $R \in I\!\!F(\mathcal{X} \times \mathcal{X})$ to be *transitive* iff

$$\sup_{z \in \mathcal{X}} \min\{\mu_R(x, z), \mu_R(z, y)\} \leq \mu_R(x, y) \quad \text{for all } x, y \in \mathcal{X} \tag{3.39}$$

holds true. More precisely, in this case R is called sup-min-*transitive*. With reference to the relational product one immediately gets as a further characterisation

$$R \text{ sup-min-}transitive \Leftrightarrow R \circ R \subseteqq R.$$

This careful terminology depends also on the fact that (3.39) sometimes is a very strong property. Thus e.g. our fuzzy relation R_0 with membership function (2.55) is not sup-min-transitive. To prove this one chooses $a = 1$ and has

$$1/2 = \sup_z \min\{\mu_R(4, z), \mu_R(z, 5)\}, \quad \text{but} \quad \mu_R(4, 5) = 0.$$

Application oriented as well as theoretical considerations already forced ZADEH (1971) as well as KLAUA (1966, 1966a), to consider modified notions of transitivity of fuzzy relations. Once again the main point of these modifications has been the replacement of the min-operator in (3.39): ZADEH uses the product instead of it and KLAUA refers to the operation $*$, which was already used implicitly in (2.99) and which for all $r, s \in [0, 1]$ is characterised by

$$r * s =_{\text{def}} [r + s - 1]^+. \tag{3.40}$$

But this is exactly the t-norm t_2 of Section 2.4. Thus as further defining conditions one has

$$\sup_{z\in\mathcal{X}}(\mu_R(x,z)\cdot\mu_R(z,y)) \leq \mu_R(x,y) \quad \text{for all } x,y\in\mathcal{X} \tag{3.41}$$

to characterise the sup-·-*transitivity*, and one has

$$\sup_{z\in\mathcal{X}}(\mu_R(x,z)*\mu_R(z,y)) \leq \mu_R(x,y) \quad \text{for all } x,y\in\mathcal{X} \tag{3.42}$$

to characterise the sup-*-*transitivity* of a fuzzy relation. Further types of transitivity can be introduced along these lines too.

A more formalised view allows for a very simple formulation of the general principle behind these modifications: the "outer" appearance of the sup-operator remains unchanged but the "inner" appearance of the min-operator is changed into an appearance of some t-norm (of the product in (3.41), of the operation $*$ in (3.42)). Essentially this corresponds to a change from the intuitive transitivity condition $R\circ R \subseteq R$ to the condition $R\circ_t R \subseteq R$, behind the transitivity definition for R, i.e. it corresponds to another interpretation of the conjunction sign in (3.23). In general then a fuzzy relation R for which $R\circ_t R \subseteq R$ holds true will be called t-*transitive* or usually even sup-t-*transitive*.

3.2.2 A Description of Distances of Fuzzy Sets*

Our sup-*-transitivity, i.e. the sup-t_2-transitivity is of special interest because of an unexpected connection with distances for fuzzy sets, more specifically with pseudo-metrics. The main fact is that for each fuzzy relation $R\in\mathbb{F}(\mathcal{X}\times\mathcal{X})$ which is reflexive, symmetric, and sup-*-transitive by

$$\varrho(x,y) =_{\text{def}} 1-\mu_R(x,y) \tag{3.43}$$

on $\mathcal{X}\times\mathcal{X}$ a function ϱ is defined which is a *distance function* with the characteristic properties

(M1) $\varrho(x,y)=0,$ if $x=y$,   (identity property)
(M2) $\varrho(x,y)=\varrho(y,x)$,   (symmetry)
(M3) $\varrho(x,z)+\varrho(z,y)\geq\varrho(x,y)$. (triangle inequality)

Additionally ϱ has the property that for any two "points" of $\mathcal{X}$ their ϱ-distance is ≤ 1.

Here the identity property (M1) is an immediate consequence of the reflexivity of R. Also the symmetry property (M2) is a direct consequence of the symmetry of the fuzzy relation R. Finally, the sup-*-transitivity of R has to be used in the proof of the triangle inequality (M3) for ϱ. It is remarkable that $* = t_2$ is not the only t-norm t for which by (3.43) a distance function ϱ_t results with the properties (M1), ..., (M3) if one starts to form a fuzzy relation R which is reflexive, symmetric, and sup-t-transitive. But t_2 is the smallest one of these t-norms. Indeed one has the following lemma which essentially is proved e.g. in GOTTWALD (1993).

Lemma: *Let be t a t-norm and R a fuzzy relation which is reflexive, symmetric, and* sup-t-*transitive. Suppose also that for this fuzzy relation by (3.43) a function $\varrho_t : \mathcal{X} \times \mathcal{X} \to [0,1]$ is defined. Then this function ϱ_t has the properties* (M1), ..., (M3) *iff*

$$r \, t \, s \geq r \, t_2 \, s \qquad \text{for all } r, s \in [0,1]$$

holds true.

Looking back at (2.55) and the fuzzy relation R_0, then via (3.43) this fuzzy relation can be defined as starting from a pseudo-metric, viz. the usual distance on the real line multiplied by a. Therefore R_0 is sup-$*$-transitive.

This point of view can be much extended. To do this one has to remember the fuzzified, i.e. graded inclusion relation $A \subseteqq B$ defined in (2.39). Of course, the implication connective $\to$ used there can now be understood as being based upon some t-norm t via (3.50) as the corresponding residuation operation satisfying condition (2.162). Hence from this point of view this graded inclusion relation becomes

$$A \subseteqq_t B = \forall x \, (x \, \varepsilon \, A \to_t x \, \varepsilon \, B).$$

This inclusion relation gives the basis of introducing a graded equality relation for such fuzzy sets as

$$A \equiv_t B =_{\text{def}} A \subseteqq_t B \wedge_t B \subseteqq_t A. \qquad (3.44)$$

This graded equality relation $\equiv_t$ for fuzzy sets $A, B \in \mathbb{F}(\mathcal{X})$ itself is a fuzzy equivalence relation in $\mathbb{F}(\mathcal{X})$ which is sup-t-transitive. The corresponding pseudo-metric (3.43) now can be written as

$$\varrho_t^*(A, B) = [\![\neg(A \equiv_t B)]\!]$$

and thus be understood as a kind of *distinguishability function*.

For fuzzy sets $A, B \in \mathbb{F}(\mathcal{X})$ in the case of the t-norm $t = t_0 = \min$ one gets by simple calculations the corresponding distinguishability function

$\varrho_0^* = \varrho_{t_0}^*$ as

$$\varrho_0^*(A, B) = \sup_{\substack{x \in \mathcal{X} \\ [\![x \, \varepsilon \, A]\!] \neq [\![x \, \varepsilon \, B]\!]}} (1 - [\![x \, \varepsilon \, A \cap B]\!])$$

$$= \sup_{\substack{x \in \mathcal{X} \\ [\![x \, \varepsilon \, A]\!] \neq [\![x \, \varepsilon \, B]\!]}} ([\![x \, \varepsilon \, (A \cap B)^c]\!])$$

and in the case of the t-norm $t = t_2$ one gets after some elementary transformations the distinguishability function $\varrho_2^* = \varrho_{t_2}^*$ as

$$\varrho_2^*(A, B) = \min \left\{ 1, \max\{0, \sup_{x \in \mathcal{X}} ([\![x \, \varepsilon \, A]\!] - [\![x \, \varepsilon \, B]\!])\} + \right.$$
$$\left. + \max\{0, \sup_{x \in \mathcal{X}} ([\![x \, \varepsilon \, B]\!] - [\![x \, \varepsilon \, A]\!])\} \right\}.$$

This function $\varrho_2^*(A, B)$ is loosely related to the Čebyšev distance of the membership functions μ_A, μ_B defined as

$$d_C(\mu_A, \mu_B) = \sup_{x \in \mathcal{X}} |\mu_A(x) - \mu_B(x)|$$

in the sense that one always has

$$d_C(\mu_A, \mu_B) \leq \varrho_2^*(A, B) \leq 2 \cdot d_C(\mu_A, \mu_B)$$

and especially using the original crisp, i.e. not graded implication relation $\subseteqq$ for fuzzy sets,

$$A \subseteqq B \quad \Rightarrow \quad \varrho_2^*(A, B) = d_C(\mu_A, \mu_B).$$

3.2.3 Fuzzy Equivalence Relations

Now, by a *fuzzy equivalence relation* one means any fuzzy relation which is reflexive, symmetric, and transitive in one of the versions we have discussed. Hence, the fuzzy relation R_0 of (2.55), (2.56) is a fuzzy equivalence relation.

Each fuzzy proximity relation R with the additional property that its kernel is a usual equivalence relation, is itself a fuzzy equivalence relation. In this case one has to refer to sup-t_3-transitivity and the drastic product (2.100) as the t-norm t_3 in $[0, 1]$ with its characterisation

$$r t_3 s = \begin{cases} \min\{r, s\}, & \text{if } \max\{r, s\} = 1, \\ 0 & \text{otherwise.} \end{cases}$$

This fact together with the intuitive idea that proximities formalise a kind of "similarity" is reflected in that sometimes fuzzy equivalence relations are also called (fuzzy) *similarity relations* (cf. Chapter 6).

For any real numbers $r, s \in [0, 1]$ the inequalities $r * s \leq r \cdot s \leq \min\{r, s\}$ hold true. Therefore each fuzzy relation which is sup-min-transitive is also sup-·-transitive, and each fuzzy relation which is sup-·-transitive is also sup-∗-transitive. And therefore each fuzzy equivalence relation $R \in I\!F(\mathcal{X} \times \mathcal{X})$ which is transitive in the sense of any one of these types of transitivity produces via (3.43) a distance function in $\mathcal{X}$. Hence each such fuzzy equivalence relation can also be considered as a fuzzy *indistinguishability relation*.

Now we proceed to define for any fuzzy equivalence relation $R \in I\!F(\mathcal{X} \times \mathcal{X})$ their equivalence classes as fuzzy subsets of the universe $\mathcal{X}$. For each $a \in \mathcal{X}$ let its *fuzzy R-equivalence class* $\langle a \rangle_R$ be characterised by the membership function

$$A := \langle a \rangle_R : \quad \mu_A(x) =_{\text{def}} \mu_R(a, x) \qquad \text{for all } x \in \mathcal{X}. \tag{3.45}$$

Thus the fuzzy R-equivalence class of a is the fuzzy set of all those elements of $\mathcal{X}$ which are R-equivalent with a. Each such fuzzy R-equivalence class is a normal fuzzy set because for $A = \langle a \rangle_R$ one has $\mu_A(a) = 1$ by the reflexivity of R. Using the language of qualitative data analysis this means that $\langle a \rangle_R$ is a fuzzy neighbourhood (relative to R) of the "crisp" point a.

But contrary to the situation with crisp equivalence relations the fuzzy R-equivalence classes of a fuzzy equivalence relation R may overlap in the sense that

$$\langle a \rangle_R \neq \langle b \rangle_R \quad \text{together with} \quad \langle a \rangle_R \cap \langle b \rangle_R \neq \emptyset \tag{3.46}$$

may happen. (In any case, for different R-equivalence classes their intersection $\langle a \rangle_R \cap \langle b \rangle_R$ is a subnormal fuzzy set. The reason is that condition $\text{hgt}(\langle a \rangle_R \cap \langle b \rangle_R) = 1$ by transitivity of R gives $\mu_R(a, b) = 1$, and hence yields $\langle a \rangle_R = \langle b \rangle_R$ by definition.) This possibility of overlap is really welcome: because if we look at a fuzzy equivalence relation as a basis for a fuzzy classification then now classes of such a fuzzy classification may have common elements – to some degree.

It is obvious that each (strong) α-cut of a reflexive or symmetric fuzzy relation again is – in the standard sense – a reflexive or a symmetric relation. But for transitive fuzzy relations their (strong) α-cuts need not be transitive relations in the usual sense.

The kernels of each equivalence class of any fuzzy equivalence relation R are pairwise disjoint and hence the equivalence classes of some crisp equivalence relation, viz. the kernel $R^{\geq 1}$ of R. Furthermore, all the elements of the kernel of a fuzzy R-equivalence class $\langle a \rangle_R$ are related to all the elements of the kernel of another fuzzy R-equivalence class $\langle b \rangle_R$ to the same degree w.r.t. R: therefore the membership degree of b in that class of the classification described by R which is represented by a, this membership degree is the same as the membership degree of each $c \in \langle b \rangle_R^{\geq 1}$ in this class which is represented by a. Thus for all R-equivalence classes $\langle a \rangle_R \neq \langle b \rangle_R$ one has $\mu_R(a, b) < 1$. Even in the case that one has $\mu_R(a, b) = 0$ neither the sup-min-transitivity nor the sup-·-transitivity of R allow an overlap of the R-equivalence classes $\langle a \rangle_R, \langle b \rangle_R$: in both cases one has $\mathrm{supp}(\langle a \rangle_R) \cap \mathrm{supp}(\langle b \rangle_R) = \emptyset$. But if R is sup-*-transitive, then $\mu_R(a, b) = 0$ forces only $\mathrm{hgt}(\langle a \rangle_R \cap \langle b \rangle_R) \leq 1/2$, i.e. in this case the R-equivalence classes $\langle a \rangle_R, \langle b \rangle_R$ may overlap. Assuming $0 \neq \mu_R(a, b) < 1$ then allows overlap of those R-equivalence classes not only in case of sup-*-transitivity but also in the cases of sup-min-transitivity and of sup-·-transitivity of the fuzzy equivalence relation R.

The choice of the type of transitivity of a fuzzy equivalence relation hence allows to control the possible overlap of the corresponding equivalence classes: sup-min-transitivity as well as sup-·-transitivity allow overlap only for such equivalence classes $\langle a \rangle_R, \langle b \rangle_R$ whose representatives a, b are R-equivalent with a nonzero degree, sup-*-transitivity instead allows an overlap of $\langle a \rangle_R, \langle b \rangle_R$ even in the case that a, b are not at all R-equivalent, i.e. if $\mu_R(a, b) = 0$ holds true.

3.2.4   Fuzzy Ordering Relations*

The ordering relations are an important class of transitive relations. Any fuzzy relation $R \in \mathbb{F}(\mathcal{X} \times \mathcal{X})$ which is reflexive and transitive (in any one of the meanings given before) is called a *fuzzy quasiordering* or a *fuzzy preference relation*. If for some t-norm t the relation R is a sup-t-transitive fuzzy quasiordering, thus e.g. if t is one of the t-norms $t_0 = \min, t_2 = *$, or $t_1 = \cdot$, then by

$$\mu_Q(x, y) =_{\mathrm{def}} \mu_R(x, y)\, t\, \mu_R(y, x) \quad \text{for all } x, y \in \mathcal{X} \tag{3.47}$$

a fuzzy relation $Q \in \mathbb{F}(\mathcal{X} \times \mathcal{X})$ is defined which is a sup-t-transitive fuzzy equivalence relation in $\mathcal{X}$.

The antisymmetric quasiorderings are the partial orderings. The most suitable way to define the antisymmetry of a fuzzy relation is to do it by a condition of the form

$$\mu_R(x, y)\, t\, \mu_R(y, x) \leq (x \doteq y) \quad \text{for all } x, y \in \mathcal{X}. \tag{3.48}$$

Here t is any t-norm and $\doteq$ understood as in (2.108). In the case that $R \in \mathbb{F}(\mathcal{X} \times \mathcal{X})$ satisfies condition (3.48), then R is called *antisymmetric*. And R is called *fuzzy partial ordering* in $\mathcal{X}$ iff R is reflexive, transitive (in some sense), and antisymmetric.

The usual, i.e. crisp partial orderings in finite universes $\mathcal{X}$ are often visualised by HASSE-diagrams which are special types of directed graphs. The same can be done for fuzzy partial orderings. But then such a generalised HASSE-*diagram* of a fuzzy partial ordering has to be a weighted directed graph – in such a way that its (suitably defined) transitive hull is the original fuzzy partial ordering. Of course, the weights of the edges of that graph which are numbers from $[0, 1]$ themselves can be read as membership degrees of those edges w.r.t. that graph, i.e. that weighted directed graph itself can be considered as a *fuzzy graph*.

3.2.5 Toward Fuzzified Relation Properties*

Using the language of many-valued logic to reformulate all these properties of fuzzy relations immediately shows, once again, that they are standard generalisations of the usual properties of crisp relations. For transitivity e.g. this procedure leads to

$$\models \forall x \forall y \forall z \, ((x, z) \, \varepsilon \, R \, \wedge \, (z, y) \, \varepsilon \, R \, \rightarrow \, (x, y) \, \varepsilon \, R), \tag{3.49}$$

with $\models$ to denote the satisfaction relation of many-valued logic. This condition hence states that the formula which follows $\models$ always has to have truth degree 1. What this really means essentially depends on how the sentential connectives $\wedge$ and $\rightarrow$ are interpreted in (3.49). Usually, the satisfaction statement $\models (H_1 \rightarrow H_2)$ means that $[\![H_1]\!] \leq [\![H_2]\!]$ holds true (w.r.t. all possible valuations). It therefore remains to discuss the interpretation of the conjunction connective $\wedge$ in (3.49). And this proves to be of great importance. Indeed, (3.39), (3.41), (3.42) are special cases of (3.49) with $\wedge$ interpreted by suitable t-norms. A more detailed study of the relations between the connectives $\wedge$ and $\rightarrow$ is basic for the work of e.g. GOTTWALD (1986, 1986a, 1993). It proves preferable to start with a t-norm t as (generalised) truth function of the conjunction connective $\wedge$ and to define from it a truth function φ_t of the implication connective $\rightarrow$ by

$$u \, \varphi_t \, v =_{\text{def}} \sup\{z \mid u \, t \, z \leq v\} \quad \text{for all } u, v \in [0, 1]. \tag{3.50}$$

From an algebraic viewpoint this is just the operation of taking the pseudo-complement in $[0, 1]$ relative to the t-norm t, i.e. φ_t is the residuation operation which corresponds to the "product" t in the sense of the residuation condition (2.162).

Accordingly, antisymmetry is most naturally defined by

$$\models \forall x \forall y \, ((x, y) \, \varepsilon \, R \, \wedge \, (y, x) \, \varepsilon \, R \, \rightarrow \, x = y). \tag{3.51}$$

Here there is an additional problem alongside that one of the interpretation of the connectives $\wedge$, $\rightarrow$: a many-valued interpretation of the equality sign $=$. Our approach (3.48) because of (2.108) is a very elementary version; more involved discussions are given e.g. in GOTTWALD (1989, 1993), and mainly based on the graded equality relations (3.44).

There is a further possible generalisation along the present lines, i.e. to use many-valued logic as in (3.49) and (3.51). The point is that up to now properties of fuzzy relations have been introduced in a "crisp" way: fuzzy relations either do have or they do not have each one of these properties. But in the realm of fuzziness it is natural also to have the possibility that some fuzzy relation has one of these properties to some degree. Looking at the transitivity property this more general approach could mean to introduce a many-valued, i.e. graded predicate Trans_t defined for fuzzy relations e.g. by

$$\text{Trans}_t(R) =_{\text{def}} \forall x \forall y \forall z \, (\, (x, y) \, \varepsilon \, R \wedge (y, z) \, \varepsilon \, R \to (x, z) \, \varepsilon \, R \,) \qquad (3.52)$$

and to use it instead of the crisp property introduced in (3.49). This idea is discussed in more detail in GOTTWALD (1991).

3.3 Fuzzy Relationships between Variables

It is of central importance for applications of fuzzy relations that they formalise fuzzy, i.e. vague relationships between variables. Of course, the arity of the relation and the number of variables which are vaguely related have to be equal.

3.3.1 Fuzzily Related Variables

In this way e.g. the fuzzy equality R_0 – according to (2.55) or (2.56), (2.57) – formalises the relationship between two variables u, v so that the (actual) values of u and v are nearly the same. And in (3.30) a relation K is defined which formalises the relationship between two variables u, v so that their corresponding values are nearly the coordinates of a point of the unit circle. Extending this point of view and considering a relationship between three variables u, v, w which means that the values of the first two variables are nearly the coordinates of a point of the unit circle is formalised not by K itself but by the cylindrical extension $\mathsf{c}_{(1,2)}(K)$ of $K \in I\!\!F(I\!\!R^2)$ to $I\!\!R^3$.

A further example of a vague relationship between three real variables u, v, w is provided by the relation S with membership function

$$\mu_S(x, y, z) = [\, 1 - a \, ((x^2 + y^2 + z^2)^{1/2} - 1)^2 \,]^+ \qquad (3.53)$$

for all $x, y, z \in I\!\!R$. Here the value triples (x, y, z) of the variables u, v, w are nearly the coordinates of a point of the unit sphere. If one now poses the problem of which relationship this determines for the variables u, v, then this relationship is formally represented by the fuzzy relation $T = \mathsf{pr}_{2,3}(S)$ with membership function

$$\mu_T(y,z) = \sup_{x \in R} \mu_S(x,y,z) \tag{3.54}$$

$$= \begin{cases} 1, & \text{if } z^2 + y^2 \leq 1; \\ \left[1 - a\left((y^2 + z^2)^{1/2} - 1\right)^2\right]^+, & \text{if } z^2 + y^2 > 1. \end{cases}$$

That means that the values of v, w have to be the coordinates of a point which essentially belongs to the interior of the unit circle.

Intuitively it is obvious that in all these examples the values of the involved variables do not vary independently, assuming that the considered relationships apply. Formally this means that the fuzzy relations which formalise these relationships are not separable ones. Furthermore now we shall denote variables as *interactive* iff between them there holds true a relationship which formally has to become represented by a fuzzy relation which is not a separable one. In the case that this representing fuzzy relation is a separable one, the corresponding variables are called *non-interactive*.[1]

Supposing that a fuzzy relation $R \in \mathbb{F}(\mathcal{X} \times \mathcal{Y})$ between variables u, v is given and additionally also a value x_0 of the variable u, then by

$$\mu_B(y) = \mu_R(x_0, y) \quad \text{for all } y \in \mathcal{Y} \tag{3.55}$$

a *fuzzy constraint* B is determined for the values of the variable v (cf. Section 2.2). Conversely, if for each possible value $x_0 \in \mathcal{X}$ of the variable u a fuzzy constraint $B \in \mathbb{F}(\mathcal{Y})$ is given for the values of the variable v, then by (3.55) a fuzzy relation R is determined which relates the values of u and v. As a special case, such an imprecise relationship between two variables u and v can be a fuzzy functional dependency, formally realised by a fuzzy function as well as by a fuzzy set of functions (cf. Section 2.2 for these notions).

Formula (3.55) in each such case allows connection with any crisp value of any one of the variables, which are involved in the fuzzy relationship R, a fuzzy constraint for the values of the other variables.

To overcome cumbersome notations one sometimes "collects" different variables into a new, multidimensional variable. Consider, as the simplest case, two variables u_1, u_2 for elements of $\mathcal{X}_1, \mathcal{X}_2$. Then it is equivalent either to look simultaneously at values of u_1 and u_2, or to consider a new variable u for elements of $\mathcal{X}_1 \times \mathcal{X}_2$ and to look for their values. This "new" variable u shall be denoted by $u = (u_1, u_2)$. Accordingly one allows the "splitting" of

---

[1]The present terminology parallels the terminology which in Chapter 2 was used for operations in $\mathbb{F}(\mathcal{X})$ and $[0,1]$. But the meaning obviously is a different one. This (ab)use of language is a bit sloppy but common. The context, however, will always provide enough information to avoid a misunderstanding.

some given (multidimensional) variable u with values in $\mathcal{X} = \mathcal{X}_1 \times \mathcal{X}_2$ into two variables u_1, u_2 with values in $\mathcal{X}_1$, $\mathcal{X}_2$, respectively.

In this way one can always combine any (finite) number of variables u_i with values in $\mathcal{X}_i$, $i = 1, \ldots, k$, respectively, into one new variable $u = (u_1, \ldots, u_k)$ with values in the (crisp) cartesian product $\mathcal{X}_1 \times \ldots \times \mathcal{X}_k$. Hence in any case one can assume to have the same situation as for formula (3.55): that a fuzzy relation R has to be considered which relates the values of two variables u, v, and that a crisp value x_0 of u is given. Then always by (3.55) a fuzzy constraint B for the values of v is determined.

3.3.2   The Possibility Interpretation of Fuzzy Sets

In such a situation that one has given a fuzzy relation R between variables u, v together with a fuzzy constraint $B \in \mathbb{F}(\mathcal{Y})$ for the values of v, then each membership degree $\mu_B(y) = \mu_R(x_0, y)$ is interpreted as the *degree of possibility* for $y \in \mathcal{Y}$ to be the true value of v given $x_0 \in \mathcal{X}$ as the true value of the variable u. If one, more generally, asks for constraints of the values of v, independent of any true, or actual value of u, then this global fuzzy constraint is provided by the projection $\mathrm{pr}_2(R)$.

This alteration of the viewpoint, from looking at $\mu_B(y)$ as membership degrees to interpret $\mu_B(y)$ as a degree of possibility, is very important for applications as well as for theoretical understanding. It presupposes viewing the fuzzy sets $B \in \mathbb{F}(\mathcal{Y})$ as fuzzy constraints for the values of some variable v with domain $\mathcal{Y}$. Thus the fuzzy sets B become conditions to be satisfied by the possible values of some variable v. These degrees of possibility usually are denoted by

$$\mathrm{Poss}\,\{v = a \mid B\} =_{\mathrm{def}} \mu_B(a) \tag{3.56}$$

in accordance with the usual notation for conditional probabilities. It is even more accurate than (3.56), but a bit more difficult, to write instead

$$\mathrm{Poss}\,\{\mathrm{value}(v) = a \mid B\} =_{\mathrm{def}} \mu_B(a). \tag{3.57}$$

The main idea with (3.56) is that a degree of possibility equal to one,

$$\mathrm{Poss}\,\{v = a \mid B\} = 1, \tag{3.58}$$

expresses the fact that the variable v can have the value a without any restriction. Accordingly,

$$\mathrm{Poss}\,\{v = a \mid B\} = 0 \tag{3.59}$$

means that it is completely impossible for v to assume the value a. The other degrees of possibility between 1 and 0 graduate the possibility that the variable v assumes the value a, as these numbers up to now did for membership.

But the degree of possibility Poss $\{v = a \mid B\}$ of (3.56) is essentially different from the well-known conditional probability

$$\text{Prob} \{v = a \mid B\} \tag{3.60}$$

that v assume the value a under the condition B. Let us assume that v is the production time of a modern engine-tool at some arbitrary working day. Under these conditions degrees of possibility as well as conditional probabilities for v may look as in Fig. 3.1: the degree of possibility (3.56) is not always smaller than the corresponding conditional probability (3.60). The degrees of

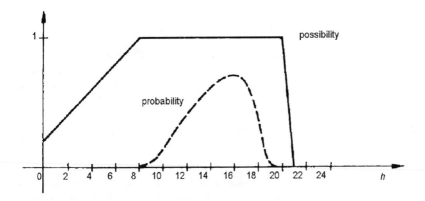

Figure 3.1: Possibility vs. probability

possibility $= 0$ where ≥ 21 hours of production time indicates the necessity of stoppage times for attendance or repairment. And the degrees of possibility < 1 where < 8 hours of production time is caused by economical constraints of profit management.

In all the cases where the fuzzy constraint B is determined by the context, the degree of possibility (3.56) is a function only of $y \in \mathcal{Y}$. Therefore ZADEH (1978) in analogy with (3.57) writes

$$\pi_v = \mu_B \tag{3.61}$$

for this function, and he calls π_v the *possibility distribution* induced by B on the variable v. Because v may be a "multidimensional" variable "collecting" other variables, i.e. because v may have the form $v = (v_1, \ldots, v_k)$, formula (3.61) also covers the case that the fuzzy constraint B itself is a fuzzy relation, and that the possibility distribution π_v is a simultaneous possibility distribution for several variables. Possibility distributions are of central importance for the representation of imprecise information in the area of approximate reasoning (cf. Section 4.4).

Having fixed a fuzzy relation(ship) R between variables u, v, then for crisp values of u by (3.55) one gets fuzzy constraints for the values of v, and hence by (3.61) possibility distributions for the possible values of the variable v. But it is often an exaggeration to suppose that a crisp value x_0 of u is given. If such a value e.g. has to be determined from observations, then usually it will be determined only imprecisely or even vaguely, depending on the type of observation. Therefore it is necessary to have, for any fuzzy relation R between the variables u, v, some way to extract information concerning the possible true values of v in those cases where a value of u is given only fuzzily.

3.3.3   Fuzzy Variables and Fuzzy Implications

As *fuzzy variables* we shall further on denote such variables which have fuzzy subsets of some suitable universe of discourse $\mathcal{X}$ as their values. Often one additionally assumes that these fuzzy values vaguely indicate "true" values of these variables which are points of the universe $\mathcal{X}$. For fuzzy variables u, v with fuzzy values in $I\!\!F(\mathcal{X}), I\!\!F(\mathcal{Y})$ and with their "true" values in $\mathcal{X}, \mathcal{Y}$, respectively, by a *fuzzy relation(ship) R between* u and v we understand a fuzzy relation $R \in I\!\!F(\mathcal{X} \times \mathcal{Y})$.

It is, however, not necessary to look at the points of the universe of discourse $\mathcal{X}$ of a fuzzy variable u as the vaguely determined "true" values of u Sometimes it is much more suitable to take the fuzzy values from $I\!\!F(\mathcal{X})$ as the genuine values of u. The hair colour with fuzzy values like blond and greying (over a universe of wavelengths) is a simple example of this situation. A slight complication in such cases, however, may result from the fact that – contrary to the situation with vaguely determined "true" background values of a fuzzy variable – now there need not be a good intuition behind the single points of the universe of discourse $\mathcal{X}$: the choice of $\mathcal{X}$ may even be only a matter of mathematical convenience.

For the case of fuzzy variables u, v with "true" background values, (3.55) can be interpreted as determining via the fuzzy relation R for each "true" value $x_0 \in \mathcal{X}$ of the variable u a fuzzy value $B \in I\!\!F(\mathcal{Y})$ of the fuzzy variable v. This fuzzy value of course is, if suitable, again interpreted as a fuzzy constraint for "true" values of v determining via (3.61) a possibility distribution of these "true" values. If instead one, is considering fuzzy variables u, v without such "true" background values, and with fuzzy values from $I\!\!F(\mathcal{X}), I\!\!F(\mathcal{Y})$, respectively, then a fuzzy relation S between (the values of) these variables more suitably has to be taken as a fuzzy subset of $I\!\!F(\mathcal{X}) \times I\!\!F(\mathcal{Y})$, i.e. as $S \in I\!\!F(I\!\!F(\mathcal{X}) \times I\!\!F(\mathcal{Y}))$.

Now, more generally, let us look at the situation that some (fuzzy) value

$A \in \mathbb{F}(\mathcal{X})$ of the fuzzy variable u is given together with a fuzzy relation $R \in \mathbb{F}(\mathcal{X} \times \mathcal{Y})$ between the fuzzy variables u, v. In this situation, w.r.t. the corresponding value B of v, the possibility degree $\mu_A(x_0)$ of some possible "true" value x_0 of u together with the degree $\mu_R(x_0, y)$ shall determine the degree of possibility $\mu_B(y)$. As a definition of this degree ZADEH (1973) chooses the following *compositional rule of inference*:

$$\mu_B(y) = \sup_{x \in \mathcal{X}} \min\{\mu_A(x), \mu_R(x, y)\} \quad \text{for all } y \in \mathcal{Y}. \tag{3.62}$$

Using this rule, for any variables u, v related by a fuzzy relationship R one is able to connect with each (fuzzy) value A of u a (fuzzy) value B of v. This connection which is based on the compositional rule of inference is often expressed in the form of a conditional expression

$$\text{IF } u = A \text{ THEN } v = B. \tag{3.63}$$

Such conditional expressions usually are called *fuzzy implications* or *fuzzy IF ...THEN-rules*. It is interesting and important that (3.63) supports the understanding that an assignment $u := A$ via a fuzzy relation R or a fuzzy implication (3.63) produces an assignment $v := B$.

There is a far reaching analogy of formulas (3.62) and (3.3). Therefore (3.62) as a characterisation of $B \in \mathbb{F}(\mathcal{Y})$ is also written

$$B = A \circ R. \tag{3.64}$$

This analogy for finite universes of discourse $\mathcal{X}, \mathcal{Y}$ goes further. Choosing according to (3.1) for R the matrix representation $R \hat{=} ((r_{ij}))$, and according to (2.3) for A, B the corresponding vector representations $A \hat{=} (a_i)$, $B \hat{=} (b_j)$, yields for $A \circ R$ in analogy with (3.14) just the product "vector $\times$ matrix" – again with supremum instead of the sum, and with minimum instead of the arithmetic product:

$$b_j = \sup_i \min\{a_i, r_{ij}\}. \tag{3.65}$$

In real world applications, as e.g. in fuzzy control problems or in the field of approximate reasoning (cf. Chapter 4), the situation quite often is the converse one: IF ...THEN-rules (3.63) are intuitively motivated, and a fuzzy relation R has to be found to base these rules via the compositional rule of inference (3.62) on R. If one has given *only one* fuzzy implication of type (3.63) then this problem of determining a suitable fuzzy relation R has simple solutions. Usually one additionally assumes that A, B are normal fuzzy sets or that at least $\text{hgt}(B) \le \text{hgt}(A)$ holds true. Then the formally simplest approach is to take

$$R = A \otimes B, \tag{3.66}$$

cf. MAMDANI/ASSILIAN (1975). But this is not the only possible approach. Other versions to transform one IF...THEN-rule (3.63) into a fuzzy relation have been proposed too, sometimes together with smaller variations of the compositional rule of inference (3.62). Some interesting choices out of a huge class of versions refer to the universal fuzzy sets X, Y over the universes of discourse $\mathcal{X}, \mathcal{Y}$ and take

$$R \;=\; (A \otimes B) \cup (A^c \otimes Y), \tag{3.67}$$
$$R \;=\; (A^c \otimes Y) + (X \otimes B), \tag{3.68}$$

cf. ZADEH (1973). A lot more such variants are discussed in MIZUMOTO (1982) and MIZUMOTO/ZIMMERMANN (1982). They usually have their motivation in analogies with usual propositional logic: in this way e.g. (3.68) is based on the understanding that

$$\text{NOT } (u = A) \text{ OR } (v = B)$$

should be a formulation equivalent with the fuzzy implication

$$\text{IF } (u = A) \text{ THEN } (v = B).$$

And (3.67) can be seen as the special case $C = Y$ of the more general rule

$$\text{IF } (u = A) \text{ THEN } (v = B) \text{ ELSE } (v = C) \tag{3.69}$$

which in a natural way is seen as to be based on the fuzzy relation

$$R = (A \otimes B) \cup (A^c \otimes C). \tag{3.70}$$

The present problem becomes much more difficult in the cases where one has to start from a whole family of fuzzy implications (3.63). Then to this family of fuzzy implications there corresponds a whole system of (fuzzy) *relational equations* (3.64) which all contain the unknown fuzzy relation R. And the problem of determining such a fuzzy relation R then becomes the problem of solving a system of relational equations (cf. Section 4.3).

3.4   Fuzzy Programming

3.4.1   Fuzzy Objectives and Constraints

Many problems in applications are formulated as *programming problems*. Over a universe $\mathcal{X}$, the *decision space* (the set of all alternatives or theoretical possibilities) some *objectives* (targets)

$$G_j(x) = \text{opt !} \quad (= \min_x !, \;\; \text{w.l.o.g.}) \quad j = 1, \ldots, m \tag{3.71}$$

are specified, which are to be satisfied under a series of *constraints*

$$C_i(\mathcal{X}), \qquad i = 1, \ldots, n. \qquad (3.72)$$

These constraints C_i are each equivalent with that subset of $\mathcal{X}$, on which they are satisfied. An example of such a constraint is the well-known condition that a certain variable must be non-negative, what corresponds to the set $\mathcal{C} = \{x \in \mathcal{X} \mid x \geq 0\}$. However, for a mathematical treatment of such programming problems (3.71) and (3.72) with usual methods of operations research we have to assume that the objectives as well as the constraints are formulated crisply and that all the structure elements, as, e.g., coefficients and algebraic connections, are known precisely. But these assumptions are satisfied in real-world applications at best approximately, which reduces the relevance of the so obtained results frequently.

It is general experience that bringing out and formulating of crisp objectives and constraints, called components of the programming problem in the following, are seldom performed without any arbitrariness and are much more complicated than the solution of the obtained crisp problem. Hence BELLMAN/ZADEH (1970) suggested to formulate and specify the objectives and constraints as fuzzy sets, starting at the practical conditions as they are. In such a way fuzzy objectives can be specified in demanding that certain elements, assumed to be approximately optimum, should be fitted as well as possible. Within the constraints equalities and bounds can be interpreted as fuzzy. So we can come to a better modelling of the practical decision situation.

Let G_j be the statement, corresponding to the j-th objective, expressed as a subset of $\mathcal{X}$. Then the solution set $\mathcal{D}$ of the crisp programming problem can be formally stated as the condition of satisfying all the objectives and all the constraints simultaneously:

$$\mathcal{D} = \left(\bigcap_{i=1}^{n} C_i \right) \cap \left(\bigcap_{j=1}^{m} G_j \right). \qquad (3.73)$$

Let μ_{C_i} and μ_{G_j} be the membership functions of the constraints and objectives now assumed to be *fuzzy*. Temporarily we leave open how the objectives can become fuzzy ones, we will go into this problem later. Moreover, for the moment we will assume that all the components of the problem are of equal importance with respect to their realisation. Different grades of importance could be taken into account e.g. by suitable factors of relevance. Whereas for crisp programming problems the condition of simultaneous fulfilment makes sense only by expressing it by the intersection $\cap$ in (3.73), for fuzzy problems we have available the whole arsenal of t-norms (see Section 2.4), with which we can model combinations of objectives and constraints, perhaps even within a preceding process of learning. Possibly the used t-norm can change from one connection to the next in (3.73). In the simplest case, if all objectives and constraints are of equal importance and if they do not show any interactivity, then we can choose, e.g., the minimum as t-norm and obtain the fuzzy solution D as

$$\mu_D(x) = \min\{\min_i \mu_{C_i}(x), \min_j \mu_{G_j}(x)\} \quad \text{for all } x \in \mathcal{X}. \tag{3.74}$$

For an evaluation of such a fuzzy solution, representing a *fuzzy decision*, we can use *fuzziness measures* as treated in Section 5.5. In this respect the situation is similar to that in fuzzy control (see Chapter 4). If *fuzzy* decisions D_k; $k \in \mathcal{K}$ are possible, then we can (as with fuzzy controllers) optimise further with respect to k. Let ϱ be a suitable distance, then this means

$$\varrho(D_k, D) = \min_k \,! \,. \tag{3.75}$$

However, if a *crisp* decision x is demanded, then we can interpret $\mu_D(x)$ as the *degree of satisfaction* of the crisp solution x for the fuzzy programming problem. Usually we will choose the crisp solution from the *set of maximum decisions*

$$\mathcal{D}^* = \{x^* \in \mathcal{X} \mid \mu_D(x^*) \geq \mu_D(x) \text{ for all } x \in \mathcal{X}\}. \tag{3.76}$$

If the components of the programming problem can compensate each other, possibly only partially, then t-norms can no longer reflect the situation adequately. It is possible to take *compromises* into account through the determining of weight functions α_i, β_j with

$$\sum_i \alpha_i(x) + \sum_j \beta_j(x) = 1, \qquad \text{for all } x \in \mathcal{X}, \tag{3.77}$$

and construction of a fuzzy solution $D(\alpha, \beta)$ by

$$\mu_D(x; \alpha, \beta) = \sum_{i=1}^n \alpha_i(x)\mu_{C_i}(x) + \sum_{j=1}^m \beta_j(x)\mu_{G_j}(x). \tag{3.78}$$

In this way we obtain a family of aggregations *between* non-interactive intersection and union

$$\left(\bigcap_{i=1}^n C_i\right) \cap \left(\bigcap_{j=1}^m G_j\right) \subseteqq D(\alpha, \beta) \subseteqq \left(\bigcup_{i=1}^n C_i\right) \cup \left(\bigcup_{j=1}^m G_j\right), \tag{3.79}$$

which allows already proper adaptations to specific connections and experts' ideas. However, also other settings are possible and useful, like, e.g., (2.98), (2.99) instead of (2.71), among them also those, which take into account interactivity of the variables belonging to the components, in the sense of

Section 3.3. With respect to even compensatory and averaging connections, which are not based on t-norms, we refer to ZIMMERMANN (1985) and ROMMELFANGER (1994). In the following we will denote the respective fuzzy solution set by D.

If the membership value $\mu_D(x^*)$ in (3.76) is very small when compared with 1, then this means that the objectives and the constraints are conflicting, in some sense, and do not allow a satisfying solution of the problem. For this case ASAI/TANAKA/OKUDA (1975) suggest a procedure, leading to a satisfying solution in practical cases by modelling a certain behaviour of tolerance of the components of the programming problem. With this procedure it is first investigated, which of the components is "responsible" for the low degree of satisfaction. Then this component is defused, e.g. by reducing the coefficient of relevance or by changing the weight function or the bounds in the constraint.

Formulation of fuzzy objectives and constraints has general importance for the development of decision theory and control theory on the basis of fuzzy set theory.

For an illustration of the performance we choose the *linear programming problem* with only one objective G:

$$G = g^\top x = \min !$$
$$Ax \leq b \tag{3.80}$$
$$x \geq 0 \quad \text{for } x \in \mathbb{R}^k.$$

In this problem the vectors $g \in \mathbb{R}^k, b \in \mathbb{R}^n$ and the $(n \times k)$-matrix A are given. Whereas demanding non-negativity $x \geq 0$ is justified by the real problem, as a rule, the other conditions, e.g. the constraints $Ax \leq b$, are mostly meant only fuzzily. Hence ZIMMERMANN (1976, 1978, 1985) suggests replacing these bounds by suitable fuzzy relations "more or less smaller". In the simplest case this is performed by introducing linear membership functions on the interval $[b_i, b_i + d_i]$, where b_i is the component of b and d_i is the component of a given vector d, which indicates the amount, to which the bounds b_i in (3.80) can be exceeded each at the utmost. Moreover, it is suggested replacing the objective by the demand that G should fall below a given bound g_0. This bound can be specified, e.g., from the situation directly or by the solution of the crisp programming problem in the "least favourable case": $Ax = b + d$. Also the so obtained bound $G \leq g_0$ is modelled as a fuzzy relation, e.g., by a linear membershp function. Here we have an example of how the objective is modelled by a fuzzy set, as mentioned and assumed already in the introduction of this section. Obviously this way remains practicable for several (linear) objectives. So, the programming problem becomes symmetric, i.e., objectives and constraints are of the same mathematical structure:

$$G \leq g_0,$$
$$\boldsymbol{A}\boldsymbol{x} \leq \boldsymbol{b}, \quad \boldsymbol{x} \geq \boldsymbol{0}. \tag{3.81}$$

The fuzzy solution D of (3.81) can now be obtained according to (3.74) or (3.78). From this solution a set $\mathcal{D}^*$ of maximum decisions according to (3.76) can be deduced, which can be used as crisp decisions. In the case, when *all* the membership functions are *linear*, we can obtain $\boldsymbol{x}^* \in \mathcal{D}^*$ directly by solving the crisp programming problem:

$$\lambda = \max !,$$
$$\lambda \boldsymbol{d} + \boldsymbol{A}\boldsymbol{x} \leq \boldsymbol{b} + \boldsymbol{d}, \tag{3.82}$$
$$\lambda d_0 + \boldsymbol{g}^{\mathsf{T}} \boldsymbol{x} \leq g_0 + d_0,$$
$$\boldsymbol{x} \geq \boldsymbol{0},$$

where d_0 is the bound of maximum exceeding for g_0.

When also non-linear membership functions occur, the determination of x^*, by this way, requires the solution of non-linear programming problems, which can be transformed into linear ones in certain cases (cf. GEYER-SCHULZ (1986)).

3.4.2   Optimising over a Fuzzy Region

If it is not possible to replace the objective by a constraint-like condition containing a certain bound, then we have the problem of optimising a crisp function over a fuzzy region C, which is determined by the constraints C_i, e.g., by $C = \bigcap_{i=1}^{n} C_i$ (see ORLOVSKY (1977)).

For every α-cut $C^{\geq \alpha}$ we consider the solution set

$$S(\alpha) = \left\{ \boldsymbol{x} \in C^{\geq \alpha} \mid G(\boldsymbol{x}) = \inf_{y \in C^{\geq \alpha}} G(\boldsymbol{y}) \right\} \tag{3.83}$$

and compute from this the solution D with

$$\mu_D(\boldsymbol{x}) = \begin{cases} \sup_{x \in S(\alpha)} \alpha & \text{for } \boldsymbol{x} \in \bigcup_{\alpha > 0} S(\alpha), \\ 0 & \text{otherwise.} \end{cases} \tag{3.84}$$

From this we obtain for the fuzzy optimum value G^* of G the membership function

$$\mu_G(r) = \begin{cases} \sup_{x \in G^{-1}(r)} \mu_D(\boldsymbol{x}) & \text{for } G^{-1}(r) \neq \emptyset, \\ 0 & \text{for all other } r \in \mathbb{R}. \end{cases} \tag{3.85}$$

The solution sets $S(\alpha)$ can be computed for all $\alpha \in (0, 1]$ by methods of parametric programming from

$$G(\boldsymbol{x}) = \min !,$$
$$\alpha \leq \mu_{C_i}(\boldsymbol{x}). \tag{3.86}$$

For practical use a finite selection of α-values will suffice.

Uncertainty w.r.t. $\boldsymbol{A}$ and $\boldsymbol{b}$ in (3.80) can be taken into account, in principle, by specifying fuzzy numbers. The term $\boldsymbol{Ax}$ must be realised via extended addition and subtraction, whereas the order relation ($\geq$) can be left as a sharp one or be replaced by a suitable fuzzy relation. In this way fuzzy constraints C_i are specified, which, aggregated to a crisp set C, can be handled further according to the above explained concept (cf. RAMIK/RIMANEK (1985)). Practicability of this procedure depends on the competitiveness of the computers available. For particular cases, so for equations as constraints and for fuzzy numbers in L/R-representation, there are some suggestions by DUBOIS/PRADE (1978, 1980).

For the procedures presented here for fuzzification of problems of linear programming the linearity of the problems is of importance for the numerical treatment of the problems to be solved as, e.g., in (3.82) and (3.83). In principle also non-linear programming problems can be handled analogously. However, the numerical work can grow essentially.

With respect to a detailed and extensive presentation of fuzzy programming we can recommend the monograph by ROMMELFANGER(1994).

Finally mentioned, also problems of dynamic programming can be fuzzified in this way and handled (cf. e.g. DUBOIS/PRADE (1980), ZIMMERMANN (1985)). However, in such cases today frequently the programming problem is replaced by a linguistic description of the problem, which is treated with methods of approximate reasoning, since this approach yields, possibly, a more comprehensible solution of the original problem, and which is frequently obtainable more easily by computers, so if the problem is from optimal control (cf. Section 4.2).

4 Linguistic Variables and Their Applications

4.1 The Notion of a Linguistic Variable

The traditional mathematical modelling of industrial processes as well as of processes in nature is based on the quantitative description of those processes. Such a quantitative description either uses crisp, i.e. exact numerical data, or such data together with error bounds. Unfortunately, from the point of view of the applications these crisp numerical data as well as their error bounds are often only pseudo-exactly determined data. Contrary to this situation, in everyday life or even in everyday industrial work, processes and algorithmic, or "rule based" behaviour are usually described much more qualitatively, using in general some more or less imprecise pieces of information, often in the form of vague data. As typical examples the reader may remember the instructions for driving a car he got at driving school, especially e.g. the instructions governing the process of parking a car into a (small) parking space parallel to the traffic direction. Other typical examples are cooking recipes with their vague data of "a teaspoon of ..." etc., others are some characteristic effects for diagnosing some specific kinds of illness, and evaluations of the quality of scientific work or of welding seams, to mention also finally a severe industrial problem.

All these non-mathematical examples typically refer to essential data, instructions, characteristic features etc. (also) in some imprecise, rough, vague, qualitative way. The problem is whether such rough descriptions can become implementable for a computer, and thus for automated treatment only via their transformation into traditional mathematical models. And the actual answer, in our context of fuzzy sets, is that e.g. the fuzzy variables of Section 3.3 provide quite natural means to convert such qualitative descriptions into implementable forms without detouring through traditional mathematical models. The main idea is to have an almost direct correspondence between qualitative data of the rough models and (fuzzy) values of fuzzy variables. Of course, in relation to the rough model one still has to fix for each significant fuzzy variable the universe of discourse of its values together with some fuzzy subsets of this universe which really should be used as values.

There is still another aspect of the fuzzy values of fuzzy variables: to become utilisable they have to be named. But the difference with real numbers is that standard names for fuzzy sets do not exist (as they do for numbers). Therefore it seems to be advisable to use the intuitive relations of the fuzzy variables to some applicational background to select names for the values under consideration – and to select names which also occur in the rough model that constitutes the applicational background.

This point of view, of naming the values of fuzzy variables using suitable words in our everyday language, was already explained by ZADEH (1975) who created this idea of fuzzy variables to call them *linguistic variables*, e.g. to distinguish them from numerical variables with imprecisely determined values. But one has to be very careful here: it is as inessential for the true character of a fuzzy variable whether their values are named by linguistic terms or not, as it is inessential for a real variable to have their values denoted using decimal notation or using hexadecimal notation.

For applications the most interesting aspect of linguistic variables is the possibility of using these variables to "translate" nearly immediately some rough description of some industrial process – of course a description of such a process which can successfully be used by a human operator – into a formalised, non-traditional mathematical model to be implemented almost directly. The main problem which remains is to specify the membership functions of the "linguistic" values of the linguistic variables which are involved into the modelling process. Actually it is one of the main lines of research to try to determine these membership functions by automatic learning processes, or even to learn control rules, e.g. by the use of neural net techniques or by using genetic algorithms; cf. TAKAGI/HAYASHI (1991), BERENJI (1992), BERENJI/KHEDKAR (1992), HAYASHI et al. (1992), NAUCK/KLAWONN/KRUSE (1993) as well as the books by NAUCK/KLAWONN/KRUSE (1994) and by GEYER-SCHULZ (1994). Besides these approaches the only other hints one has in general is able to give are that these membership functions have to be chosen according to the special knowledge of the expert – and that they perhaps have to be tuned via trial and error.

There is general agreement that usually a fuzzy variable with values in a class $I\!F(\mathcal{X})$ does not have all the fuzzy subsets of $\mathcal{X}$ as its values. A remarkable additional idea, already explained in ZADEH (1975), is that all the values of some fuzzy variable (which is under consideration for some specific application) could be supposed to be determined by a *generative grammar* out of some few basic linguistic values. Each such generative grammar then has to start from the linguistic terms which denote these basic linguistic values, and proceeds to further linguistic terms mainly via sentential connectives like "and", "or", "not" etc. and by the use of *linguistic modifiers* like "very", "more or less". Iterated applications of these tools then give the whole expressive power of sentential logic, but also further modifiers like "not very much", "very very" etc. Also these more complicated linguistic terms are names of fuzzy values of the linguistic variable with which the grammar is related. On the side of the fuzzy values to the "linguistic" combinations of the grammar there are corresponding operations on fuzzy sets. If a linguistic combination of the names of fuzzy values is realised by one of the sentential connectives then obviously there is a corresponding set algebraic operation: this is obvious for "and", "or", and "not" – and all the other sentential connectives can be equivalently represented, intuitively, using only these connectives. More difficult is the situation for the linguistic modifiers. They have to be represented by unary operations on fuzzy sets, but there do not exist any commonly accepted candidates for such corresponding operations on fuzzy sets.

For an illustration of the problem let us look at an example. We consider a linguistic variable to describe the age of some object. Possible fields of application here are medical or psychological modelling, but also the problem of wearing out of tools e.g. in (automated) production lines. According to common usage we denote this linguistic variable by AGE. Its fuzzy values shall be subsets of the real interval $[0, 100]$. As basic linguistic values we consider, cf. Fig. 4.1, fuzzy sets named: young, middle-aged, old. Then it is easy to show the results of sentential combinations of these names. So e.g. the fuzzy value named not old is the complement of the fuzzy set named old,

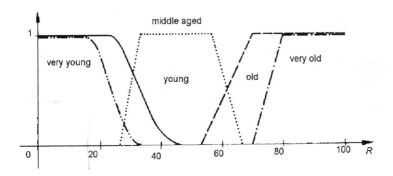

Figure 4.1: Linguistic values of AGE

and the same holds true for not middle-aged. The fuzzy set named young or old is of course the union of the fuzzy sets named young and named old. And the fuzzy set named young but (and) not middle-aged is the intersection of the fuzzy sets named young and not middle-aged.

As discussed in Sections 2.3 and 2.4 here intersection and union can be understood as t-norm based. But, if there is no mentioning of a t-norm in this context, the min-based operations are always intended.

Possible linguistic modifiers for this fuzzy variable AGE surely are the hedges very and more or less which allow to built up the linguistic terms very young, not very old, more or less middle-aged, very very young etc. But not all formally possible combinations seem to be acceptable: intuitively not acceptable are e.g. very middle-aged, very (young or old), very more or less young. For the generative grammar this means that usually the generating rules have to be combined with some restrictions. But such restrictions have to be imposed specifically for each single case. More interesting and more important is looking e.g. for the unary operator on fuzzy sets connected with the hedge very. In the present case this operator has to produce a fuzzy subset of $[0, 100]$ out of some – preferably: each – fuzzy subset of $[0, 100]$. Without giving any details Fig. 4.1 shows some resulting fuzzy sets which an application of this operator may have produced.

Our example illustrates two main problems: Neither gives the usual intuitive approach sufficient information to uniquely determine the membership functions which correspond to the basic linguistic terms, nor does it determine sufficiently well the operators which correspond to the linguistic modifiers. To overcome the last mentioned problem at least partially, ZADEH (1975) offered the proposal to uniformly interpret very as squaring of the membership degrees (and more or less as taking the square roots). In our example, yet, this approach gives e.g.

$$\mu_{\text{very old}}(x) =_{\text{def}} (\mu_{\text{old}}(x))^2, \qquad\qquad (4.1)$$

which seems quite inappropriate. For, starting from our obviously acceptable choice $\mu_{\text{old}}(70) = 1$, cf. Fig. 4.1, i.e. agreeing with the approach that a 70 years old person is an old one really, this approach toward the understanding of the hedge very forces also $\mu_{\text{very old}}(70) = 1$ which is not really at all plausible, and forces even $\mu_{\text{very very old}}(70) = 1$ which is obviously unacceptable. Therefore in Fig. 4.1 instead of (4.1) a combination of a "translation" of the membership function and an enlargement of its slope has been used. (The mathematical details are once again not important here.)

In general, each application of fuzzy variables needs separate, and at least partially independent decisions concerning the basic linguistic terms, the fuzzy sets named by them, and the choice and mathematical understanding of the linguistic modifiers. As a simplification, therefore, in not too complicated cases, e.g. if some linguistic variable has only few linguistic values, one tends to avoid the creation of these values by a generative grammar and prefers to define them all separately.

Nevertheless, this theoretical deficit is not so severe as to turn down the idea of using linguistic variables, especially for applications which tend to combine rough modelling with fuzzy sets techniques. It is much more important for any application to know about these theoretical deficiencies and thus to be able to circumvent them. The method of choice, actually, in all such applications is to define the relevant fuzzy sets (and sometimes also the fuzzy set operations) with reference to some parameters, and finally to tune these parameters by trial and error – or by neural net techniques (or even some other method from the field of automatic learning). For suitable applications this is still a much more efficient procedure than trying to develop a traditional mathematical model.

4.2 Fuzzy Control

Now we shall take a closer look at a methodology of rough, imprecise modelling which has proven its suitability in a lot of very interesting cases, cf. Section 4.5. The main field of applications is actually in the area of automatic control: in closed loop as well as in open loop control situations. The goal is to use fuzzy set tools to devise rough models of processes in a way which allows one to implement such rough models almost straightforwardly on a computer – and to use the implementation either for automatic control or in man-machine dialogues. Also a combination of both these types of usage is possible: to have completely automatic control in "normal" situations, and the man-machine dialogue in "extremal" situations of the process behaviour.

4.2.1 Fuzzy Controller

This methodology of fuzzy control as a way to process fuzzy information, the result of which is called a *fuzzy controller,* is characterised by the following two basic ideas:

1. A fuzzy controller has to be able to act on fuzzy input data to create – usually again fuzzy – output data.

2. The design of a fuzzy controller in general is supposed to be rule based. And this design has to allow the treatment of only qualitatively given process information, like a human operator is able to do (if he knows some – usually likewise qualitative – rules for his control behaviour).

If one directly links a fuzzy controller with a process and its control, then the first one of these ideas is often considered as of minor importance, despite the fact that even the measurement outputs of sensors can often realistically only be understood as fuzzy data. The background for this point of view is the quite traditional understanding, that physical or chemical sensors produce crisp output values as actual control inputs, and that automatic control tools really act as if they would realise crisp values (precisely). But idea 1 is closely related to idea 2. Nevertheless, for true applications one has to be careful to allow not only "truly fuzzy" but also crisp (maybe pseudo-exact) input data – e.g. the outputs of some standard measuring devices – as well as to provide additional methods to convert (automatically) a fuzzy output of the fuzzy controller into a crisp – and thus usually pseudo-exact – one, which again an automatic control tool may realise. (Again here, from the more theoretical point of view one has to have in mind that de facto any such automatic, i.e. usually mechanical tool, that realizes a control output, works only with approximate preciseness.) Thus true automatic control idea 2 is often seen as to have superiority over idea 1. But idea 1 is at least very important (i) for the internal process of developing a fuzzy controller, and (ii) for all fuzzy control systems which act within man-machine dialogues – and moreover in all the cases where the idea of fuzzy control or of fuzzy rule based information processing is used in expert systems.

Both these ideas force a fuzzy controller to be able to cope with qualitative information. Therefore one assumes that the input as well as the output variables of such a fuzzy controller are fuzzy or even linguistic variables. Furthermore, the fact that the design of a fuzzy controller aims at rule basing is usually seen as intending that one starts from a kind of "linguistic protocol" which collects the relevant process (control) information in the form of rules. And, of course, these rules connect characteristic values of the main input and output variables of the process.

Basically therefore a fuzzy controller realises a fuzzy relationship between its input and its output variables. This fuzzy relationship models either the behaviour of the process to be controlled or the necessary control actions.

Formally the preferred understanding of this fuzzy relationship is to take it as a fuzzy relation; cf. Section 3.3. Therefore, to design a fuzzy controller means to design a rule base which connects (linguistic) values of the fuzzy input and output variables, i.e. which sums up the relevant process information in more or less qualitative form, and afterwards to transform this rule base into a fuzzy relation.

This transformation of a rule base into a fuzzy relation may happen in two different ways: either explicitly in determining some fuzzy relation, or implicitly in fixing some method to "join" the partial information about the overall fuzzy relationship between input and output variables contained in each single rule into a global one. The latter way obviously very much imitates the usual interpolation strategy for only partially, e.g. pointwise, determined functions.

The first one of these approaches, to build up a fuzzy relation R out of a list (4.2) of control rules, was initially used by MAMDANI/ASSILIAN (1975) for the control of an engine-boiler combination and is therefore often referred to as the MAMDANI approach – or this type of fuzzy controller is termed MAMDANI controller.

The second one of these approaches, the more direct "combination" of all the control rules – which are supposed to "act" in parallel – was first used by HOLMBLAD/ØSTERGAARD (1982) and later on in a modified form by SUGENO/NISHIDA (1985).

Despite the fact that both these approaches look quite different at first glance, each one of them may be interpreted in terms of the other one, as a more detailed study will show later on.

The fact, cf. Section 3.3, that one is always able to collect several (input as well as output) variables into one – with a more complex, multi-dimensional universe of discourse – enables one to restrict the following considerations to the case of one (linguistic) input variable u and one (linguistic) output variable v. Furthermore, in this case the rule base which comprises the qualitative process information becomes the form

$$\text{IF } u = A_i \text{ THEN } v = B_i, \quad i = 1, \ldots, n \qquad (4.2)$$

of a list of *control rules* (3.63). (Of course, instead of these rules, control rules of type (3.69) or of further, more complicated types can be taken into consideration. But usually one restricts to systems (4.2) of control rules, and substitutes for a rule of type (3.69) two rules of type (3.63).)

For the whole process of designing a fuzzy controller the problem of the transformation of the rule base (4.2) into a fuzzy relation is only one of several important problems. Even more important for an engineer who designs a fuzzy controller is the choice of the input and output variables u, v, of their – fuzzy or linguistic – values, and of the whole list (4.2) of control rules. Another decision connected with these choices is whether the process to be controlled shall be controlled by a single fuzzy controller – or by several fuzzy controllers which act in parallel. It is always possible to approach this aspect of the design problem as was supposed in (4.2): with one input and one output variable.

Even in a case where one does not have, from the very beginning, k independent output variables $v_1, \ldots, v_k$ which could be treated by parallel controllers, but if one has only one output variable v initially, then one should test if this output variable can be "split" into several. This splitting test should already be done for the system (4.2) of control rules. Having in mind that for a complex output variable $v = (v_1, \ldots, v_k)$ all the output values B_i in (4.2) themselves are fuzzy relations, i.e. code fuzzy relationships between $v_1, \ldots, v_k$, then the crucial formal splitting condition for a system (4.2) of control rules into independent systems for $v_1, \ldots, v_k$, is just the condition that $v_1, \ldots, v_k$ are non-interactive w.r.t. all the fuzzy relations $B_1, \ldots, B_n$, i.e. is that $B_1, \ldots, B_n$ are separable fuzzy relations.

Quite often this *splitting* into several fuzzy controllers acting in parallel has further advantages besides the simplification of the corresponding list of control rules. One point is that often not every one of these "split" controllers needs each one of the input variables. Another one is that different ones of these single controllers may act with quite different frequencies in their input measurements and in their control actions. And finally the smaller size of the single fuzzy controller allows for high frequencies in their control actions, a fact that may prove decisive for some control processes which need high frequency control actions – and which only may become controllable in true time with this splitting strategy.

4.2.2   The MAMDANI Approach

As already mentioned in Section 3.3, by now the standard understanding is that each control rule of the list (4.2) is interpreted as producing a value assignment $v := B_i$ out of a value assignment $u := A_i$. In the MAMDANI approach one is then using a fuzzy relation R which is supposed to be "coded" by (4.2), and refers to the compositional rule of inference (3.62). But, such a fuzzy controller shall also be able to act for (fuzzy) input data, i.e. values $u = A$ of the input variable which have not explicitly been mentioned in system (4.2), i.e. which are characterised by $A \neq A_i$ for $i = 1, \ldots, n$. Even in such cases in the MAMDANI approach one is able to use the fuzzy relation R coded by (4.2), and additionally refers to the compositional rule of inference. Hence, having given as an input the value assignment $u := A$, one assigns, using the notation of (3.64), to the output variable v the value

$$v := A \circ R, \tag{4.3}$$

i.e. one chooses according to (3.62)

$$\mu_{A \circ R}(y) = \sup_{x \in \mathcal{X}} \min\{\mu_A(x), \mu_R(x, y)\} \quad \text{for all } y \in \mathcal{Y}. \tag{4.4}$$

It is (4.3) or (4.4), together with the determination of a fuzzy relation R by a system of control rules (4.2), which makes the MAMDANI type fuzzy controllers as useful as they really are. Of course, (4.3) presupposes that the system (4.2) of control rules is chosen in such a way that it is "representative" for the actual process (or its control).

To get an idea of how to proceed in getting a fuzzy relation R which may code the system (4.2) of control rules, let us first consider the case $n = 1$ of a system (4.2) of only one control rule. In this situation one can immediately use

$$R_1 = A_1 \otimes B_1, \tag{4.5}$$

i.e. can take R_1 as the fuzzy cartesian product of the fuzzy data A_1, B_1. With this choice

$$\mu_{R_1}(a, b) = \min\{\mu_{A_1}(a), \ \mu_{B_1}(b)\}, \tag{4.6}$$

and the compositional rule of inference (3.62) one has for each $y \in \mathcal{Y}$ the membership degree in the output fuzzy set $D := A_1 \circ R_1$ determined as:

$$
\begin{aligned}
\mu_D(y) &= \sup_{x \in \mathcal{X}} \min\{\mu_{A_1}(x), \min\{\mu_{A_1}(x), \mu_{B_1}(y)\}\} \\
&= \sup_{x \in \mathcal{X}} \min\{\mu_{A_1}(x), \mu_{B_1}(y)\} = \mu_{B_1}(y).
\end{aligned} \tag{4.7}
$$

Assuming only that one has $\mathrm{hgt}\,(A_1) \geq \mathrm{hgt}\,(B_1)$, this yields

$$B_1 = A_1 \circ R_1. \tag{4.8}$$

In general, according to (4.5) with each control rule of a system (4.2) one can connect a fuzzy relation $R_i = A_i \otimes B_i$, and then one can use all these "single" fuzzy relations to "compose" out of them one fuzzy relation R related to the whole system (4.2). MAMDANI/ASSILIAN (1975) start just in this way with (4.5) and then use the composition

$$R = \bigcup_{i=1}^{n} R_i = \bigcup_{i=1}^{n}(A_i \otimes B_i). \tag{4.9}$$

This gives them a very simple possibility to determine a fuzzy relation R out of the system (4.2) of control rules and their input/output data A_i, B_i. Written down in a more explicit manner, their approach results in a superposition of the minimisation (4.6) with a maximisation as

$$\mu_R(a, b) = \max_{1 \leq i \leq n} \min\{\mu_{A_i}(a), \mu_{B_i}(b)\}. \tag{4.10}$$

The whole fuzzy controller which is based on this fuzzy relation thus, according to the compositional rule of inference (3.62), connects with each fuzzy input $u := A$ the fuzzy output $v := A \circ R$ determined as

$$
\begin{aligned}
\mu_{A \circ R}(y) &= \sup_{\substack{x \in \mathcal{X} \\ i=1,\ldots,n}} \min\{\mu_A(x), \mu_{A_i}(x), \mu_{B_i}(y)\} \\
&= \max_{i=1,\ldots,n} \min\{\mathrm{hgt}\,(A \cap A_i), \mu_{B_i}(y)\}.
\end{aligned} \tag{4.11}
$$

From the mathematical point of view, determining a fuzzy controller via this MAMDANI approach means to determine the fuzzy relation R which characterises it out of the system (4.2) of control rules. And via (4.4) this system (4.2) can be understood as a system

$$B_i = A_i \circ R, \qquad i = 1, \ldots, n \tag{4.12}$$

of relational equations (3.64). Here the fuzzy sets A_i, B_i are given data, and the fuzzy relation R has to be determined. This type of mathematical problem is treated in Section 4.3.

With regard to the problem of the splitting of one fuzzy controller into several ones, which have to act in parallel, one has to have in mind that for automation one perhaps has to implement the fuzzy relation R on a computer according to (4.12) or (4.9) or some other choice of R, and has to use it via (4.3) together with the compositional rule of inference (3.62) as an "inference mechanism" to get a value assignment for the output variable from a value assignment to its corresponding input variable. In practice R often is implemented as a matrix, and the compositional rule of inference is implemented in the form (3.65). But in this situation having collected several output variables $v_1, \ldots, v_k$ into one $v = (v_1, \ldots, v_k)$ may result in an enormous increase of the necessary storing capacity. Because, by (3.1) the number l of rows of the matrix R is the cardinality of the universe of discourse $\mathcal{X}$ of the input variable u, and the number m of columns is the cardinality of the universe of discourse $\mathcal{Y}$ of the output variable v. Thus, having a multi-dimensional output variable $v = (v_1, \ldots, v_k)$ and for the universes $\mathcal{Y}_j$, $j = 1, \ldots, k$ of the variables v_j the cardinalities m_j, then the product $m = m_1 \cdot \ldots \cdot m_k$ is the number of columns of R – and each output value $v = B$ is itself a fuzzy relation in $\mathcal{Y} = \mathcal{Y}_1 \times \cdots \times \mathcal{Y}_k$. But if one takes into consideration here instead of one fuzzy controller with output variable $v = (v_1, \ldots, v_k)$ just k fuzzy controllers with the output variables $v_1, \ldots, v_k$, respectively, for parallel work then these controllers determine matrices R_j, $j = 1, \ldots, k$, with m_j columns for the j-th controller. Thus, on the one hand one has the matrix R with $l \cdot (m_1 \cdot \ldots \cdot m_k)$ elements, on the other hand in case of a parallel handling only the much smaller number $l \cdot (m_1 + \cdots + m_k)$ of elements of all the matrices $R_1, \ldots, R_k$.

This *splitting* of the control output into independent output variables was already realised in the very first application of the fuzzy control methodology by MAMDANI/ASSILIAN (1975): they considered (in a laboratory environment) a combination of a steam engine with a boiler in such a way that with two input variables for the steam pressure in the boiler and the speed of the engine they controlled two control variables with parallel fuzzy controllers: the heat input at the boiler and the throttle opening at the input of the engine cylinder.

4.2.3 The Method of Activation Degrees

The understanding of a fuzzy controller R as a tool to determine to each input value $u := A$ an output value $v := B$ via (4.3), (4.4), i.e. the specification of R as a fuzzy relation together with the choice $B = A \circ R$, this is only one way to implement a fuzzy control strategy. Another way, a more direct use of the system (4.2) of control rules, a way without a direct detour on a fuzzy relation, first was used by HOLMBLAD/ØSTERGAARD (1982): the *method of degrees of activation.*

This method avoids combining explicitly with (4.2) a fuzzy relation. Instead one has to have another possibility to treat an input value $u := A$ which does not appear in any one of the control rules (4.2) as a value of u. Hence, for such a situation one now has to determine how the single rules of (4.2) have to "react" for any possible input value assignment $u := A$.

For the traditional rule based systems our present problem has a very simple solution: a rule becomes applicable just in those cases where the input condition of this rule is satisfied. This understanding is still not the right one in the fuzzy field: here we also have to discuss the case that the input condition of a rule (3.63) is actually satisfied only "to some degree". This degree of satisfaction of the input condition of a rule (3.63) under some specific input value A is taken as the degree to which this input value A "activates" the rule under consideration.

This degree of activation of the j-th rule of (4.2) for a given input $u := A$ then acts as a parameter which influences a degree to which the output value B_j of rule j determines the actual output $v := B$ of the fuzzy controller for the input A. In a suitable sense hence the actual output B for the input A is determined as a kind of weighted superposition of the output values of the single rules. Of course there are a lot of possibilities of defining a degree to which an actual input value $u := A$ activates the j-th control rule of (4.2), as well as for this kind of weighted superposition which has to refer to the degrees of activation and the outputs of the rules of (4.2).

The choice of HOLMBLAD/ØSTERGAARD (1982) is that they define as a *degree of activation* of rule j of (4.2) in case of input $u := A$ the number

$$\beta_j = \mathrm{hgt}\,(A \cap A_j) = \sup_{x \in \mathcal{X}} \min\{\mu_A(x), \mu_{A_j}(x)\}. \tag{4.13}$$

Intuitively, this degree of activation can be seen as a very simple "degree of coincidence" between the actual input value A and the "standard" input A_j of rule j. The weighted superposition then means in this case, that the output B_j of rule j influences the total output B only to the "degree" β_j, i.e. that a product of B_j and β_j, a new fuzzy set C_j defined by

$$C_j := \beta_j \cdot B_j : \quad \mu_{C_j}(y) = \beta_j \cdot \mu_{B_j}(y) \quad \text{for all } y \in \mathcal{Y}, \tag{4.14}$$

is considered instead of B_j and used for determining the total output B as

$$\mu_B(y) = \max_{1 \leq j \leq n} \mu_{C_j}(y)$$

$$= \max_{1 \leq j \leq n} \left(\sup_{x \in \mathcal{X}} \min\{\mu_A(x), \mu_{A_j}(x)\} \right) \cdot \mu_{B_j}(y). \tag{4.15}$$

The degree of activation β_j of the j-th control rule w.r.t. some fuzzy input value $u := A$ measures a kind of "deviance" of the actual input value $u = A$ and the j-th rules input value $u = A_j$ (the "standard input situation" for that rule). Hence, the method of degrees of activation in this respect is analogous to standard *interpolation* procedures where one refers to interpolation nodes and the distances of the actual argument to (some of) these nodes – and where one then (often linearly) combines the weighted function values at the nodes to get the interpolated value at the actual argument place. Obviously, here the fuzzy input values are taken into consideration instead of argument values of a function. The weighted superposition of the rules outputs to determine the actual output (4.15) again clearly parallels the standard interpolation behaviour.

4.2.4   Comparing Both Approaches*

In more set theoretic terms the output value $v = B$ for the input value $u = A$ according to the approach of HOLMBLAD/ØSTERGAARD (1982) can be written down as

$$B = \bigcup_{j=1}^{n} \beta_j \cdot B_j = \bigcup_{j=1}^{n} \mathrm{hgt}\,(A \cap A_j) \cdot B_j. \tag{4.16}$$

Using the class term notation (2.40) this means

$$B = \{y \,\|\, \bigvee_{j=1}^{n} (\exists x (x \,\varepsilon\, A \,\wedge\, x \,\varepsilon\, A_j) \,\&_1\, y \,\varepsilon\, B_j)\} \tag{4.17}$$

where $\&_1$ denotes the conjunction connective of many-valued logic with the t-norm t_1 of (2.112) as its corresponding truth degree function.

Changing the product $\beta_j \cdot B_j$ in (4.14), (4.16) into another modification $\beta_j \sqcap B_j$ defined as

$$D_j := \beta_j \sqcap B_j : \quad \mu_{D_j}(y) = \min\{\beta_j, \mu_{B_j}(y)\} \quad \text{for all } y \in \mathcal{Y},$$

then by routine calculation one can show that the MAMDANI approach follows the same pattern. Having $R_M = \bigcup_{j=1}^{n}(A_j \otimes B_j)$ determined from the list (4.2) of control rules, the fuzzy output $A \circ R_M$ for a fuzzy input $u = A$ as given in (4.4) can be written as

$$A \circ R_M = \bigcup_{j=1}^{n} \beta_j \sqcap B_j, \tag{4.18}$$

because one has

$$
\begin{aligned}
A \circ R_M &= \{y \,\|\, \exists x (x \,\varepsilon\, A \,\wedge\, (x,y) \,\varepsilon\, \bigcup_{j=1}^{n} (A_j \otimes B_j))\} \\
&= \{y \,\|\, \exists x (x \,\varepsilon\, A \,\wedge\, \bigvee_{j=1}^{n} (x \,\varepsilon\, A_j \,\wedge\, y \,\varepsilon\, B_j))\},
\end{aligned}
\tag{4.19}
$$

which, finally, can be written as

$$B = \{y \,\|\, \bigvee_{j=1}^{n} (\exists x (x \,\varepsilon\, A \,\wedge\, x \,\varepsilon\, A_j) \,\wedge\, y \,\varepsilon\, B_j)\}. \tag{4.20}$$

And this, clearly, parallels formula (4.17).

Thus, both these approaches toward fuzzy control can be understood as variants of interpolation between given control rules.

On the other hand, to compare these two approaches toward fuzzy controllers from the point of view of the MAMDANI approach, based on the more "global" attitude to represent a list of control rules by one fuzzy relation, we use again the class term notation (2.40) and our reference to the language of many-valued logic. Based on a system (4.2) of control rules the output value $v := B$ for an input value $u := A$ in case of the MAMDANI/ASSILIAN (1975) approach is easily found to be determined as

$$B = \left\{ y \in \mathcal{Y} \,\|\, \exists x \,(x \,\varepsilon\, A \,\wedge\, (x,y) \,\varepsilon\, \bigcup_{j=1}^{n} (A_j \otimes B_j)) \right\}. \tag{4.21}$$

Here conjunction $\wedge$ means the min-operator, and the min-operator is also used in the definition of the fuzzy cartesian product $\otimes$. Set theoretically, in (4.21) the fuzzy set B is the (generalised, i.e. fuzzified) full image of the fuzzy (input) set A under a fuzzy relation.

Approach (4.16), (4.17) of the method of activation degrees does not directly follow this pattern. Formula (4.17) obviously can be rewritten as

$$B = \{y \,\|\, \exists x \bigvee_{j=1}^{n} ((x \,\varepsilon\, A \,\wedge\, x \,\varepsilon\, A_j) \,\&_1\, y \,\varepsilon\, B_j)\} \tag{4.22}$$

which is still analogous to formula (4.20). But the way "back" to a formula which parallels formula (4.19) is blocked: To get formula (4.20) from formula (4.19) one needs, among others, the associativity of $\wedge$, but actually there does not hold any kind of associativity w.r.t. a common appearance of both connectives $\wedge$ and $\&_1$. Instead, a distributivity law holds true enabling reformulation of (4.22) as

$$B = \{y \,\|\, \exists x \bigvee_{j=1}^{n} ((x \,\varepsilon\, A \,\&_1\, y \,\varepsilon\, B_j) \wedge (x \,\varepsilon\, A_j \,\&_1\, y \,\varepsilon\, B_j))\},$$

but this does not seem to be an interesting reformulation. Nevertheless, there is a slight variation of formula (4.17) which does follow the pattern of the MAMDANI approach. Having in mind the multiplication in (4.14) one can change (4.13) into

$$\gamma_j = \mathrm{hgt}\,(A \bullet A_j), \tag{4.23}$$

i.e. one can in (4.13) exchange the intersection operation according to (2.71) for the intersection according to (2.98). Again via (4.14) this new degree γ_j of activation of the j-th control rule provides the modified rule output

$$C_j := \gamma_j \cdot B_j : \quad \mu_{C_j}(y) = \gamma_j \cdot \mu_{B_j}(y) \quad \text{for all } y \in \mathcal{Y}. \tag{4.24}$$

Superposition of these modified outputs as before gives then instead of (4.15) the result

$$B = \left\{ y \in \mathcal{Y} \,\|\, \exists x \,(x \,\varepsilon\, A \,\&_1\, (x, y) \,\varepsilon\, \bigcup_{j=1}^{n} (A_j \otimes_{t_1} B_j)) \right\}. \tag{4.25}$$

Hence also from the point of view of MAMDANI's approach toward fuzzy control the two approaches of MAMDANI/ASSILIAN (1975) and of HOLMBLAD/ØSTERGAARD (1982) are more deeply related than would seem on the surface. Furthermore, even the choice of the degree of activation (4.13) can be understood as a kind of inconvenience of the HOLMBLAD/ØSTERGAARD approach.

4.2.5   The Problem of Defuzzification

Both the MAMDANI approach via (4.3), (4.4) and the method of degrees of activation accept crisp inputs and thus can be used on-line for automatic control together with direct inputs from standard sensors. The approach via (4.3), (4.4) takes such a crisp input value $x_0 \in \mathcal{X}$ as the fuzzy singleton $A = \langle\!\langle x_0 \rangle\!\rangle_1$ with support $\mathrm{supp}\,(\langle\!\langle x_0 \rangle\!\rangle_1) = \{x_0\}$ and membership degree $\mu_{\langle\!\langle x_0 \rangle\!\rangle_1}(x_0) = 1$. The method of degrees of activation follows essentially the same idea. Most important now is that the determination of the activation degrees β_j becomes extremely simple because the singleton input $A = \langle\!\langle x_0 \rangle\!\rangle_1$ in (4.13) reduces this formula (4.13) to

$$\beta_j = \mu_{A_j}(x_0).$$

The output $v := B$ which a fuzzy controller produces for an input $u := A$ is a fuzzy set B. This output value can be offered directly to any user. In the case, however, that v is a linguistic variable with some standard linguistic values one likes to get such a standard value instead of B. Thus in such a case one additionally needs some "linguistic approximation" of B, i.e. one has to find some of the standard linguistic values for v which optimally coincides with B.

For this last mentioned approximation problem the extremely simple "degree of coincidence" β_j of (4.13) is not, in general, the right measure of coincidence. Instead one is going to compare the membership function μ_B with the membership functions of the standard linguistic values for v as functions, i.e. one will compute the distances of these function w.r.t. some suitable metric for functions. But this transforms the problem of linguistic approximation of μ_B by one of the standard linguistic values of v completely into a problem of traditional function approximation.

Linguistic approximation is often seen as a problem only for expert system applications or man-machine dialogues. The motivation given for this point of view is that for automated on-line control neither the fuzzy output B nor its linguistic approximation would be of central importance. Instead, in this situation a control action should consist of giving some control parameter a crisp value. (This point of view disregards the fact that such a crisp output, usually a real number, can only pseudo-exactly become realised by some technical tool intended to automatically realise it. Thus, this point of view still represents some mixture of a truly fuzzy approach and the old one of traditional, crisp mathematical modelling. Some considerations of how to handle final decisions as normalised fuzzy sets, e.g. as fuzzy numbers, are contained in BANDEMER (1990).)

For this, actually almost standard, understanding one has to *defuzzify* the fuzzy output $B \in I\!F(\mathcal{Y})$ into a crisp value $y_0 \in \mathcal{Y}$. For this defuzzification process some different procedures are under discussion. A general theory determining the defuzzification value $y_0(B)$ of any fuzzy set B is actually lacking.

The max-*procedure* in its most simple form assumes that the membership function μ_B of the fuzzy output B has a single maximal point and then takes as defuzzification value $y_0(B)$ the argument value at this maximal point

$$
\begin{aligned}
y_0(B) &= \ \text{arg} \ \max\{\mu_B(y) \mid y \in \mathcal{Y}\} \\
&= \ \mu_B{}^{-1}(\max\{\mu_B(y) \mid y \in \mathcal{Y}\}).
\end{aligned}
$$

But this assumption is quite specific. If μ_B has maximal values then more often it will have more then one maximal point. In this situation one may start with the set $\mathcal{B}_{\max}$ of all the arguments of maximal points of μ_B

$$
\begin{aligned}
\mathcal{B}_{\max} &= {\mu_B}^{-1}(\{\max_{z \in \mathcal{Y}} \mu_B(z)\}) \\
&= \{y \in \mathcal{Y} \mid \mu_B(y) = \max_{z \in \mathcal{Y}} \mu_B(z)\}. \qquad (4.26)
\end{aligned}
$$

The idea is that $\mathcal{B}_{\max}$ is the set of optimal control decisions. But, finally one of them has to be chosen.

One way to reach a final control decision now is to choose one element of $\mathcal{B}_{\max}$ randomly. But this uses the presupposition that all the elements of $\mathcal{B}_{max}$ are equally good decisions. The interpretation, however, that points outside $\mathcal{B}_{max}$ are not optimal often is also read as a hint that $y_0(B)$ should not be chosen from the borderline region of $\mathcal{B}_{\max}$ but preferably from the "middle" of $\mathcal{B}_{\max}$.

If one assumes additionally that the universe of discourse $\mathcal{Y}$ of the output variable v is a set of numbers, i.e. $\mathcal{Y} \subseteq R$, then another proposal favours some mean value of $\mathcal{B}_{\max}$, i.e. in case of a finite set $\mathcal{B}_{\max}$ e.g. the value

$$
y_0(B) = \frac{1}{N} \sum_{y \in \mathcal{B}_{\max}} y \qquad (4.27)
$$

with N the cardinality of $\mathcal{B}_{\max}$. In case, $\mathcal{B}_{\max}$ is a "continuous" set then

$$
y_0(B) = \frac{1}{\int\limits_{\mathcal{B}_{\max}} dy} \cdot \int\limits_{\mathcal{B}_{\max}} y \, dy \qquad (4.28)
$$

is the substitute for (4.27), of course assuming existence and convergence of the integrals involved here.

But one has to be careful here. Such a mean value of $\mathcal{B}_{\max}$ may be a "preferable" decision in the case that $\mathcal{B}_{\max}$ is an interval in $\mathcal{Y}$. Otherwise one can have $y_0(B) \notin \mathcal{B}_{\max}$ and reach even an extremely bad decision. To see this one simply has to imagine automated driving of a car, an obstacle in the middle of the road, and thus two equally good possibilities of circumventing this obstacle right or left. A mean value decision in such a situation would be the worst case.

Another disadvantage of any kind of max-procedure is that it ignores all the information concerning the membership function μ_B outside $\mathcal{B}_{max}$. This whole membership function μ_B is instead taken into consideration in the *center-of-gravity* (COG) procedure. Here in the background one also has a mean value strategy. But the mean value which determines $y_0(B)$ is now taken as a weighted mean over all of $\text{supp}(B)$. Therefore for a "discrete" universe of discourse $\mathcal{Y}$ one has $y_0(B)$ determined as

$$y_0(B) = \frac{1}{\text{card}(B)} \sum_{y \in \mathcal{Y}} y \cdot \mu_B(y) \tag{4.29}$$

with $\text{card}(B)$ according (2.18) as the sum of all the membership degrees $\mu_B(y)$. In the case of a "continuous" universe of discourse $\mathcal{Y}$ one has $\text{card}(B)$ to read as in (2.19) and gets

$$y_0(B) = \frac{1}{\text{card}(B)} \int_{\mathcal{Y}} y \cdot \mu_B(y) \, dy. \tag{4.30}$$

The fact that also this COG procedure is a mean value method causes here the same trouble we previously discussed with the worst case scenario of an automated car driving round an obstacle. Therefore, in all the cases where B is not a convex fuzzy set the COG procedure may yield a worse control decision via (4.29) or (4.30).

The final control decision $y_0(B)$ is in the case of the COG procedure (4.29) and (4.30) only determined to a small amount by the point $y \in \mathcal{Y}$ with a "very small" membership degree $\mu_B(y)$. Sometimes it may even be preferable to neglect all the points $y \in \mathcal{Y}$ with a membership degree which is "too small", i.e. which is below some threshold level. A reason may be that these very small membership degrees are different of zero only because of some noise. Therefore PEDRYCZ (1989) introduced the *center-of-gravity procedure with threshold*: here one starts with a threshold λ and determines the control decision $y_0{}^\lambda(B)$ only with those $y \in \mathcal{Y}$ with $\mu_B(y) \geq \lambda$. Therefore in the "discrete" case one has

$$y_0{}^\lambda(B) = \frac{1}{\text{card}(B^{\geq \lambda})} \sum_{y \in B^{\geq \lambda}} y \cdot \mu_B(y), \tag{4.31}$$

with $\text{card}(B^{\geq \lambda})$ the usual cardinality of the crisp λ-cut $B^{\geq \lambda}$. And in the "continuous" case one has

$$y_0{}^\lambda(B) = \frac{1}{\int_{B^{\geq \lambda}} \mu_B(y) \, dy} \cdot \int_{B^{\geq \lambda}} y \cdot \mu_B(y) \, dy. \tag{4.32}$$

Obviously, $\lambda = 0$ gives back the unrestricted COG procedure. On the other hand, $\lambda = \max_{y \in \mathcal{Y}} \mu_B(y)$, realises the max-procedure with mean of maxima added to determine the final control decision. (Of course, this holds true only in case that some maximum exists.)

Nevertheless, COG with a threshold is also a mean value strategy and hence burdened with the same problems we discussed before twice. That also means

$y_0^\lambda(B)$ in general looks acceptable only in those cases where the "restriction" of B to $B^{\geq\lambda}$ is a convex fuzzy set.

4.2.6   The SUGENO Approach

This problem of defuzzification avoids another strategy of fuzzy control, first considered by SUGENO/NISHIDA (1985) and now often referred to as SUGENO controller.   Here the control rules (4.2) are slightly modified in such a way that their outputs are (crisp) numbers, the inputs remain fuzzy values. For an actual input value the output is determined by using the activation degrees of the single rules as coefficients for a weighted linear combination of the rules outputs. Thus, having the control rules

$$\textsf{IF} \quad u = A_i \quad \textsf{THEN} \quad v = y_i, \quad i = 1, \dots, n \tag{4.33}$$

and an actual input value $u := A$ with the activation degrees β_j of rule j, then the actual output becomes

$$v := \sum_{j=1}^n \beta_j \cdot y_j \Big/ \sum_{j=1}^n \beta_j. \tag{4.34}$$

But usually with the SUGENO approach one connects two additional presuppositions. The first one is that the actual values of the input variables are always supposed to be crisp ones – despite the fact that the control rules refer to fuzzy values of the input variables. And the second one is that each actual crisp output value is even taken as – in the standard sense – functionally dependent from the (actual) crisp input values. Remembering that the input variable u may be a k-dimensional one, viz. $u = (u_1, \dots, u_k)$, this means that for a SUGENO controller the list of control rules becomes

$$\textsf{IF} \quad u = A_i \quad \textsf{THEN} \quad v = f_i(u_1, \dots, u_k), \quad i = 1, \dots, n. \tag{4.35}$$

As for the method of activation degrees, the total output y^* of the SUGENO controller for a fixed input $u^* = (u_1^*, \dots, u_k^*)$ is the "superposition" of the single rules outputs, with superposition understood here usually as the weighted sum

$$y^* = \sum_{j\geq 1}^n \beta_j \cdot f_j(u_1^*, \dots, u_k^*) \tag{4.36}$$

or as the corresponding normalised version

$$y^* = \sum_{j=1}^n \beta_j \cdot f_j(u_1^*, \dots, u_k^*) \Big/ \sum_{j=1}^n \beta_j \tag{4.37}$$

with the degrees of activation

$$\beta_i = \mu_{A_i}(u^*), \qquad i = 1, \ldots, n \tag{4.38}$$

as the membership degrees of the actual input w.r.t. the control rules fuzzy input values.

Practically, hence, such a fuzzy controller of the SUGENO type is the weighted superposition of n "traditional" controllers with output functions $f_i(u_1, \ldots, u_k)$ given over the supports $\mathrm{supp}\,(A_i)$. Outside the kernels $A_i^{\geq 1}$ these traditional control functions $f_i(u_1, \ldots, u_k)$ are also modified according to the weights (4.38). And moreover, of course, this whole method additionally realises a – possibly non-linear – interpolation between these different control functions (at those points of the input space which belong to the supports $\mathrm{supp}\,(A_i), \mathrm{supp}\,(A_j)$ of the fuzzy input values A_i, A_j of different control rules).

4.3 Relational Equations and Fuzzy Control

4.3.1 Solutions of Systems of Relational Equations

The (re)formulation of a system (4.2) of control rules as a system (4.12) of relational equations transforms the problem to determine a fuzzy relation which realises the control rules (4.2) into the problem to solve the system (4.12) of equations. Here, an engineering problem is transformed into a mathematical problem.

Let us first consider the most simple case of only one relational equation

$$B = A \circ R. \tag{4.39}$$

Here $A \in I\!\!F(\mathcal{X})$, $B \in I\!\!F(\mathcal{Y})$ are given fuzzy sets; and a fuzzy relation $R \in I\!\!F(\mathcal{X} \times \mathcal{Y})$ has to be determined as a solution. It is not hard to prove that the set of solutions

$$\boldsymbol{R} = \{R \in I\!\!F(\mathcal{X} \times \mathcal{Y}) \mid B = A \circ R\} \tag{4.40}$$

is an upper semilattice w.r.t. inclusion for fuzzy sets, i.e. with any two solutions R', R'' of (4.39) also their union $R' \cup R''$ is a solution of (4.39):

$$R', R'' \in \boldsymbol{R} \ \Rightarrow \ R' \cup R'' \in \boldsymbol{R}, \tag{4.41}$$

and $R' \cup R''$ is w.r.t. the inclusion relation $\subseteq$ the smallest solution of (4.39) which is bigger than R' and R''. Therefore the set $\boldsymbol{R}$ of solutions has at most one maximal element w.r.t. $\subseteq$, the *biggest solution* of (4.39), but there may exist several minimal solution w.r.t. $\subseteq$.

The problem of determination of minimal solutions of (4.39), i.e. of smal-
est elements (w.r.t. $\subseteqq$) of the set $\boldsymbol{R}$, has been discussed occasionally but
seems to be of minor importance. Minimal solutions have been studied e.g.
by SANCHEZ (1977), SESSA (1984), DINOLA (1984, 1985); a good survey is
given in the book DINOLA/SESSA/PEDRYCZ/SANCHEZ (1989).

It is, however, more important – and even easier – to treat the biggest solution
of (4.39). For doing this we introduce a new set algebraic operation $\oslash$ for
fuzzy sets. Having given fuzzy sets $A \in \mathbb{F}(\mathcal{X})$, $B \in \mathbb{F}(\mathcal{Y})$ this new operation
yields a fuzzy relation $A \oslash B \in \mathbb{F}(\mathcal{X} \times \mathcal{Y})$, which is defined as

$$R := A \oslash B :$$

$$\mu_R(x, y) =_{\text{def}} \begin{cases} 1, & \text{if } \mu_A(x) \leq \mu_B(y) \\ \mu_B(y), & \text{if } \mu_A(x) > \mu_B(y). \end{cases} \tag{4.42}$$

Now, following the treatment by SANCHEZ (1984), cf. also GOTTWALD (1986a),
one has a very simple solvability criterion for equation (4.39).

Theorem 4.1: *A relational equation $B = A \circ R$ is solvable iff $A \oslash B$ is
a solution of this equation; and if $A \oslash B$ is a solution of this equation, then
$A \oslash B$ is additionally the biggest one w.r.t. $\subseteqq$.*

Let us look at an example. The universes of discourse $\mathcal{X}, \mathcal{Y}$ shall have
three and four elements, respectively. The fuzzy subsets A_0 of $\mathcal{X}$ and B_0 of
$\mathcal{Y}$ shall be represented by the vectors of membership degrees

$$A_0 \,\hat{=}\, (0.9 \,;\, 1 \,;\, 0.7), \quad B_0 \,\hat{=}\, (1 \,;\, 0.4 \,;\, 0.8 \,;\, 0.7). \tag{4.43}$$

In this case then via (4.42) one gets the fuzzy relation

$$R_0 \,\hat{=}\, \begin{pmatrix} 1 & 0.4 & 0.8 & 0.7 \\ 1 & 0.4 & 0.8 & 0.7 \\ 1 & 0.4 & 1 & 1 \end{pmatrix} \tag{4.44}$$

as the biggest solution (w.r.t. $\subseteqq$) of the relational equation $B_0 = A_0 \circ R$.
Another solution of this equation is

$$R_1 \,\hat{=}\, \begin{pmatrix} 0 & 0.4 & 0.8 & 0 \\ 1 & 0 & 0 & 0 \\ 0 & 0 & 0 & 0.7 \end{pmatrix}, \tag{4.45}$$

and this is even a minimal solution w.r.t. $\subseteqq$. Therefore also each other
matrix with elements coordinatewise in between the corresponding elements
of R_0 and R_1 is a solution of this equation $B_0 = A_0 \circ R$. This is caused by the

fact that the relational product ∘ is monotonous w.r.t. $\subseteq$. A further solution of our equation is

$$R_2 \hat{=} \begin{pmatrix} 0 & 0 & 0 & 0.7 \\ 1 & 0.4 & 0.8 & 0 \\ 0 & 0 & 0 & 0 \end{pmatrix}. \tag{4.46}$$

Obviously one has $R_1 \subseteq R_0$ and $R_2 \subseteq R_0$; but the solutions R_1, R_2 are incomparable w.r.t. $\subseteq$.

Even for systems (4.12) of relational equations one has the result (4.41), with $\boldsymbol{R}$ now the set of solutions of the system (4.12). Therefore the set $\boldsymbol{R}$ of solutions of a system of equations (4.12) has a biggest element w.r.t. $\subseteq$, of course assuming $\boldsymbol{R} \neq \emptyset$, i.e. assuming the solvability of the system (4.12). And again now in the case $\boldsymbol{R} \neq \emptyset$ there exist in general different w.r.t. $\subseteq$ minimal elements, i.e. in general (4.12) has w.r.t. $\subseteq$ incomparable minimal solutions.

There are not only these structural analogies between the set of solutions of single relational equations (4.39) and whole systems (4.12) of them. There also holds true a solvability criterion corresponding to the above one, cf. GOTTWALD (1984, 1986a, 1993). And this solvability criterion additionally reduces the biggest solution of system (4.12) to the biggest solutions of its single equations.

Theorem 4.2: *A system $B_i = A_i \circ R$, $i = 1, \ldots, n$, of relational equations is solvable iff the fuzzy relation*

$$C = \bigcap_{i=1}^{n} (A_i \oslash B_i)$$

is a solution of this system; and if C is a solution of the system $B_i = A_i \circ R$, $i = 1, \ldots, n$, then this fuzzy relation C at the same time is the biggest solution w.r.t. the inclusion relation $\subseteq$.

The importance of both these solvability results reduces to the cases that equation (4.39) or system (4.12) of equations really have solutions. In a lot of applicationally relevant cases, systems (4.2) of control rules instead lead to systems (4.12) of relational equations which do not have solutions – or at least to systems for which one has no information concerning their solvability.

Therefore besides these results one is interested in solvability conditions for systems (4.12) of relational equations. Caused by the fact that solvability of (4.12) means that the system (4.2) of control rules on which this system

of equations is based can be realised by a fuzzy relation without any "inter-action" of the control rules, solvability of (4.12) is equivalent with the "true" realisability of the system (4.2) of control rules.

The problem of solvability of a system (4.12) of relational equations (4.12) in a natural way splits into two problems of the solvability of systems of rela-tional "inequalities"

$$B_i \subseteq A_i \circ R, \qquad i = 1, \dots, n, \tag{4.47}$$

$$B_i \supseteq A_i \circ R, \qquad i = 1, \dots, n. \tag{4.48}$$

The solvability of (4.47) is known as the *superset property* of R and is a relatively weak condition: for having (4.47) solvable it is sufficient to have

$$\mathrm{hgt}\,(B_i) \leq \mathrm{hgt}\,(A_i) \quad \text{for } i = 1, \dots, n \tag{4.49}$$

satisfied. And one way to have this condition satisfied is to suppose that in the system (4.2) of control rules all the input data A_i have to be normal fuzzy sets.

The solvability of (4.48) is known as the *subset property* of R. This prop-erty is the more difficult one of the two. Accordingly, only sufficient conditions of a relatively strong nature are known, cf. GOTTWALD (1984a, 1993). The most simple one of them is the pairwise disjointness of the input data of the system (4.2) of control rules:

$$A_j \cap A_k = \emptyset \quad \text{for all } 1 \leq j < k \leq n. \tag{4.50}$$

But this condition (4.50) is quite restrictive from the viewpoint of the appli-cations. Yet all the other sufficient conditions given in GOTTWALD (1984a, 1993) for the subset property (4.48) are not much weaker.

4.3.2   Approximate Solutions and Their Evaluation

Nevertheless, these difficulties do not prove the absurdity of the methodology of transfering a system (4.2) of control rules into a system (4.12) of relational equations and of accepting a solution of (4.12) as a fuzzy relation realising (4.2). The crucial point is, instead, allowing the consideration of approxi-mate solutions of systems (4.12) of relational equations. Fortunately, this idea works in analogy with our earlier results and leads to the following result (cf. GOTTWALD (1986a)).

Theorem 4.3: *For any system (4.12) of relational equations the fuzzy relation*

$$\hat{R} = \bigcap_{i=1}^{n} (A_i \oslash B_i)$$

is not only the biggest solution in the case of solvability of (4.12), *but in any case it is a best possible approximate solution.*

This result is a corollary of a generalised solvability criterion for systems of relational equations proven in GOTTWALD (1986a). The basic idea which was the starting point for this generalised solvability criterion was to take the sentence G: "there exists a solution of system (4.12)" as a sentence of the language of a suitable system of many-valued logic – and to determine the truth degree of G. The main problem for this approach to (4.12) was to have a suitable many-valued version of the equality relation. It was not the simple version (2.109), however, which could do this job, but a version which resulted from (2.39) by defining

$$A \equiv B =_{\text{def}} A \subseteq B \wedge B \subseteq A.$$

This "fuzzified" equality for fuzzy sets is a sup-∗-transitive equivalence relation. Thus via (3.43) this generalised equality $\equiv$ determines a metric ϱ_0, and the above mentioned approximate solution $\hat{R}$ of Theorem 4.3 is an optimal solution in the sense that the ∗-composition, i.e. the composition based on the t-norm t_2, of all the distances $\varrho_0(B_i, A_i \circ \hat{R})$, $i = 1, \ldots, n$, takes a minimal value. Here this metric ϱ_0 is for all fuzzy sets $C, D \in I\!F(\mathcal{Y})$ given as

$$\varrho_0(C, D) = \sup_{\substack{y \in \mathcal{Y} \\ \mu_C(y) \neq \mu_D(y)}} \left(1 - \min\{\mu_C(y), \mu_D(y)\}\right), \tag{4.51}$$

and thus not one of the preferred metrics for functions. If one, instead, is interested to consider e.g. the Cebyshev distance

$$\varrho^*(C, D) = \sup_{y \in \mathcal{Y}} |\mu_C(y) - \mu_D(y)| \tag{4.52}$$

and to have an optimal approximate solution of (4.12) w.r.t. this Cebyshev distance, then this situation itself can be approximated by choosing in the conditional rule of inference (3.62) and otherwise for the min-operator the ∗-operator, i.e. the t-norm t_2. In this case Theorem 4.3 holds true approximately in the same form as given above, cf. GOTTWALD (1986a, 1993), and the distance ϱ_2 resulting from this reference to the t-norm t_2 lies in between the Cebyshev distance and its doubled values.

Even more generally, in Theorems 4.1 and 4.2 one can already base the relational product operation ∘ on any (left continuous) t-norm t and thus use

$$\mu_{A \circ R}(y) = \sup_{x \in \mathcal{X}} \left(\mu_A(x) \, t \, \mu_R(x, y)\right) \quad \text{for all } y \in \mathcal{Y}.$$

instead of (4.4). Writing in this case more precisely $\circ_t$ for $\circ$, and defining additionally a fuzzy relation $A \oslash B \in I\!F(\mathcal{X} \times \mathcal{Y})$ by

$$R := A \oslash_t B : \qquad \mu_R(x, y) =_{\text{def}} \mu_A(x) \, \varphi_t \, \mu_B(y) \tag{4.53}$$

instead of (4.42), then both of Theorem 4.1 and Theorem 4.2 remain true with $\circ_t$, $\oslash_t$ instead of $\circ$, $\oslash$.

Approximate solvability of system (4.12) can not only be understood, as was done for Theorems 4.3 and 4.2, as demanding to have (4.47) and (4.48) satisfied as well as possible. There is also another way of looking at these conditions (4.47), (4.48) and their approximate satisfaction: one can substitute for the fuzzy sets B_i in (4.47) subsets $\underline{B_i}$ of them, i.e. fuzzy sets with $\underline{B_i} \subseteqq B_i$, and substitute for them in (4.48) supersets $\overline{B_i}$ with $B_i \subseteqq \overline{B_i}$ – and then again one can ask for a fuzzy relation R which simultaneously satisfies all these weakened conditions (4.47), (4.48). This idea is carried through in WAGENKNECHT/HARTMANN (1986, 1986a). These authors get their *tolerance sets* $\underline{B_i}, \overline{B_i}$ in such a way that they determine pointwise tolerances for all the membership degrees $\mu_{B_i}(y)$, $y \in \mathcal{Y}$ and $i = 1, \ldots, n$, as

$$c_i(y) \le \mu_{B_i}(y) \le d_i(y)) \tag{4.54}$$

and thus have their tolerance sets $\underline{B_i}, \overline{B_i}$ defined as

$$\mu_{\underline{B_i}}(y) = c_i(y), \quad \mu_{\overline{B_i}}(y) = d_i(y) \quad \text{for all } y \in \mathcal{Y}. \tag{4.55}$$

Now system (4.12) of relational equations is transformed into a system of *tolerance "equations"*

$$\underline{B_i} \subseteqq A_i \circ R \subseteqq \overline{B_i}, \quad i = 1, \ldots, n. \tag{4.56}$$

Obviously, here the choice of the local tolerances (4.54) is crucial for the solvability of (4.56). Quite large tolerance intervals $[c_i(y), d_i(y)]$ cause solvability of (4.56). The larger one chooses these tolerance intervals, the more inaccurately any solution R of the tolerance "equations" (4.56) realises the control rules (4.2) one was starting from.

Of course, having (4.49) satisfied and hence the superset property (4.47), one can always take $\underline{B_i} = B_i$ in (4.56) supposing (4.49). Furthermore, the fuzzy relation $\hat{R}$ of Theorem 4.3 can always be used to determine tolerances (4.54) in such a way that with these tolerances (4.56) becomes solvable. Moreover, each fuzzy relation other than $\hat{R}$ also yields such tolerances.

Along these lines there is still another way to approach approximate solvability. The main problem, again, is to have the subset property (4.48) satisfied. For this, one can try to make the fuzzy sets A_i "bigger" and, at the same time, to make the fuzzy sets B_i "smaller" (both in the sense of the $\subseteqq$-ordering in $\mathbb{F}(\mathcal{X}), \mathbb{F}(\mathcal{Y})$, respectively), as is done by KLIR/YUAN (1994) extending an idea of WU (1986).

The crucial point is to consider a fuzzy relation R^* as an approximate solution of a relational equation $B = A \circ R$ iff the following requirements are satisfied:

(i) there exist $A^* \in I\!\!F(\mathcal{X})$ with $A \subseteq A^*$ and $B^* \in I\!\!F(\mathcal{Y})$ with $B^* \subseteq B$ such that $A^* \circ R^* = B^*$;

(ii) if there exist $A' \in I\!\!F(\mathcal{X})$ and $B' \in I\!\!F(\mathcal{Y})$ such that $A \subseteq A' \subseteq A^*$ and $B^* \subseteq B' \subseteq B$, and that $A' \circ R = B'$ has a solution, then one has $A' = A^*$ and $B' = B^*$.

Also in this modified sense, the fuzzy relation $A \oslash B$ of (4.42) remains the biggest approximate solution.

And this result, too, can not only be generalised to fuzzy relational equations $A \circ_t R = B$, t any left continuous t-norm, as Theorems 4.1 and 4.2 before: it can also be generalised in the sense of Theorem 4.3.

Sometimes one is not even interested in good approximate solutions, but accepts any kind of approximate solution which one can get in some simple way, e.g. with only few simple computations, or based on quite simple theoretical ideas. In such a situation, of course besides

$$\hat{R} = \bigcap_{i=1}^{n}(A_i \oslash B_i)$$

one has a lot of further possibilities to connect a fuzzy relation R with (4.2) to be taken via (3.62) as a "realisation" of (4.2).

An extremely simple method of connecting the control rules (4.2) with a fuzzy relation R has already been chosen by MAMDANI/ASSILIAN (1975) for their fuzzy controller, and has since been used more often.

Thus, MAMDANI/ASSILIAN (1975) starting with a system (4.2) of control rules determine a rough approximate solution (4.9) of the corresponding system (4.12) of relational equations. And the same, obviously, holds true for the method of degrees of activation introduced by HOLMBLAD/ØSTERGAARD (1982); cf. Section 4.2.

Furthermore, this approach of HOLMBLAD/ØSTERGAARD (1982) shows that one is not forced in starting from a system (4.2) of control rules to refer back to the compositional rule of inference (3.62) and some fuzzy relation determined by (4.2). Instead, (3.62) can be substituted by other ways of composition to get from some fuzzy input value $u := A$ a fuzzy output value $v := B$ via the system (4.2) of control rules. But, up to now besides the approaches via the compositional rule of inference (3.62) and the idea of degrees of activation (4.15) there is essentially no further competing method.

In any case, if one is able to formulate the procedure of getting the fuzzy output for a fuzzy input with reference to equations of type (4.12) – with a suitably interpreted "composition" $\ldots \circ R$ – then the determination of a fuzzy controller as a fuzzy relation out of control rules can always be seen as the problem to solve some system of relational equations. If one only has available an approximate solution of these equations, as in (4.9), or if a solution does not exist at all, then one meets the problem of determining the "quality" of such a solution w.r.t. (4.2), i.e. to determine how well such an "approximate solution" realises the control rules (4.2). In the same way, if one bases the determination of the fuzzy output directly on the control rules and on some idea to "interpolate" between them, then either the rules are realised without interaction – or otherwise again one is confronted only with some approximate realisation of the rules. In this last case, again, the problem of evaluating the "quality" of this approximation is present.

Writing – independent of the type of the "composition" $\circ - v := A \circ R$ for the output value of the fuzzy controller given via (4.2) for the input value $u := A$ then the "quality" of this realisation of the control rules (4.2) has to be evaluated w.r.t. the pairs $(B_i, A_i \circ R)$ for all $i = 1, \ldots, n$. Being confronted with different fuzzy relations R as realisations (4.2) then this type of evaluation of intended vs. realised outputs allows one to evaluate these relations and to fix an optimal one. If on the other hand, as e.g. in (4.9), one has a fixed algorithm to connect some approximate solution of (4.12) with a system (4.2) of control rules, then one can look for variations of (4.2) which allow for a better realisation.

Exactly this last idea has been considered several times: to use the data $(B_i, A_i \circ R)$, $i = 1, \ldots, n$, to optimise the system (4.2) of control rules. Here one should have in mind that often in systems (4.2) the fuzzy input and output data A_i, B_i are determined only heuristically out of linguistic or qualitative information on the values of fuzzy variables u, v. And some intuitively inessential changes may then sometimes cause a much better realisation of (4.2) by the intended formal method. Even more may be possible: caused by the fact that (4.2) is often itself based on rough, qualitative process informations, the whole structure of (4.2) may be changed – e.g. by eliminating some of the control rules from this list of rules.

The simplest type of evaluation refers to some distance function ϱ for fuzzy sets and uses the numbers $\varrho(B_i, A_i \circ R)$, $i = 1, \ldots, n$, for some numerical "index" which characterises the quality of the fuzzy controller based on (4.2) – an index which e.g. results via averaging or via summation of these distances $\varrho(B_i, A_i \circ R)$. Inspired by theoretical considerations in connection with Theorem 4.3, GOTTWALD/PEDRYCZ (1986) instead use some solvability index for the system (4.12) of relational equations resulting from the control rules (4.2), and discuss optimisations of (4.2) on that basis. Another approach to evaluate the data $(B_i, A_i \circ R)$, $i = 1, \ldots, n$, refers to some fuzzy measure (cf. Section 5.1) and integration related to it – in the sense of a Sugeno integral.

And this approach even allows one to realise different degrees of precision of the realisation of (4.2) over different parts of the output universe of discourse $\mathcal{Y}$; cf. GOTTWALD/PEDRYCZ (1986). And still another idea was discussed in GOTTWALD/PEDRYCZ (1988): to look at the data $(B_i, A_i \circ R)$, $i = 1, \ldots, n$, as a kind of sample to evaluate how well the list (4.2) of control rules can be realised at all. (It has to be admitted that they do not discuss whether this sample in some reasonable sense may count as a representative one.)

But for an evaluation of a list of control rules (4.2) it is, not even necessary to look for some fuzzy relation which "realises" (4.2). Already the simple idea that rules of (4.2) with "nearly equal" input data should not have "too different" output data – i.e. some kind of consistency requirement for the system of control rules – opens ways to discuss the quality of as well as optimisations for the system of control rules under discussion; cf. GOTTWALD/PEDRYCZ (1985).

Nevertheless, up to now there is no common agreement whether any one of these ideas of evaluating systems of control rules deserves special attention. Thus, for each specific application of the fuzzy control strategy, i.e. for each specific system (4.2) of control rules one has to test the behaviour of the fuzzy controller which is based on this system of control rules against the real process to be controlled. Hence, the test and adaptation process refers most often to trial and error optimisation using parameters inherent in the system of control rules and its input and output data. This trial and error adaptation sometimes can itself become automated. For doing so one has to suppose that one knows of a suitably good list of pairs of process states and successful control actions. Then one can use e.g. neural net techniques to optimise or even to learn the list of control rules; cf. NAUCK/KLAWONN/KRUSE (1994).

4.4 Approximate Reasoning

4.4.1 The General Idea

Once again we will look at the process of designing a fuzzy controller as discussed in Section 4.2. The essential steps there, from the present point of view, have been: (i) the introduction of linguistic or fuzzy variables and their use in control rules, (ii) the translation of these control rules into a fuzzy relation, and (iii) the treatment of any fuzzy input information via this fuzzy relation and the compositional rule of inference or via some kind of very special interpolation process. This whole procedure is nothing but a simple special case of a much more general situation: the treatment of vague or qualitative information in (designing and using of) expert systems. The most characteristic case for introducing fuzzy set based methods into expert systems (design) is the need to use expert knowledge which is not usually given in a numerical way, or for which one does not have a possibility for a numerical treatment – either because no measurement exists at all or because it actually is (practically) impossible to measure some of the crucial values.

In the special case of a system (4.2) of control rules with only one rule, i.e. with $n = 1$, the input/output behaviour of the fuzzy controller can be seen as subsumed under an application of the inference schema

$$\begin{array}{l} \text{IF } u = A_1 \text{ THEN } v = B_1 \\ \underline{u = A} \\ v = B = A \circ R \end{array}. \tag{4.57}$$

In this case, here the fuzzy relation R has to be assumed as being determined by the input/output data A_1, B_1 such that $A_1 \circ R = B_1$. Obviously, this schema (4.57) is formally nearly equal to the well-known *modus ponens* or *rule of detachment*. The difference lies in the present use of linguistic or fuzzy values $u = A_1$ in the antecedent as well as $v = B_1$ in the consequent of the *fuzzy implication*

$$\text{IF } u = A_1 \text{ THEN } v = B_1 \tag{4.58}$$

and moreover also in the most remarkable fact that, contrary to the usual applications of the rule of detachment, the antecedent of the fuzzy implication (4.58), i.e. the first premise of schema (4.57), is not necessarily identical with the second premise $u = A$ of that schema.

This approximate equality of both these schemata as well as this quite specific difference are the main reasons to call schema (4.57) a *schema of approximate reasoning*.

For advanced expert systems it is one of the more characteristic features that they should be able to proceed qualitative, vague, fuzzy information: as input data as well as inside their inference engines and knowledge bases. From this point of view schema (4.57) is only *one* example for "approximate" ways to reach conclusions in everyday or *common sense reasoning*. It was mainly ZADEH (1978, 1978a, 1979, 1981, 1982, 1983, 1984) who initiated the development of a theory of approximate reasoning. Despite the fact that such a theory is actually far from complete we shall sketch some of the basic ideas.

Qualitative information or uncertain data, once again, are formally treated by fuzzy – or even linguistic – variables. And again the interpretation of these fuzzy – or linguistic – values proceeds by reference to the possibility interpretation of the membership degrees as explained in Section 3.3. Therefore one assumes to consider variables u, v with their "true" values in some universes of discourse $\mathcal{X}, \mathcal{Y}$, respectively, and with their fuzzy values as "elastic constraints" for these "true" values – and sometimes one also assumes to know some fuzzy relationships between the values of these variables. The essential goal of *approximate reasoning* is now to suitably treat pieces of fuzzy information given via fuzzy data, i.e. via fuzzy values of fuzzy variables and via fuzzy relation(ship)s between their values. Additionally one presupposes that this treatment happens in some (perhaps even structural) analogy with everyday reasoning.

As preliminary steps for such a methodology of approximate reasoning up to now we used to write fuzzy relationships as fuzzy relations and sometimes even as equations involving such fuzzy relations. But this together with the possibility interpretation, i.e. the interpretation of qualitative information and fuzzy data via possibility distributions (3.56), (3.61) for the "true" values of suitable variables, has to be completed by further methods to treat such fuzzy data to reach the goal of a theory of approximate reasoning.

Essentially it seems to be necessary to add many more rules for approximate reasoning. ZADEH (1978a) does this and introduces four types of rules for approximate reasoning:

(1) rules pertaining to modification,
(2) rules pertaining to composition,
(3) rules pertaining to quantification,
(4) rules pertaining to qualification.

4.4.2 Rules for Modification

The *rules for modification* are related to a situation that one starts with a fuzzy information "$u = A$" of type (3.56) and aims at transforming it into a fuzzy information of type "$u = m\text{-}A$". Here by $m\text{-}A$ a modifier application is meant which linguistically is to be represented by some hedge like

$$\text{very, more or less, approximately, } \ldots \tag{4.59}$$

or their iterations. Therefore, such rules for modification have e.g. to cover what we discussed earlier (cf. Fig. 4.1 in Section 4.1) as changes from fuzzy sets representing linguistic values like young, old to fuzzy sets representing very young, very old. For the modifier, i.e. the set theoretic operator related with the hedge very ZADEH (1973) already proposes the definition (4.1), and additionally in ZADEH (1975) he defines a modifier related to the hedge more or less by

$$\mu_{\text{more-or-less-}A}(x) = (\mu_A(x))^{1/2}. \tag{4.60}$$

Yet, the same reservations we mentioned w.r.t. definition (4.1) in Section 4.1 now apply to this new definition.

Unfortunately, however, besides these critical remarks this problem was up to now almost completely neglected. A very first approach toward it by KÖHLER (1994) discusses e.g. a combination of the main idea behind (4.1), (4.60), i.e. the understanding of a modifier as a (usually monotonous) function over the membership degrees, with some transformation of the universe of discourse. In the special case that the universe of discourse $\mathcal{X}$ is the real line and that the fuzzy set $A \in I\!\!F(\mathcal{X})$ to be modified has as its support $\operatorname{supp}(A) = (a, b)$ some interval, then a modification $\operatorname{mod}-A \in I\!\!F(\mathcal{X})$ of $A \in I\!\!F(\mathcal{X})$ may be determined by some monotonic bijection $t : (a, b) \to (a, b)$ as

$$\mu_{\operatorname{mod}-A}(x) = \begin{cases} \mu_A(t(x)) & \text{for } x \in \operatorname{supp}(A), \\ 0 & \text{for } x \notin \operatorname{supp}(A) \end{cases}$$

but it may even be determined by reference to such a bijection t together with some additional modification $\sigma : [0, 1] \to [0, 1]$ of the membership degrees as

$$\mu_{\operatorname{mod}-A}(x) = \begin{cases} \sigma(\mu_A(t(x))) & \text{for } x \in \operatorname{supp}(A), \\ \sigma(0) & \text{for } x \notin \operatorname{supp}(A). \end{cases} \tag{4.61}$$

Using the bijection $t^* : \mathcal{X} \to \mathcal{X}$ defined as

$$t^*(x) = \begin{cases} t(x) & \text{for } x \in \operatorname{supp}(A), \\ x & \text{for } x \notin \operatorname{supp}(A), \end{cases}$$

this last mentioned definition (4.61) can, much more compactly, be written as

$$\mu_{\operatorname{mod}-A} = \sigma \circ \mu_A \circ t^*.$$

Surely, this is a very first approach of the general problem of modifiers. However further investigations, are somewhat lacking.

Thus, in each concrete application one has to decide separately if one accepts (4.1), (4.60) or if one chooses other definitions instead; and in the same way one has to define modifiers for other hedges of type (4.59) one intends to use. At present, however, it seems to be recommendable to use such modifiers
basic fuzzy values for the fuzzy variables under consideration.

4.4.3   Rules for Composition

The *rules for composition* concern primarily the combination of qualitative information, i.e. fuzzy data using conjunction, disjunction, and implication connectives as well as some sort of negation related to such data. Thus schema (4.57) is already an example of such a rule for composition. In general, each fuzzy implication (4.58) is seen as yielding, as in the case of fuzzy controllers, a fuzzy relation R and thus as in (3.61) a *conditional possibility assignment* $\pi_{(v|u)}$ as

$$\pi_{(v|u)} = \mu_{A \oslash B} = \mu_{(A^c \otimes Y) + (X \otimes B)} \tag{4.62}$$

or as

$$\pi_{(v|u)} = \mu_{(A \otimes B) \cup (A^c \otimes Y)}. \tag{4.63}$$

For getting from any possibility assignment π_u and every conditional possibility assignment $\pi_{(v|u)}$ a further possibility assignment π_v once again one uses the compositional rule of inference (3.62), and thus has

$$\pi_v = \mu_{A \circ R} \quad \text{if} \quad \pi_u = \mu_A \quad \text{and} \quad \pi_{(v|u)} = \mu_R. \tag{4.64}$$

From the mathematical point of view, such a conditional possibility assignment is just a common possibility assignment for both variables u, v, i.e. a possibility assignment for the combined variable $w = (u, v)$.

The most essential point with this treatment of qualitative information and fuzzy data is the fact that approaches as in (4.42) or (3.67), (3.68) for a formalization of fuzzy implications (3.63) as expressing some fuzzy relation become interpreted as fixing some possibility assignment.

Conjunctive as well as disjunctive combination of fuzzy data "$u = A$" and "$v = B$" are again read as providing common possibility assignments for u, v, i.e. with the fuzzy information

$$u = A \quad \text{and} \quad v = B \tag{4.65}$$

one connects, assuming that u and v are distinct variables, the possibility assignment

$$\pi_{(u,v)} = \mu_{A \otimes B} = \mu_{(A \otimes Y) \cap (X \otimes B)}. \tag{4.66}$$

And with the fuzzy information

$$u = A \quad \text{or} \quad v = B \tag{4.67}$$

one connects, again for distinct variables u and v, the possibility assignment

$$\pi_{(u,v)} = \mu_{(A \otimes Y) \cup (X \otimes B)}. \tag{4.68}$$

In the case that v is the same variable as u, i.e. if (4.65) is the fuzzy information

$$u = A \quad \text{and} \quad u = B, \tag{4.69}$$

then instead of (4.66) this is understood as describing the possibility assignment

$$\pi_u = \mu_{A \cap B}. \tag{4.70}$$

And accordingly in this case, that v is the same variable as u, fuzzy information (4.67) becomes

$$u = A \quad \text{or} \quad u = B \tag{4.71}$$

and is understood as the possibility assignment

$$\pi_u = \mu_{A \cup B}. \tag{4.72}$$

Essentially the same type of "translation" is being done in the case of a negation connective: the fuzzy information

$$u = \text{non-}A \tag{4.73}$$

is translated into the possibility assignment

$$\pi_u = \mu_{A^c}. \tag{4.74}$$

Therefore, Boolean combinations of fuzzy data for the values of different variables are always transformed into common possibility assignments for these variables. In general, thus, for the processing of fuzzy information this poses the problem of how to combine, in a single inference process, fuzzy data related to (common) possibility assignments of multidimensional fuzzy variables with fuzzy data related to "single" fuzzy variables which appear as components of the multidimensional ones, i.e. how to combine possibility assignments which are related to variables $u = (u_1, \ldots, u_k)$ together with fuzzy data related only to "single" variables u_j that appear as "components" of u. The principal treatment shall be explained for the case $k = 2$.

Given possibility assignments

$$\pi_{(v|u)} = \mu_R, \qquad \pi_u = \mu_A, \tag{4.75}$$

with $R \in \mathbb{F}(\mathcal{X} \times \mathcal{Y})$ and $A \in \mathbb{F}(\mathcal{X})$, the combination of the two pieces of information, provided by these assignments (4.75), into an information concerning the value of v is done as

$$\pi_v = \mu_{\mathrm{pr}_1(R \cap (A \otimes Y))} = \mu_{A \circ R}. \tag{4.76}$$

This means that, once again, one applies the compositional rule of inference in the form (4.64) to combine the fuzzy data (4.75).

4.4.4   Rules for Quantification

The *rules for quantification* are designed to treat fuzzy quantificational information as indicated by expressions like

many, most of, almost all, a few, not very many, about 5, ...

Here again, the basic understanding is to read such fuzzy quantificational information as fuzzy data related to the values of some suitably chosen numerical variables, i.e. variables with "numbers" as their "true" values. With these numerical variables one has to be careful because fuzzy quantificational information of the indicated types may either refer to absolute numerical data (about 5, much more than 20, a few, many,...) or may refer to relative numerical data (most of, almost all, many of, a large part of, ...). The problem is usually that this distinction is not given by the words used to formulate fuzzy quantificational information, but has to be extracted from the whole context. Some typical examples of such a fuzzy quantificational information are:

– Very few parts are of bad quality.
– Many Swedes are blond.
– Most of those who overeat are obese.
– Almost all modern trucks have diesel engines, but only a few of them are very clean.

In the majority of cases, after some slight reformulation, such fuzzy quantificational information can quite often be given in the form

$$Q \ N \text{ are } A \tag{4.77}$$

or as a Boolean combination of such simple quantificational statements. Here, Q is a fuzzy quantification, and by A one refers to a – usually again fuzzy – property of the objects named N. Of course, for the formal treatment the objects named by N have to constitute the universe of discourse $\mathcal{X}$ for the fuzzy sets A – these are the (produced) parts in our first example, the Swedes in the second etc. As a special case it may even happen that the objects named N themselves are systems of other objects, i.e. $\mathcal{X}$ may e.g. be a cartesian product, as is the case for: "About 50% of the student couples have their children at the campus."

To treat a fuzzy quantificational information (4.77) in approximate reasoning, this information (4.77) again has to be transformed into a possibility assignment. To do this one introduces a fuzzy variable u to denote the (absolute or relative) number of objects of $\mathcal{X}$ with the fuzzy property A – and this number is just a suitably chosen cardinality of the fuzzy set $A \in \mathbb{F}(\mathcal{X})$. Thus (4.77) becomes transformed into the possibility assignment

$$\pi_{\text{card}(A)} = \mu_Q \quad \text{or} \quad \pi_{\text{card}_{\mathcal{X}}(A)} = \mu_Q, \tag{4.78}$$

additionally assuming here that the fuzzy quantification Q in (4.77) is simultaneously understood as a fuzzy subset of some suitable universe of discourse of numbers.

Then looking again at the first one of our examples, the universe of discourse $\mathcal{X}$ e.g. shall be the set of all parts (perhaps produced during some fixed time interval, e.g. one day) and the fuzzy property A formalised as its fuzzy subset of all parts of bad quality. Then according to (4.78) it results in the possibility assignment

$$\pi_{\mathrm{card}(A)} = \mu_{\mathrm{very-few}},\qquad(4.79)$$

for the case of an absolute understanding of the fuzzy quantification.

This method of transformation of fuzzy quantificational information (4.77) into the form (4.78) opens the door to considering inference schemata typical for the treatment of such quantifications. Such schemata shall e.g. be analogous to the traditional syllogisms.[1] An example of syllogistic reasoning is

> Most students are single.
> A little more than half of single students are male.
> ―――――――――――――――――――――――――――
> (?Q) students are single and male.

Here (?Q) symbolises a fuzzy quantification which has to be determined – either by some "direct calculation" or by subsuming this example under some general schema of syllogistic approximate reasoning. (The problem with such general schemata, nevertheless, is that not even the intuition of everyday reasoning provides clear hints of how to determine this fuzzy quantification (?Q).) As examples of such general schemata of "approximate syllogisms" ZADEH (1983, 1985) discusses e.g. schemata of the forms

$$
\begin{array}{ll}
\begin{aligned}
&Q_1 \ N \text{ are } M\\
&\underline{Q_2 \ M \text{ are } P}\\
&(?Q) \ N \text{ are } P
\end{aligned}
&
\begin{aligned}
&Q_1 \ N \text{ are } A\\
&\underline{Q_2 \ N \text{ are } B}\\
&(?Q) \ N \text{ are } A \cap B
\end{aligned}
\end{array}
\qquad(4.80)
$$

and proposes for them "resulting" fuzzy quantifications (?Q). Of course, much more such schemata can be written down and studied. Because of this wealth of possibilities we shall not look into more details here but refer the interested reader to ZADEH's papers. It must, however, be mentioned that these papers only give intuition-based proposals, no general theory of approximate syllogisms. As with the rules for modifications, in the present situation also a sound theoretical foundation is lacking on which to decide which schemata

---

[1] In traditional logic syllogisms are special types of first order inference schemata, i.e. schemata with quantifications in a crucial position. Any syllogism has two premises, each of one of the types: all A are B, some A are B, some A are not B, no A is B. Here A, B are usual notions/properties. Characteristic for syllogisms is furthermore that both their premises have a common notion. Syllogistic, the theory of syllogisms, was a central part of traditional logic. Actually, syllogisms are only seen as quite special cases of inference schemata of first order logic.

of type (4.80) have to be accepted and which have to be abandoned. Some functional dependency is especially lacking up to now, given a fixed inference schema of type (4.80), which allows one to determine the fuzzy quantification (?Q) out of the fuzzy quantifications Q_1, Q_2.

4.4.5 Rules for Qualification

Finally, the *rules for qualification* are related to the evaluation of the truth of sentences by linguistic truth values like

$$\text{true, absolutely false, not very true, more or less false,}\dots, \tag{4.81}$$

i.e. they are related to types of fuzzy information like:

It is more or less false,

that a lot of private cars have diesel engines. (4.82)

The *linguistic truth values* (4.81) are fuzzy subsets of the set $[0,1]$ of all membership degrees, and hence of the set of truth degrees of the many-valued logic one always has behind these membership degrees. Linguistic truth values are thus (linguistic) values of a linguistic variable TRUTH. The use of such a linguistic variable TRUTH is, however, not as much common usage as the use of linguistic variables like AGE or TEMPERATURE. Nevertheless, a sufficient intuitive understanding results if one looks at the linguistic truth values as providing fuzzy information about the "true" truth degree of a sentence H, a truth degree which belongs to $[0,1]$. Thus, linguistic truth values indicate a possibility assignment to the truth degree of some sentence written down in the language of (a suitable system of) many-valued logic – or even of some fuzzy information itself.

Assuming that fuzzy information "$u = A$" is given and evaluated by some linguistic truth value $\tau \in I\!\!F([0,1])$, then this situation (which is exactly the situation of example (4.82)) is usually written down as *truth qualification* of "$u = A$" in the form

$$(u = A) \quad \text{is} \quad \tau. \tag{4.83}$$

To transform (4.83) back into the usual form of fuzzy information, one has to determine some fuzzy information "$u = B$" which is equivalent with (4.83) and such that $B \in I\!\!F(\mathcal{X})$ is a function of $A \in I\!\!F(\mathcal{X})$ and $\tau \in I\!\!F([0,1])$. For this ZADEH (1976) and BELLMAN/ZADEH (1977) propose

$$\pi_u(x) = \mu_B(x) = \mu_\tau\left(\mu_A(x)\right) \quad \text{for all } x \in \mathcal{X} \tag{4.84}$$

and thus a method which easily can be extended to structurally more complicated types of qualitative, i.e. fuzzy information.

For a derivation of this formula (4.84) we start with a special case, information provided by the fuzzy datum "$u = A$" which, contrary to the situation in (4.83), is not qualified by some linguistic truth value but by a truth degree $r \in [0, 1]$. That means, instead of (4.83) we, consider for the moment, a truth qualification

$$(u = A) \quad \text{has truth degree} \quad r. \tag{4.85}$$

This truth qualification means for the "true", i.e. actual crisp value x_0 of u that

$$\mu_A(x_0) = r \tag{4.86}$$

or, using the possibility assignment equation corresponding to (4.85), that

$$\pi_u(x_0) = r.$$

The method to start from (4.85) and to determine those "true" values of the fuzzy variable u which satisfy (4.85), this method means – having in mind that usually not only one such "true" value shall satisfy (4.85) – to determine the (crisp) set $\mathcal{B}$ of all these values. With reference to the inverse mapping of the membership function μ_A, i.e. with reference to $\mu_A{}^{-1}$, this set is determined as

$$\mathcal{B} = \mu_A{}^{-1}(r) = \pi_u{}^{-1}(r), \tag{4.87}$$

i.e. it is the full image of the crisp singleton $\{r\}$ under the mapping $\mu_A{}^{-1}$:

$$\mathcal{B} = \{x \in \mathcal{X} \mid \mu_A(x) = r\} = \{x \in \mathcal{X} \mid \mu_A(x) \in \{r\}\}. \tag{4.88}$$

But now it is equivalent with (4.87) and (4.88) to have satisfied the condition

$$x \in \mathcal{B} \quad \Leftrightarrow \quad \mu_A(x) \in \{r\} \tag{4.89}$$

for all $x \in \mathcal{X}$. And with this last mentioned formulation it becomes obvious how to generalise this consideration from (4.85) to the more general case of (4.83): the usual membership relation in (4.89) has to be exchanged for membership functions, the crisp set $\mathcal{B}$ becomes a fuzzy set B, and the fuzzy singleton $\{r\}$ has to be substituted by the linguistic truth value τ. This immediately gives (4.84):

$$\mu_B(x) =_{\text{def}} \mu_\tau(\mu_A(x)).$$

Looking at fuzzy information of the type "$u = A$" as a fuzzy datum A in the sense of Chapter 6, the idea of the truth qualification (4.83) by the linguistic truth value τ is closely related to the idea of the fuzzily evaluated datum A with fuzzy evaluation τ. And indeed, this idea of truth qualification motivated the idea of the data transformation (6.105) via a kind of chain-rule. Nevertheless, there is a severe difference: here the truth qualification w.r.t. a fuzzy datum $A \in I\!F(\mathcal{X})$ is used to transform it into a fuzzy datum $B \in I\!F(\mathcal{X})$, in Section 6.4 a fuzzily evaluated datum $A \in I\!F(\mathcal{X})$ is transformed into a fuzzy datum $C \in I\!F(I\!F(\mathcal{X}))$.

From an intuitive point of view, this last mentioned approach looks even more satisfactory than the approach (4.84): the main idea behind (6.105) is that a truth qualification (4.83) indicates that the value assignment "$u = A$" is true only to some (fuzzy) degree, i.e. that besides A a whole fuzzy class of other fuzzy(!) values are also acceptable as fuzzy values of the variable u.

BELLMAN/ZADEH (1977) explain another use of linguistic truth values. They use them to evaluate one piece of fuzzy information on the basis of another one. Let e.g. the (fuzzy) information "$u = B$" be given for some fuzzy variable u with "true" values in $\mathcal{X}$. In this case one can use this information to evaluate further fuzzy information "$u = A$". As usual, "$u = B$" according to (3.56), (3.61) is understood as a possibility assignment $\pi_u = \mu_B$ for the "true" values of the variable u. Now the mapping $\pi_u : \mathcal{X} \to [0, 1]$ from the universe of discourse of A, B to the universe of discourse of some linguistic truth value $\tau_{A,B}$ provides, in accordance with the extension principle (2.105), a way to connect with the fuzzy sets A, B another fuzzy set $\tau_{A,B} \in \mathbb{F}([0, 1])$ defined for all $z \in [0, 1]$ by

$$\mu_{\tau_{A,B}}(z) = \sup_{\substack{x \in \mathcal{X} \\ z = \pi_u(x)}} \mu_A(x) = \sup_{\substack{x \in \mathcal{X} \\ z = \mu_B(x)}} \mu_A(x). \tag{4.90}$$

Thus they achieve the (conditional) truth qualification:

$$(u = A) \text{ is } \tau_{A,B} \quad \text{provided} \quad u = B. \tag{4.91}$$

Obviously, for getting (4.84) one can immediately generalise (4.88) by reference to the generalised class terms (2.40). In a natural way thus one gets the modified fuzzy value B in "$u = B$" as

$$B =_{\text{def}} \{x \,\|\, \mu_A(x) \,\epsilon\, \tau\}$$

and hence has directly arrived at (4.84).

Theoretically it is a much more interesting problem whether, in proceeding via (4.90) to connect with given fuzzy information "$u = B$" the (conditional) truth qualification $\tau_{A,B}$ of the fuzzy information "$u = A$", one is conversely able to start from the truth qualification

$$(u = A) \text{ is } \tau_{A,B} \tag{4.92}$$

and to get back via (4.84) the initial fuzzy information "$u = B$".

In general, this proves to be impossible. However, there is a necessary and sufficient condition for getting back from (4.92) via (4.84) the membership function μ_B, i.e. the fuzzy information "$u = B$", viz. that

$$\mu_A(x_1) = \mu_A(x_2) \Rightarrow \mu_B(x_1) = \mu_B(x_2) \quad \text{for all } x_1, x_2 \in \mathcal{X} \tag{4.93}$$

holds true. The reason is that condition (4.93) implies that equation (4.84) can be "solved" for μ_τ and that by

$$\mu_\tau(z) =_{\text{def}} \mu_B(x) \quad \text{for some } x \in \mu_A^{-1}(z)$$

a *function* μ_r is defined. Approaching (4.90) avoids this mathematical problem but has the disadvantage that $\mu_B \neq \mu_{\tau_{A,B}} \circ \mu_A$ holds true in the case that (4.93) does not hold true [∘ here means the composition, i.e. the superposition of these functions].

Defining the fuzzy truth value $\tau_{A,B}$ for this conditional truth qualification as in (4.90) often poses the problem of a *linguistic approximation* of $\tau_{A,B} \in IF([0, 1])$, i.e. the problem of determining for the fuzzy set $\tau_{A,B} : [0, 1] \to [0, 1]$ a suitable name out of the list (4.81) of linguistic truth values. But this, again, can usually be realised only approximately.

Together with these truth qualifications ZADEH (1978) also discusses qualifications, i.e. linguistic evaluations of probabilities and of possibilities, thus also enabling in approximate reasoning the treatment of pieces of information like:

- It is quite probable that fever and headache indicate influenza.

- It is neither very probable nor very unprobable that a marriage divorces after 10 years.

- There is only a small possibility that a bad student earns good marks simply by copying another guy's work.

- There is a high possibility that high-speed driving in foggy weather causes a car accident.

As with truth qualification (4.83), probability qualifications and possibility qualifications are read as possibility assignments for the values of suitably chosen variables; cf. ZADEH (1978a, 1979), DUBOIS/PRADE (1985). For probability as well as possibility qualifications through linguistic probabilities or linguistic possibilities it is obvious that – more than in the case of truth qualifications – they express possibility assignments for the probabilities or possibilities out of [0,1], respectively. The treatment of these resulting possibility assignments is then the same as for the possibility assignments which resulted from truth qualification. And again here, as for truth qualifications, these other types of qualifications can be read as fuzzily evaluated fuzzy data in the sense of Section 6.4 and be treated as discussed there; cf. also BANDE-MER/NÄTHER (1992) for a more detailed presentation.

The four types of rules which we introduced on p. 117 together with the standard method of transforming qualitative information, provided by some fuzzy data, into some possibility assignment (related to suitably chosen fuzzy variables) build up a framework for the inferential treatment of fuzzy information and constitute the field of approximate reasoning. Unfortunately, up to now this whole methodology is mainly based only on intuitions and heuristic ideas. What is lacking is some reliable theoretical foundation which bases these intuitions on clear principles. One main aspect of this problem e.g. is the fact that there does not exist any theoretical foundation to split the huge amount of possible inference schemata, e.g. for composition or quantification, into sound and non-sound ones as one is used to be able to do in classical (and even many-valued) logic.

Therefore, for every expert system application and each general inference one has to decide which types of inference schemata are acceptable – and why. For the fuzzy control methodology, this whole problem is not of such a severe character, because for fuzzy controllers on the one hand one is referring only to very simple inference methods or even "only" to relational equations – and on the other hand in fuzzy control applications it is not usually too hard to test the control quality directly with the process to be controlled. For expert systems applications in general, however, such a general theoretical foundation marks the most severe gap to be filled by future theoretical research.

4.5 Examples for Applications of Linguistic Variables and of Fuzzy Controllers

First true applications of the concepts of fuzzy control and of linguistic variables concerned the control of processes in the laboratory equipment. The initial example of control of a steam engine by MAMDANI/ASSILIAN (1975) proved to be of basic importance and became a treatment, which prototyped most of the later approaches. Therefore we sketch some of its details.

The process they intend to control, i.e. intend to have in a prespecified state or range of such states, is a combination of a steam engine with a boiler. Two state variables of this process are under control: the steam pressure in the boiler and the speed of the engine. The control actions proceed by influencing the heat input to the boiler and the throttle opening at the input of the engine cylinder. Thus, the whole control process splits into two separate, but related control actions. That means, the actual control is realised by two single fuzzy controllers.

We shall discuss only one of them: the control algorithm for the throttle opening. The output variable of this controller is the throttle change TC, that means that by changing this throttle opening the engine speed is changed. The input variables of the controller, two variables, are – relative to some standard value of the engine speed – the speed error SE and the change in speed error CSE.

Physically, the ranges of these variables are continuous sets of reals. Actually they are treated as fuzzy variables over discrete and finite universes of discourse with 13 elements (for SE and CSE) and with 5 elements (for TC) which represent equidistant points of some measurement scales symmetric to some origin, the set point. The linguistic values of these fuzzy variables are chosen out of the following list:

PB	positive big,	NB	negative big,
PM	positive medium,	NM	negative medium,
PS	positive small,	NS	negative small,

and completed by a zero value (NO), or sometimes two of them: (NO$^-$ for "just below the set point" and NO$^+$ for "just above the set point"). Actually, NO is used for the variable CSE, and NO$^-$, NO$^+$ are used for the variable SE. For the variable TC only PB, PS, NO, NS, NB are used. The definition of the membership functions for these linguistic values of the variable CSE is given in Table 4.1, and for the variable TC in Table 4.2.

Table 4.1: Linguistic values of the variable CSE (all empty places indicate a zero)

	-6	-5	-4	-3	-2	-1	0	+1	+2	+3	+4	+5	+6
PB										0.1	0.4	0.8	1
PM									0.2	0.7	1	0.7	0.2
PS								0.9	1	0.7	0.2		
NO						0.5	1	0.5					
NS			0.2	0.7	1	0.9							
NM	0.2	0.7	1	0.7	0.2								
NB	1	0.8	0.4	0.1									

One should however read these tables carefully because linguistic values with the same name may denote different fuzzy sets, that means, the interpretation of PB, PM, ... depends here on the fuzzy variable they are used as values of. For the fuzzy variable SE in MAMDANI/ASSILIAN (1975) a table is given which is much analogous to Table 4.1, hence this table will not be repeated here.

The system of control rules (4.2) for this fuzzy controller which controls the throttle opening consists of 9 rules which are collected in Table 4.3. Each one of these rules has the two input variables SE, CSE and the output variable TC.

The finiteness of the universes of discourse for all the fuzzy variables SE, CSE, and TC can be understood as the result of a discretisation of more basic continuous universes.

As a result, the set of membership degrees here can also be considered as a discretisation of $[0, 1]$, especially thus as one of the sets L_m. Here, L_{11} is the most preferable choice.

Table 4.2: Linguistic values of the variable TC (all empty places indicate a zero)

	-2	-1	0	+1	+2
PB				0.5	1
PS			0.5	1	0.5
NO		0.5	1	0.5	
NS	0.5	1	0.5		
NB	1	0.5			

Table 4.3: Control rules for throttle opening

	SE	CSE	TC
1	NB	not (NB or NM)	PB
2	NM	PB or PM or PS	PS
3	NS	PB or PM	PS
4	NO^-	PB	PS
5	NO^- or NO^+	PS or NS or NO	NO
6	NO^+	PB	NS
7	PS	PB or PM	NS
8	PM	PB or PM or PS	NS
9	PB	not (NB or NM)	NB

The background for this discretisation is the fact that one has only a more or less rough intuitive idea of how to understand the linguistic values which are used for the linguistic variables SE, CSE, TC. But furthermore this is also quite a common strategy for any numerical treatment and therefore the usual choice in designing fuzzy controllers.

Of course, continuous membership functions for linguistic values of suitable variables are sometimes used as well. This e.g. is the case in a paper by ADLASSNIG/KOLARZ (1982). The context there is medical diagnosis, the appearance of symptoms, and their significance for characterising types of illness. In that case the linguistic values are fuzzy subsets of the real interval $[0, 100]$, and the membership functions are the S-shaped function f_1 of (2.48) as well as the bell-shaped function f_2 of (2.49). Among others, these authors use the linguistic values always, almost always, often, unspecific, seldom characterised by the membership functions

$$\mu_{\text{always}}(x) = f_1(x; 97, 98, 99),$$

$$\mu_{\text{almost always}}(x) = f_1(x; 80, 85, 90),$$
$$\mu_{\text{often}}(x) = f_1(x; 40, 60, 80),$$
$$\mu_{\text{unspezific}}(x) = f_2(x; 20, 50),$$
$$\mu_{\text{seldom}}(x) = 1 - f_1(x; 20, 40, 60).$$

Both these examples indicate that it is not of primary importance whether one uses discrete or continuous universes of discourse for linguistic values, i.e. whether one has discrete or continuous (or even uncontinuous) membership functions. The choice of these possibilities completely depends on the actual application.

It is much more of interest to have some examples of applicational areas where linguistic variables have been used successfully. Such a list once again indicates how useful the concept of a linguistic variable really is. (Actually, the field of fuzzy control is a very rapidly growing one. Therefore we restrict the examples here to typical ones from the more initial phase of the fuzzy control applications. Nevertheless, the examples indicate well enough the broad range of applicability of these notions.)

Problems of medical diagnosis, besides ADLASSNIG/KOLARZ (1982), are the topic of SAITTA/TORASSO (1981) and LESMO/SAITTA/TORASSO (1982) too. In these cases the problems are heart diseases and of albumin concentration. Further medical problems are the background e.g. in MOON et al. (1977), CERUTTI/PIERI (1981), ADLASSNIG (1982), and in KRUSINSKA/LIEBHART (1986).

Cost-benefit analysis which uses linguistic variables is done in NEITZEL/HOFFMAN (1980), a model of social psychology in the topic of KICKERT (1979), an interactive system of risk analysis considers SCHMUCKER (1984), and more general quantitative analyses are studied in WENSTØP (1980). The same author already discussed organisational structures with the help of linguistic variables in WENSTØP (1975). And in the field of earthquake research LIU/WANG/CHEN (1985) classify intensity types by linguistic variables, as do OGAWA/FU/YAO (1985) in general with damage assessments of existing structures.

This list of examples is far from complete. But it proves that for applications which are often called "soft computing" this concept of linguistic variables and of fuzzy variables in general is extremely useful. Therefore there also exist implementations of these tools in shells for fuzzy control as well as in shells for data and knowledge bases. Research by ZEMANKOVA-LEECH/KANDEL (1984, 1985), BALDWIN (1985) and BALDWIN/BALDWIN/BROWN (1985), UMANO (1985) as well as ALEXEYEV (1985) marks the beginning of this development. Actually there are a lot of such devices sold on the software market.

For modelling of technological processes and industrial applications in general the most serious point is that fuzzy variables allow for a quite direct implementation of "informal", i.e. qualitative knowledge which is quite often the (only) basic knowledge of human operators.

Since the end of 1980 the concept of fuzzy control has shown quite a lot of remarkable applications in consumer goods as well as in advanced technological research. These applications cover a very wide range. They started with the automatic control of a cement kiln as described in HOLMBLAD/ØSTERGAARD (1982). The real breakthrough for industrial applications was the successful control of the subway system of Senday (Japan) by fuzzy controllers; cf. YASUNOBU/MIYAMOTO (1985). Other industrial applications, discussed in the mid-1980's, are presented in SUGENO (1985a,b). Since then, fuzzy control has proved its effectiveness e.g. in Minolta cameras, in Mitsubishi cars, in washing machines, rice cookers etc. The technique of fuzzy control, based on the fundamentals we presented in this chapter, has now become a kind of standard tool for control engineering; cf. also DRIANKOV/HELLENDOORN/REINFRANK (1993).

Finally, it is interesting to add that there is also a useful way to integrate fuzzy classification and fuzzy control, described e.g. in BOCKLISCH (1987), which allows one to combine the analysis of technological systems with the intention of fuzzy control. Other extensions of the fuzzy control strategy are related to a combination of fuzzy control techniques with ideas from fuzzy clustering and also from neural net techniques, e.g. to the learning and automated adaptation of fuzzy control rules, as well as to the combination of the fuzzy control strategy with ideas from the field of genetic algorithms which also aim at a kind of "automated design" of fuzzy controllers. But these topics will not be treated here in detail. Instead, the interested reader is referred to the literature, e.g. to: BEZDEK/PAL (1992), TAKAGI/LEE (1993), HOPF/KLAWONN (1994), NAUCK (1994) as well as NAUCK/KLAWONN/KRUSE (1994) and GEYER-SCHULZ (1994).

5 Measure Theory and Fuzzy Sets

5.1 Fuzzy Measures for Crisp Sets

5.1.1 Fuzzy Measures

When specifying a crisp set $\mathcal{A}$ we have to fix for *every* point of the universe $\mathcal{X}$, whether it belongs to $\mathcal{A}$ or not. If this specification is possible only gradually for every point, then the totality of all these membership degrees $\mu_A(x)$, $x \in \mathcal{X}$ will describe a fuzzy set A.

Simultaneously we could specify a certain element $x_0 \in \mathcal{X}$ by fixing for every subset $\mathcal{B}$ of $\mathcal{X}$, i.e. for all elements of the power set $I\!P(\mathcal{X})$, whether x_0 is contained in it or not. The set function Q which results from this fixing is defined as

$$Q(.,x_0) \ : \ I\!P(\mathcal{X}) \to \{0,1\} \tag{5.1}$$

and corresponds to the characteristic function when specifying common sets, i.e. for a given x_0 the function $Q(\mathcal{B}, x_0)$ is the characteristic function of the set of such $\mathcal{B}$'s, which hit x_0 (hence called hit function).

In many practical cases an interesting element of the universe can be located almost exactly, e.g. the cause of a disease, the culprit of a crime, or the affiliation of the discovered fossil to a species. This gives cause for a *fuzzy description Q of that element* by specifying a corresponding degree of assignment for every one of the sets of $I\!P(\mathcal{X})$. For the function

$$Q \ : \ I\!P(\mathcal{X}) \to [0,1] \tag{5.2}$$

it makes sense to demand that

$$Q(\emptyset) = 0 \ ; \qquad Q(\mathcal{X}) = 1 \tag{5.3}$$

and moreover

$$\forall \mathcal{A}, \mathcal{B} \in I\!P(\mathcal{X}) : \ \mathcal{A} \subseteq \mathcal{B} \Rightarrow Q(\mathcal{A}) \leq Q(\mathcal{B}) \,, \tag{5.4}$$

i.e. that the degree of assignment cannot decrease when the set becomes larger.

For *finite* universes these properties suffice already to develop a useful theory and application of such so-called *fuzzy measures*. For *infinite* universes according to SUGENO (1974, 1977) continuity with respect to set inclusion is required additionally:

Let $I\!A \subseteq I\!P(\mathcal{X})$ be a set with the property that every monotonic sequence

$$\mathcal{A}_1 \subseteq \mathcal{A}_2 \subseteq \cdots \quad \text{or} \quad \mathcal{A}_1 \supseteq \mathcal{A}_2 \supseteq \cdots$$

of sets $\mathcal{A}_i \in I\!A$; $i = 1, 2, \ldots$; converges towards an element of $I\!A$. Then this continuity means that for every one of such monotonic sequences it holds

$$\lim_{i \to \infty} Q(\mathcal{A}_i) = Q(\lim_{i \to \infty} \mathcal{A}_i). \tag{5.5}$$

The place of $I\!P(\mathcal{X})$ or $I\!A$ will usually be taken, guided by the considered problem or by mathematical convenience, by a suitable σ-algebra $I\!B$ over $\mathcal{X}$. Then, in analogy to a probability space, $[\mathcal{X}, I\!B, Q]$ is called a *fuzzy measure space*.

Since from additivity of probability, i.e. from

$$\text{Prob}\,(\mathcal{A} \cup \mathcal{B}) = \text{Prob}\,(\mathcal{A}) + \text{Prob}\,(\mathcal{B}), \text{ for } \mathcal{A} \cap \mathcal{B} = \emptyset \tag{5.6}$$

monotonicity

$$\begin{aligned} \mathcal{A} \subseteq \mathcal{B} \quad &\Rightarrow \quad \mathcal{B} = \mathcal{A} \cup (\mathcal{B} \cap \mathcal{A}^c) \\ &\Rightarrow \quad \text{Prob}(\mathcal{A}) \leq \text{Prob}(\mathcal{B}) \end{aligned} \tag{5.7}$$

and even continuity (5.5) follow, all probability measures are special fuzzy measures. They express the respective degree of assignment (to the set given as the argument) of a not yet performed realisation of the random variable, distributed according to the given probability measure.

Since KOLMOGOROV introduced probability calculus as probability theory into the canon of mathematical sciences by formulating his famous axioms for a probability measure (cf. KOLMOGOROV (1933)) it is a widespread opinion in mathematics as well as in its applications that this theory is able to model *every* kind of uncertainty properly. This opinion must be contradicted. Here we follow the reasoning of DUBOIS/PRADE (1985). The fundamental axiom is that of additivity of the probabilities of disjoint events (5.6). What does this property mean for practical cases? For the classical definition of probability, based on the calculus of chances, as the ratio of the number of favourable atoms to the number of all possible atoms, and also for the frequentistic interpretation in the sense of VON MISES (1919), this additivity is plausible. However, these approaches postulate, inter alia, that an experiment can be repeated arbitrarily often under the same conditions. In order to avoid the difficulties with this postulate when treating problems from the real world, supporters of the theory of subjective probability interpret probability as a *measure of the feeling of uncertainty*, taking up again every early ideas of probability calculus (cf. LEIBNIZ (1703), COURNOT (1843)). To quantify this feeling, as is necessary for the application and calculus, the numerical value of a probability is specified as proportional to the sum an individual would be willing to pay should a probable event, expected by him, not occur, i.e. a proposition that he asserts proves false. In so far as this sum exists, it is shown that the measure of uncertainty so defined obeys the axioms of probability theory, provided that the behaviour of the individual satisfies conditions of "rationality" (cf. SAVAGE (1972)). On this basis, the subjectivists succeeded in showing that Kolmogorov's axioms were the only reasonable basis for evaluating subjective uncertainty.

This rather extreme attitude can be contested from a philosophical and from a practical point of view.

So, it seems difficult to maintain that every uncertain judgement obeys the rules of betting. The necessary monetary commitment that forms an essential part of the model could prevent an individual from uncovering the true state of his knowledge, for fear of financial loss. Thus, a professional gambler will distribute his stakes evenly if he knows that all the options on which he is betting have equal strength. In the absence of any information, the neophyte will do the same, because it is the most prudent strategy. The subjective probability approach allows no distinction between these two states of knowledge and seems ill adapted to situations where this knowledge is sparse.

In particular, the limiting case of total ignorance is very poorly handled by the probabilistic model, which presupposes that a set of mutually disjoint events has been identified, to which are assigned, by virtue of the principle of maximum entropy, equal probabilities in the finite case. In the case of total ignorance, it seems to be ruled out that one is capable of identifying all the events, and therefore disputable that the measures of uncertainty attributed to them should depend on the number of alternatives, as is the case with probabilities.

From the practical point of view, it is clear that the numbers given by individuals to describe, in terms of probabilities, for example, the state of their knowledge must be considered for what they are, namely, approximate indications. Subjective probability theory does not seem to be concerned with this type of imprecision, considering that a rational individual must be able to furnish precise numbers, when proper procedures for their elicitation are used.

Hence, probability theory seems to be too normative a framework to take all the aspects of uncertain judgement into account. So far the reasoning by DUBOIS/PRADE (1985), which we endorse.

Readers interested in this controversy in more detail are referred to CHEESEMAN (1986) for arguments in favour of probability and to DUBOIS/PRADE (1990) for more arguments against its claim to sole rights.

There are already serious reservations about the exclusive use of probability for modelling of uncertainty, however, when evaluating elements of the power set $I\!P(\mathcal{X})$ in a principally subjective manner, its inadequacy becomes evident. When evaluating, by experts, sites with respect to their suitability for building a production plant it can quite happen that joining (union) of two disjoint and totally unworkable, but neighbouring sites (with respective evaluation 0) leads to an ideally workable site (evaluated by 1).

Hence it is interesting and necessary to look for measures, which do *not* satisfy the condition of additivity.

5.1.2   Possibility and Necessity Measures

From monotonicity (5.4) it follows immediately for all fuzzy measures that

$$Q(\mathcal{A} \cup \mathcal{B}) \geq \max\{Q(\mathcal{A}), Q(\mathcal{B})\} \tag{5.8}$$

and

$$Q(\mathcal{A} \cap \mathcal{B}) \leq \min\{Q(\mathcal{A}), Q(\mathcal{B})\}. \tag{5.9}$$

The limiting case in (5.8) ZADEH (1978) called *possibility measure* Poss:

$$\text{Poss}\,(\mathcal{A} \cup \mathcal{B}) = \max\{\text{Poss}\,(\mathcal{A}), \text{Poss}\,(\mathcal{B})\} \quad \text{for all } \mathcal{A}, \mathcal{B} \in I\!P(\mathcal{X}). \tag{5.10}$$

It denotes the *degree of possibility*, that a non-located element is situated in the set forming the argument.

One may be astonished that in contrast to (5.6) the condition $\mathcal{A} \cap \mathcal{B} = \emptyset$ is now missing. As can be shown (DUBOIS/PRADE (1980)), that if (5.10) holds for all pairs of *disjoint* sets, then it holds also for *all* pairs of sets.

If $\mathcal{X}$ is *finite*, then every possibility measure Poss can be defined by its values assumed on the elements $x \in \mathcal{X}$:

$$\forall \mathcal{A} \in I\!P(\mathcal{X}) : \text{Poss}\,(\mathcal{A}) = \max_{x \in \mathcal{A}} \pi(x) \tag{5.11}$$

where

$$\pi(x) = \text{Poss}\,(\{x\}) \tag{5.12}$$

and $\pi : \mathcal{X} \to [0,1]$ is called the *possibility distribution*. Because of the reasonable condition $\text{Poss}\,(\mathcal{X}) = 1$ the distribution π is normalised

$$\exists x \in \mathcal{X} : \pi(x) = 1 \,. \tag{5.13}$$

If $\mathcal{X}$ is *infinite*, then such a possibility distribution need not exist. However, this existence is guaranteed if the original condition (5.10) is extended to infinite unions of sets (cf. NGUYEN (1979)). In applications the existence can be always assumed and in (5.11), if necessary, max can be replaced by sup.

However, in the case of infinite universes $\mathcal{X}$, possibility measures need not satisfy the condition of continuity (5.5), and hence then be *no* fuzzy measures (cf. PURI/RALESCU (1982) for details).

Since a possibility distribution π has the property of a normalised membership function, the membership value $\mu_B(y)$ to a fuzzy set B can be interpreted as the degree of possibility that a variable v assumes the value $y \in \mathcal{Y}$. This way we used in Section 3.3. The fuzzy set B is often called the *inducing* set and carried with when specifying possibility degrees of some variable (cf. e.g. (3.56)). Hence it is possible, in the respective formal environment, to identify $\text{Poss}(\{x\})$ also with $\text{Poss}(v = x|B)$, and $\text{Poss}(\mathcal{A})$ with $\text{Poss}(v = \mathcal{A}|B)$.

Let $\mathcal{X}$ and $\mathcal{Y}$ be two universes with the respective variables u and v, and $\pi_{(u,v)}$ the possibility distribution belonging to (u, v). Then the projections

$$\pi_u(x) = \sup_y \pi_{(u,v)}(x,y); \qquad \pi_v(y) = \sup_x \pi_{(u,v)}(x,y) \tag{5.14}$$

introduce the so-called marginal distributions. In the case of separability (3.35) of the fuzzy relation corresponding to $\pi_{(u,v)}$ it holds

$$\pi_{(u,v)}(x,y) = \min\{\pi_u(x),\ \pi_v(y)\}. \tag{5.15}$$

Via

$$\begin{aligned}
\pi_u(x) &= \sup_y \pi_{(u,v)}(x,y) \\
&= \sup_y \min\{\pi_{(u,v)}(x,y), \sup_x \pi_{(u,v)}(x,y)\}
\end{aligned}$$

we obtain

$$\pi_u(x) = \sup_y \min\{\pi_{(u,v)}(x,y),\ \pi_v(y)\}. \tag{5.16}$$

When interpreting (5.15) as an analogue to the definition of *independence* in the case of probability, then (5.16) represents the respective analogue to the formula of total probability. Hence, in this context, $\pi_{(u,v)}$ is called *conditional possibility distribution*. This analogy was considered by NGUYEN (1978), who introduced the notion of a *normalised conditional possibility distribution*, which again satisfies the condition (5.13). He considers

$$\pi(x|y) = \pi_{(u,v)}(x,y)\theta(\pi_u(x), \pi_v(y)), \tag{5.17}$$

where θ is a normalising function, which is determined from

$$\text{hgt}(\pi(x|y)) = 1$$

and

$$\min\{\pi_u(x), \pi_v(y)\}\theta(\pi_u(x), \pi_v(y)) = \pi_u(x). \tag{5.18}$$

The equation (5.18) means that, in the case of separability (5.15), the normalised conditional possibility distribution equals the marginal distribution, which completes the analogy with probability distributions. The conditions (5.18) lead to

$$\pi(x|y) = \begin{cases} \pi_{(u,v)}(x,y), & \text{if } \pi_u(x) \le \pi_v(y), \\ \pi_{(u,v)}(x,y)\pi_u(x)/\pi_v(y), & \text{if } \pi_u(x) > \pi_v(y). \end{cases}$$

Because of that we arrive finally at

$$\pi_u(x) = \sup_y \min\{\pi(x|y), \pi_v(y)\}.$$ (5.19)

The other limiting case from (5.9) leads to so-called *necessity measures* Nec, which satisfy for all $A, B \in \mathbb{P}(\mathcal{X})$ the condition

$$\text{Nec}(A \cap B) = \min\{\text{Nec}(A), \text{Nec}(B)\}.$$ (5.20)

A necessity measure indicates the degree that a non-located element of $\mathcal{X}$ is situated *necessarily* in the set forming the argument. This interpretation becomes clear when we consider that (5.20) is equivalent to

$$\forall A \in \mathbb{P}(\mathcal{X}) : \text{Nec}(A) = 1 - \text{Poss}(A^c),$$ (5.21)

then (5.21) is a quantitative expression of the duality relationship, used in modal logic, between the notions of the possible and the necessary, stating that an event is *necessary* if its contrary is *impossible*.

According to (5.21) from a possibility distribution a necessity measure can also be constructed:

$$\text{Nec}(A) = \inf_{x \notin A}\{1 - \pi(x)\}.$$ (5.22)

Because of (5.13) it holds

$$1 = \text{Poss}(A \cup A^c) = \max\{\text{Poss}(A), \text{Poss}(A^c)\}$$ (5.23)

and according to (5.21) then

$$0 = \min\{\text{Nec}(A), \text{Nec}(A^c)\}.$$ (5.24)

From (5.21) and (5.24) we can conclude that

$$\forall A \in \mathbb{P}(\mathcal{X}) : \text{Poss}(A) \ge \text{Nec}(A),$$ (5.25)

which corresponds to the idea that an event becomes possible before becoming necessary. Moreover, we have

$$\text{Nec}(A) > 0 \quad \Rightarrow \quad \text{Poss}(A) = 1,$$ (5.26)
$$\text{Poss}(A) < 1 \quad \Rightarrow \quad \text{Nec}(A) = 0.$$ (5.27)

For a detailed presentation of theory and calculus of possibility and necessity measures the monograph by DUBOIS/PRADE (1985) can be recommended.

5.1.3 Sugeno Measures

The rule for computing the measure value for the union of two sets, cf. (5.6), (5.8), (5.10), is an interesting starting point for the construction of measures, e.g. from a given system of elementary sets.

In generalising of (5.6) SUGENO (1974) suggested so-called λ-*fuzzy measures* Q_λ, which obey the combining rule:

$$Q_\lambda(\mathcal{A} \cup \mathcal{B}) = Q_\lambda(\mathcal{A}) + Q_\lambda(\mathcal{B}) + \lambda Q_\lambda(\mathcal{A}) Q_\lambda(\mathcal{B}) \quad \text{for } \mathcal{A} \cap \mathcal{B} = \emptyset. \quad (5.28)$$

With $Q_\lambda(\mathcal{X}) = 1$ the measure Q_λ satisfies the conditions (5.3) to (5.5) for $\lambda > -1$. For $\lambda = 0$ then Q_λ is obviously a probability measure.

The usual rules necessary for application can be derived easily, in analogy with the performance in probability theory from (5.28), e.g.

$$Q_\lambda(\mathcal{A}^c) = \big(1 - Q_\lambda(\mathcal{A})\big) / \big(1 + \lambda Q_\lambda(\mathcal{A})\big) \quad (5.29)$$

and the generalisation of (5.28) to the case $\mathcal{A} \cap \mathcal{B} \neq \emptyset$:

$$Q_\lambda(\mathcal{A} \cup \mathcal{B}) = \frac{\big(Q_\lambda(\mathcal{A}) + Q_\lambda(\mathcal{B}) - Q_\lambda(\mathcal{A} \cap \mathcal{B}) + \lambda Q_\lambda(\mathcal{A}) Q_\lambda(\mathcal{B})\big)}{\big(1 + \lambda Q_\lambda(\mathcal{A} \cap \mathcal{B})\big)} . \quad (5.30)$$

Let $\mathcal{E}_1, \mathcal{E}_2 \ldots$ be a system of disjoint (elementary) sets, then we have

$$Q_\lambda\Big(\bigcup_{i=1}^{\infty} \mathcal{E}_i \Big) = \lambda^{-1}\Big(\prod_{i=1}^{\infty} \big(1 + \lambda Q_\lambda(\mathcal{E}_i)\big) - 1 \Big) . \quad (5.31)$$

For the special case $\mathcal{X} = \mathbb{R}$ the measure Q_λ can be defined via a function h showing properties usually required for a continuous distribution function in probability theory, i.e. monotonicity and continuity with limits 0 and 1, respectively (cf. SUGENO (1977)). Then for all intervals $[a, b]$ the following construction rule is valid

$$Q_\lambda([a, b]) = \big(h(b) - h(a)\big) / \big(1 + \lambda h(a)\big) . \quad (5.32)$$

These λ-fuzzy measures are important, since they allow one to approximate the frequent requirements from the context of the fuzzy measure very flexibly by choosing a suitable λ, and since the calculus is relatively simply to handle.

5.1.4 Dempster - Shafer Theory

Another way to generalise the usual probability is taken by DEMPSTER and SHAFER (cf. DEMPSTER (1967), SHAFER (1976)).

A probability measure is specified, if $\text{Prob}(\mathcal{A})$ is given for all events, i.e. for all elements of some σ-algebra $\mathbb{B}(\mathcal{X})$, or, more precisely, for all elements of a generating system of $\mathbb{B}(\mathcal{X})$. In application to real problems the state of knowledge frequently allows the specification of the probability values only for some events, i.e. for the elements of a certain subset $I\!\!A \subseteq \mathbb{B}(\mathcal{X})$. In certain cases, e.g. if $I\!\!A$ contains a generating system of $\mathbb{B}(\mathcal{X})$, the probability for all events $\mathcal{B}$ outside of $I\!\!A$ can be computed. In every case the specifying of $\mathrm{Prob}(\mathcal{A})$ for all $\mathcal{A} \in I\!\!A$ restricts the set of possible values for $\mathrm{Prob}(\mathcal{B})$ for $\mathcal{B} \notin I\!\!A$. Possibly the first mentioning of such a problem is due to BOOLE (1854), who considered the case that for two events $\mathcal{A}, \mathcal{B}$ only the probabilities

$$\mathrm{Prob}\,(\mathcal{A}) = p \quad \text{and} \quad \mathrm{Prob}\,(\mathcal{A} \cap \mathcal{B}) = q \tag{5.33}$$

are given. From (5.33) we obtain the bounds for $\mathrm{Prob}\,(\mathcal{B})$:

$$q \leq \mathrm{Prob}\,(\mathcal{B}) \leq q + 1 - p. \tag{5.34}$$

Another approach to bounds for probabilities is due to CHOQUET (1954), who considered upper and lower measures, P and S say, such that for all events $\mathcal{A} \in \mathbb{B}(\mathcal{X})$ it holds

$$P(\mathcal{A}) \leq \mathrm{Prob}(\mathcal{A}) \leq S(\mathcal{A}). \tag{5.35}$$

He showed, among other things, how to compute with such *capacities* (P, S). A special case, namely, that the probability measure is given on a coarser algebra, is treated by PAWLAK (1984) in some detail.

The fact that the values of the probabilities can be given only for a subset $I\!\!A$ not sufficient for generation of the σ-algebra $\mathbb{B}(\mathcal{X})$ expresses the given state of knowledge, or rather, of ignorance, hence called *partial ignorance*, with respect to the probability distribution.

For *finite* universes $\mathcal{X}$ SHAFER (1976) (cf. also DUBOIS/PRADE (1987)) presented an interesting concept, according to which we can construct fuzzy measures starting from such incomplete specifications. The weight 1 is distributed amongst the sets of $I\!\!P(\mathcal{X})$ (or $\mathbb{B}(\mathcal{X})$), i.e. a mapping

$$p : I\!\!P(\mathcal{X}) \to [0, 1] \tag{5.36}$$

is specified. Because of the normalisation to 1, i.e. besides of $p(\emptyset) = 0$, we demand

$$\sum_{\mathcal{B} \in I\!\!P(\mathcal{X})} p(\mathcal{B}) = 1. \tag{5.37}$$

The mapping p is called *basic probability assignment* . The sets with $p(\mathcal{A}) > 0$ are *focal subsets* of p. The set of all focal sets, so to speak the support of p, will be denoted by supp p. The pair (supp p, p) SHAFER (1976) called a *body of evidence*.

The weight $p(\mathcal{A})$ is sometimes also called *global probability assignment* to $\mathcal{A}$. However, this notation is somewhat misleading, since this value represents only some *remainder* of the probability Prob $(\mathcal{A})$, which, according to the given state of knowledge, cannot be distributed further to subevents of $\mathcal{A}$ (and, in this sense, remains "global"). The value $p(\mathcal{A})$ is also interpreted, frequently, as the relative level of confidence in $\mathcal{A}$ as a representation of the available information. It represents the "probability" that this information is described correctly and completely by $x \in \mathcal{A}$. The focal sets need not be disjoint, nor form a covering of $\mathcal{X}$. Even $\mathcal{X}$ can be a focal set. Then $p(\mathcal{X})$ means that portion of confidence which is owed to ignorance. Hence total ignorance is expressed by $p(\mathcal{X}) = 1$. This interpretation rests on the assumption that the focal set $\mathcal{A}$ describes all possible positions, which the value of a certain variable can assume, e.g. $\mathcal{A}$ can be a fuzzy observation or measurement. In this context the information is called *disjunctive*, in such a sense that the actual value of the variable is unique. Hence the focal sets represent mutually excluding possible values of the variable.

In general, the probabilities of events $\mathcal{B} \in \mathbb{B}(\mathcal{X})$ remain unspecified by a basic probability assignment p, where, in general, it is unimportant, whether $\mathcal{B}$ is a subset of a focal set $\mathcal{A}$ or not. It is only known that the probability Prob($\mathcal{B}$) is an element of some interval $[P_*(\mathcal{B}), P^*(\mathcal{B})]$ with

$$P_*(\mathcal{B}) \;=\; \sum_{\mathcal{A} \subseteq \mathcal{B}} p(\mathcal{A}), \tag{5.38}$$

$$P^*(\mathcal{B}) \;=\; \sum_{\mathcal{A} \cap \mathcal{B} \neq \emptyset} p(\mathcal{A}). \tag{5.39}$$

So, the value $P_*(\mathcal{B})$ is computed by considering all focal sets $\mathcal{A}$, which make the event $\mathcal{B}$ a necessary one (i.e. as a consequence), whereas for $P^*(\mathcal{B})$ all focal sets are taken into account, which make the event a possible one.

Moreover, there exists a duality relation between P^* and P_*: it holds for all $\mathcal{A} \in \mathbb{P}(\mathcal{X})$

$$P^*(\mathcal{A}) = 1 - P_*(\mathcal{A}^c) . \tag{5.40}$$

However, P^* and P_*, in general, are no longer possibility and necessity measures, respectively. They are such measures iff the focal sets are nested, this case is then called the *consonant* case. More precisely, if for the focal sets it holds

$$\mathcal{A}_1 \subset \mathcal{A}_2 \subset \cdots \subset \mathcal{A}_s,$$

then the corresponding possibility distribution is defined by

$$\pi(x) = P^*(\{x\}) = \begin{cases} \sum_{j=i}^{s} p(\mathcal{A}_j), & \text{if } x \in \mathcal{A}_i \, ; \, x \notin \mathcal{A}_{i-1}, \\ 0, & \text{if } x \in \mathcal{X} \setminus \mathcal{A}_s. \end{cases} \qquad (5.41)$$

If, on the other hand, all focal sets are elementary events (respective atoms) and hence disjoint, that is the *dissonant* case, then it holds obviously

$$\forall \mathcal{B} : P_*(\mathcal{B}) = \text{Prob}\,(\mathcal{B}) = P^*(\mathcal{B}). \qquad (5.42)$$

When the state of knowledge is expressed by a body of evidence it becomes clear that probability measures address precise but differentiated items of information, whereas possibility measures reflect imprecise but coherent items. So, possibility measures are useful for subjective uncertainty: we expect from an informant no very precise data, however, we expect the greatest possible coherence among his statements. On the other hand, precise, but variable data are usually the result of carefully observing physical phenomena.

Usually the state of knowledge is neither precise nor totally coherent, i.e. P^* and P_* are neither probabilities, nor possibility and necessity degrees, respectively. Hence SHAFER (1976) called the measure P_*, defined by (5.38) for finite universes $\mathcal{X}$, in the general case, the *degree of credibility* (or of belief) of $\mathcal{B}$:

$$\text{Cr}(\mathcal{B}) = \sum_{\mathcal{A} \subseteq \mathcal{B}} p(\mathcal{A}). \qquad (5.43)$$

It represents the *weight of evidence*, the *degree of confidence*, concentrated on $\mathcal{B}$, or, as already expressed in the language of probability theory, concentrated on events, which have the occurrence of $\mathcal{B}$ as a consequence. Deducing from this measure, SHAFER defined by

$$\text{Pl}(\mathcal{B}) = 1 - \text{Cr}(\mathcal{B}^c) = \sum_{\mathcal{A} \cap \mathcal{B} \neq \emptyset} p(\mathcal{A}) \qquad (5.44)$$

the *degree of plausibility*, the degree of "understanding", which obviously coincides with P^* according to (5.39). It represents the weight of evidence, which is *not concentrated* on $\mathcal{B}$; this is, as already mentioned, equivalent with the concentration on events, which make the occurrence of $\mathcal{B}$ a possible event.

Interpreting $\text{Cr}(\mathcal{B}^c)$ as the degree, with which the affiliation of a non-located element to $\mathcal{B}$ is *doubted*, then $\text{Pl}(\mathcal{B})$ is the degree to which this is *undoubted*, thus taken for understandable or plausible.

The basic probability assignment can be obtained back from Cr as well as from Pl, e.g. we have

$$p(\mathcal{B}) = \sum_{\mathcal{A} \subseteq \mathcal{B}} (-1)^{\text{card}\,(\mathcal{B} \setminus \mathcal{A})} \text{Cr}(\mathcal{A}). \qquad (5.45)$$

Naturally, it holds always

$$Pl(\mathcal{B}) \geq Cr(\mathcal{B}) . \tag{5.46}$$

If the focal sets are one-element sets, then p is a common probability distribution on $\mathcal{X}$ and $Pl(\mathcal{B}) = Cr(\mathcal{B}) = Prob\,(\mathcal{B})$ is a probability.

The degree of credibility satisfies a weakening of the well-known general addition rule for probabilities

$$Cr(\mathcal{A} \cup \mathcal{B}) \geq Cr(\mathcal{A}) + Cr(\mathcal{B}) - Cr(\mathcal{A} \cap \mathcal{B}), \tag{5.47}$$

and, more generally, for any finite system of sets $\{\mathcal{A}_i\}$ with $\mathcal{A}_i \in I\!\!P(\mathcal{X})$ (cf. SMETS (1981), SHAFER (1976)):

$$Cr\left(\bigcup_i \mathcal{A}_i\right) \;\geq\; \sum_i Cr\,(\mathcal{A}_i) - \sum_{i<j} Cr\,(\mathcal{A}_i \cap \mathcal{A}_j) + \cdots$$
$$\cdots + (-1)^{n+1} Cr\left(\bigcap_j \mathcal{A}_j\right) . \tag{5.48}$$

Obviously then it holds (Note that $\mathcal{B}$ is a crisp set!)

$$Cr(\mathcal{B}) + Cr(\mathcal{B}^c) \leq 1 . \tag{5.49}$$

Let the non-located element of $\mathcal{X}$, for instance, be a discovered fossil. Then it can be assigned, with a certain degree of conviction, i.e. of credibility, to a certain species $\mathcal{B}$, specimens of which were found very frequently in the stratum under consideration. However, lacking confidence in this classification ($Cr(\mathcal{B}) < 1$) does not necessarily lead to a high confidence in the case that the fossil does *not* belong to $\mathcal{B}$ ($Cr(\mathcal{B}^c) > 0$).

For Pl we obtain formulae in analogy with (5.47) to (5.49), when changing the union there with the intersection and inverting the inequality signs.

For *infinite* universes we can use (5.48) and the corresponding formula for Pl, assumed for all natural numbers n, for characterising fuzzy measures Cr and Pl and thus finding a linkage to CHOQUET'S capacities (CHOQUET (1954)). A detailed investigation of this infinite case is due to KOHLAS (1994). However, this approach seems hardly practicable at present.

5.2 Fuzzy Measures for Fuzzy Sets

An argument for introducing fuzzy measures in Section 5.1 was the possibility, provided by this notion, to characterise an element of the universe $\mathcal{X}$, which cannot be located precisely, by specifying for every subset of $\mathcal{X}$, i.e. for every $\mathcal{A} \in I\!\!P(\mathcal{X})$, a degree of assignment $Q(\mathcal{A})$. By this performance a fuzzy set was introduced on $I\!\!P(\mathcal{X})$. As applications of fuzzy sets inform, when specifying sets to be evaluated by degrees of assignment, even these sets can only be defined as fuzzy sets, e.g. groups of potential customers, climatic regions, symptoms of diseases, and sets of worn out components. Hence it is reasonable to extend the range of fuzzy measures from $I\!P(\mathcal{X})$ to the set of all fuzzy sets on $\mathcal{X}$, i.e. to $I\!F(\mathcal{X})$.

5.2.1 Probability for Fuzzy Sets

Since probability measures are special fuzzy measures we will consider this case first. As is well known, when introducing probability for crisp sets $\mathcal{A}, \mathcal{B}, \ldots$ we start with the assumption that these are random events, i.e. elements of some given σ-algebra $I\!B(\mathcal{X})$. Every event $\mathcal{A}$ is assigned a probability Prob $(\mathcal{A})$, which is a value of the set function P, called the probability measure. Usually it is expressed by an integral

$$\text{Prob}\,(\mathcal{A}) = \int\limits_{\mathcal{A}} \mathrm{d}P(x). \tag{5.50}$$

Using the characteristic function $\mu_{\mathcal{A}}$ of $\mathcal{A}$ this can be written as

$$\text{Prob}\,(\mathcal{A}) = \int\limits_{\mathcal{X}} \mu_{\mathcal{A}}(x)\,\mathrm{d}P(x). \tag{5.51}$$

For finite or countable infinite universes we obtain from this the well-known representation by sums of probabilities of the elements of $\mathcal{X}$.

This representation was the starting point taken by ZADEH (1968) for defining probability also for fuzzy sets $A \in I\!F(\mathcal{X})$, e.g. for values of linguistic variables (cf. Section 4.1) by interpreting μ_A in (5.51) as a membership function.

This concept proved workable, although the usual interpretation as a probability of the event that a realisation according to P will fall into A, no longer seems possible. However, it seems reasonable to take (5.51) as an expectation value of the membership function. As usual we introduce a random variable $\mathbf{X}\colon \Omega \to \mathcal{X}$ and write

$$\text{Prob}\,(A) = \mathsf{E}_P \mu_A(\mathbf{X}) = \text{Prob}\,(\text{``}\mathbf{X} \in A\text{''})\,. \tag{5.52}$$

Let $x_1, x_2, \ldots, x_n$ be independent realisations of the random variable $\mathbf{X}$, then, on only small restrictive assumptions, we obtain statements like those known from probability theory as laws of large numbers, e.g.

$$\text{Prob}\,(A) = \lim_{n \to \infty} (1/n) \sum_{i=1}^{n} \mu_A(x_i)\,. \tag{5.53}$$

For fuzzy sets A probability can be interpreted as the *mean membership degree* of the elements of a sample of infinite size according to the probability distribution belonging to P.

Some properties of probability remain valid also for fuzzy sets, e.g.

$$A \subseteq B \quad \Rightarrow \quad \text{Prob}\,(A) \leq \text{Prob}\,(B),$$
$$\text{Prob}\,(A \cup B) \quad = \quad \text{Prob}\,(A) + \text{Prob}\,(B) - \text{Prob}\,(A \cap B).$$

However, the essential notion of *independence* of two (fuzzy) events must now be introduced in a different manner, since the intersection $A \cap B$ is combined, according to the connection used here, with the *minimum* of the corresponding membership values.

Taking the *alternative* connection of sets

$$C = A \bullet B \quad \text{with} \quad \mu_C(x) = \mu_A(x) \cdot \mu_B(x)\,, \tag{5.54}$$

cf. (2.98), then the definition

$$A, B \text{ independent} \quad \Leftrightarrow \quad \text{Prob}\,(A \bullet B) = \text{Prob}\,(A) \cdot \text{Prob}\,(B) \tag{5.55}$$

corresponds with the idea of independence in common probability theory.

This approach, e.g., clears the road for an introduction of conditional probabilities in the form (for $\text{Prob}\,(B) > 0$)

$$\text{Prob}\,(A|B) = \text{Prob}\,(A \bullet B)/\text{Prob}\,(B)\,. \tag{5.56}$$

When using (5.51) also for fuzzy events we must demand that μ_A is integrable with respect to P.

The rather heuristic character of this introduction of probability for fuzzy events caused SMETS (1982) to justify this approach theoretically. He introduced more generally

$$\text{Prob}\,(A) = \int\limits_{\mathcal{X}} g(\mu_A(x))\,\mathrm{d}P(x) \tag{5.57}$$

and put some conditions with respect to the properties of g. So e.g. g must be monotonically non-decreasing with $g(0) = 0$ and $g(1) = 1$, in order for Kolmogorov's axioms to be valid. Moreover, we can demand that the sum of the conditional probabilities of a fuzzy event and of its complement with respect to any other event must add up to 1.

When, as appropriate to (5.54), taking the union according to (2.102)

$$D = A + B \quad \text{with} \quad \mu_D(x) = \mu_A(x) + \mu_B(x) - \mu_A(x)\mu_B(x)\,,$$

for probabilities it holds again

$$\text{Prob}\,(A+B) = \text{Prob}\,(A) + \text{Prob}\,(B) - \text{Prob}\,(A \bullet B)\,, \tag{5.58}$$

which will be of interest, when, for objective reasons, we have to give up the max-min-connection.

Having defined probability we can also introduce the entropy of a fuzzy event, e.g. for finite universes $\mathcal{X} = \{x_1, \ldots, x_n\}$ by

$$H_P(A) = -\sum_{i=1}^{m} \mu_A(x_i)\text{Prob}\,(\{x_i\})\ln \text{Prob}\,(\{x_i\})\,.$$

This entropy of a fuzzy event must not be confused with the entropy measure in the sense of DeLuca/Termini (1979); cf. Section 5.5.

To illustrate this idea we will give an example from an application due to Kandel (1986), which was simplified with respect to the model used. The *process of ageing* of a component (where age means the time passed since inserting the component into the process) is essentially influenced by stochastic factors, which can be taken into account, e.g., by specifying a speed of ageing A with values $a \in [0, \infty)$. This speed is a random variable distributed according to some probability law, e.g. to a gamma distribution $\Gamma(b, p)$ with parameters $b = a_0^{-1}$ and $p = 2$, i.e. with a density f, yielding the infinitesimal probability

$$dP(a) = f(a)da = a_0^{-2}a\exp\{-a/a_0\}da\,.$$

For every individual "age" t all those components are regarded as *worn out*, which belong to the fuzzy set $A(t)$ defined, e.g., by the membership function

$$\mu_{A(t)}(a) = 1 - \exp\{-at/a_m t_m\},$$

for which the degree at of being worn out is "approximately larger " than the standard degree $a_m t_m$ computed from given evaluation constants a_m and t_m.

The probability that a component with "age" t is considered as a worn out one, is, according to (5.51),

$$
\begin{aligned}
\text{Prob}\,(A(t)) &= a_0^{-2}\int_0^\infty (1 - \exp\{-at/a_m t_m\})a\exp\{-a/a_0\}da \\
&= 1 - (1 + \lambda t)^{-2} \qquad \text{with } \lambda = a_0(a_m t_m)^{-1}\,.
\end{aligned}
$$

5.2.2   Possibility for Fuzzy Sets

By analogy we can also extend possibility measures to fuzzy sets. Starting with the possibility distribution $\pi(x)$; $x \in \mathcal{X}$; and the representation for crisp sets $\mathcal{A}$

$$\text{Poss}(\mathcal{A}) = \sup_{x \in \mathcal{A}} \pi(x), \tag{5.59}$$

we can introduce the possibility degree for fuzzy sets A by

$$\text{Poss}(A) = \sup_{x \in \mathcal{X}} \min\{\pi(x), \mu_A(x)\}. \tag{5.60}$$

For crisp sets (5.60) coincides with (5.59). The possibility degree for a fuzzy set A can be interpreted as the degree of consistency of the fuzzy "event" A with a fuzzy set B, the membership function of which is induced by the possibility distribution: $\mu_B = \pi$.

Obviously, we have also for fuzzy sets:

$$\text{Poss}(A \cup B) \quad = \quad \max\{\text{Poss}(A), \text{Poss}(B)\}, \tag{5.61}$$
$$A \subseteq B \quad \Rightarrow \quad \text{Poss}(A) \le \text{Poss}(B). \tag{5.62}$$

Two fuzzy sets A and B are called *non-interactive*, if

$$\text{Poss}(A \cap B) = \min\{\text{Poss}(A), \text{Poss}(B)\}. \tag{5.63}$$

If $\pi_{(u,v)} \in \mathbb{F}(\mathcal{X} \times \mathcal{Y})$ is *separable* (cf. (5.15)), then these fuzzy events $A \in \mathbb{F}(\mathcal{X})$, $B \in \mathbb{F}(\mathcal{Y})$ are *non-interactive*. Finally, one has some kind of Bayesian formula

$$\text{Poss}(A|B) = \min\{\text{Poss}(B|A), \text{Poss}(A)\}, \tag{5.64}$$

for which $\text{Poss}(B|A)$ is to be computed from (5.17), e.g. by

$$\text{Poss}(B|A) = \sup_{x \in \mathcal{X}, y \in \mathcal{Y}} \pi(x|y). \tag{5.65}$$

5.2.3   Fuzzy Integrals

The integral representation (5.50), as used in extending probability measures, and the formula (5.60) used when extending a possibility measure, reflect union operations as used when advancing from a measure theory to an integration theory.

Hence SUGENO (1974) considered fuzzy integrals, with which not only an extension for fuzzy measures to $\mathbb{F}(\mathcal{X})$ can be effected. Although SUGENO (1974, 1977) showed essential statements of his theory for the "fuzzily measurable" space $[\mathcal{X}, \mathbb{I}\!A]$, i.e. where $\mathbb{I}\!A$ is a subset of $\mathbb{P}(\mathcal{X})$, which is closed with respect to monotonic sequences of sets, in the following we will base our considerations, for mathematical convenience, on a *fuzzy measure space* $[\mathcal{X}, \mathbb{B}, Q]$ with a suitable σ-algebra $\mathbb{B}$ on $\mathcal{X}$.

Now, let $h : \mathcal{X} \to [0, 1]$ be some $\mathbb{B}$-measurable function and $\mathcal{A} \in \mathbb{P}(\mathcal{X})$; then Sugeno's definition of a *fuzzy integral* is equivalent with

$$\fint_{\mathcal{A}} h(x) \circ Q(.) = \sup_{\alpha \in [0,1]} \min\{\alpha, Q(\mathcal{A} \cap h^{\geq \alpha})\} \tag{5.66}$$

where $h^{\geq \alpha} = \{x \in \mathcal{X} \mid h(x) \geq \alpha\}$. The restriction to the domain $[0, 1]$ for h is essential and suited to the purpose of introducing fuzzy measures for fuzzy sets. Giving up this condition seems artificial (cf. for that KANDEL (1979), RALESCU (1982)). Sometimes we will succeed in defining the function h in such a manner that $[0, 1]$ becomes a natural or suitable range.

Because of the lacking additivity of the measure, as a rule, only statements with respect to monotonicity remain valid as properties of those integrals, e.g. for all $\mathcal{A} \in \mathbb{B}$

$$\forall x \in \mathcal{A} : h(x) \leq h'(x) \Rightarrow \fint_{\mathcal{A}} h(x) \circ Q(.) \leq \fint_{\mathcal{A}} h'(x) \circ Q(.) \tag{5.67}$$

and

$$\fint_{\mathcal{A}} \max\{h_1(x), h_2(x)\} \circ Q(.)$$

$$\geq \max \left\{ \fint_{\mathcal{A}} h_1(x) \circ Q(.), \fint_{\mathcal{A}} h_2(x) \circ Q(.) \right\} \tag{5.68}$$

(correspondingly for the minimum).

Now let $\mu_{\mathcal{A}}$ be the characteristic function of $\mathcal{A} \in \mathbb{P}(\mathcal{X})$, then, because of $(\mathcal{A} \cap (\mu_{\mathcal{A}})^{\geq \alpha}) = \mathcal{A}$ for all $\alpha \in (0, 1]$, we have

$$\fint_{\mathcal{A}} 1 \circ Q(.) = \fint_{\mathcal{X}} \mu_{\mathcal{A}}(x) \circ Q(.) = Q(\mathcal{A}) \tag{5.69}$$

and, by analogy,

$$\fint_{\mathcal{A}} h(x) \circ Q(.) = \fint_{\mathcal{X}} \min\{\mu_{\mathcal{A}}(x), h(x)\} \circ Q(.) . \tag{5.70}$$

If we replace $\mu_{\mathcal{A}}(x)$ by the membership function μ_A of a fuzzy set $A \in \mathbb{F}(\mathcal{X})$, then we can use (5.69) to introduce $Q(A)$, and (5.70) for defining integration over *fuzzy* regions.

In analogy with (5.67) and (5.68) the fuzzy Sugeno-integral (5.66) shows monotonicity also with respect to the integration region

$$\mathcal{A} \subseteq \mathcal{B} \quad \Rightarrow \fint_{\mathcal{A}} h(x) \circ Q(.) \leq \fint_{\mathcal{B}} h(x) \circ Q(.) , \tag{5.71}$$

$$\oint_{\mathcal{A} \cup \mathcal{B}} h(x) \circ Q(.) \geq \max \left\{ \oint_{\mathcal{A}} h(x) \circ Q(.), \oint_{\mathcal{B}} h(x) \circ Q(.) \right\} \tag{5.72}$$

(correspondingly for the minimum).

Further results on fuzzy integrals and, especially, on the mathematically interesting problem of interchangeability of the order of integration with other converging procedures can be found in SUGENO (1974). Only one result will be mentioned here. Let P be a probability measure, then the crisp and the fuzzy integral with respect to this measure can be determined and the following estimation is valid:

$$\left| \int_{\mathcal{X}} h(x) \mathrm{d}P(x) - \oint_{\mathcal{X}} h(x) \circ P(.) \right| \leq 1/4 . \tag{5.73}$$

Because of this analogy the fuzzy integral is also called *fuzzy expectation value* of h.

The integration theory, in the sense of SUGENO, can be used, in analogy with the performance in probability theory, for establishing a theory of conditional measures. Let $\Phi : \mathcal{X} \to \mathcal{Y}$ be a mapping of the universe $\mathcal{X}$ into the universe $\mathcal{Y}$ of the measurable space $[\mathcal{Y}, \mathbb{B}^{\Phi}]$, then Q^{Φ} denotes the induced measure of the $(\mathbb{B}, \mathbb{B}^{\Phi})$-measurable mapping Φ in the usual manner

$$\forall \mathcal{A} \in \mathbb{B}^{\Phi} : \quad Q^{\Phi}(\mathcal{A}) = Q\left(\Phi^{-1}(\mathcal{A}) \right) .$$

When now introducing an *equivalence* among all functions which are measurable over $[\mathcal{X}, \mathbb{B}, Q]$ by the relation

$$\forall \mathcal{A} \in \mathbb{B} : \quad \oint_{\mathcal{A}} h(x) \circ Q(.) = \oint_{\mathcal{A}} h'(x) \circ Q(.),$$

then, over $\mathbb{B}$, a *conditional fuzzy measure* $Q(.|\Phi = y)$ can be defined by choosing for $Q(\mathcal{E}|\Phi = y)$ a representative in the class of all those measurable functions h, which are equivalent with respect to Q and satisfy the condition

$$Q(\mathcal{E} \cap \Phi^{-1}(\mathcal{F})) = \oint_{\mathcal{F}} h(y) \circ Q^{\Phi}(.),$$

where we have to insert

$$\Phi^{-1}(\mathcal{F}) = \{ x \in \mathcal{X} \mid \Phi(x) \in \mathcal{F}, \, \mathcal{F} \subseteq \mathcal{Y} \}.$$

Then $Q(. \mid \Phi = y)$ connects the measure space $[\mathcal{Y}, \mathbb{B}^{\Phi}, Q^{\Phi}]$ with $[\mathcal{X}, \mathbb{B}, Q]$ instead of Φ. Even if two measure spaces are connected with each other in such a way, Φ

cannot always be determined explicitly. Then we will write $Q(.|\Phi = y)$ as $Q_{\mathcal{X}}(.|y)$ and call it a *conditional fuzzy measure* of $\mathcal{Y}$ to $\mathcal{X}$.

The Sugeno integral (5.66) can be specified also for possibility measures. Within an integral theoretic approach, even more general in a setting of complete lattices and of other t-norms within the integral, in a similar manner as with the Lebesgue integral, a theory for product measures and conditional measures was developed by DeCooman/Kerre/Vanmassenhove (1992). This allows, among other statements, a unified presentation of possibility theory.

5.2.4   Credibility for Fuzzy Sets

The approach by Sugeno is not the only possible one for defining integrals with respect to fuzzy measures and to generalise these to fuzzy sets. An example is given by Zadeh (1968), who started with the definition (5.51) of the probability of a fuzzy set, which, according to (5.73), can deviate only up to $1/4$ from the probability introduced in analogy with (5.69).

From the diversity of other approaches, which are mentioned e.g. by Weber (1984), we will present a suggestion from Smets (1981) for generalising credibility and plausibility measures to fuzzy sets. For an overview of fuzzy measure theory we refer to Wang/Klir (1992).

Smets considers the set $\mathcal{C}$ of all probability measures P over $[\mathcal{X}, I\!B]$ satisfying, for a given degree of credibility Cr and the corresponding degree of plausibility Pl (cf. (5.43) and (5.44)), the condition:

$$\forall \mathcal{A} \in I\!B : \ \mathrm{Cr}(\mathcal{A}) \leq P(\mathcal{A}) \leq \mathrm{Pl}(\mathcal{A}). \tag{5.74}$$

$\mathcal{C}$ is called the set of *probability measures compatible with* Cr.

Let now $f : \mathcal{X} \to I\!R$ be a function, for which

$$\mathrm{E}(f, P) = \int\limits_{\mathcal{X}} f(x) \mathrm{d}P(x) \tag{5.75}$$

exists for all $P \in \mathcal{C}$. Then we introduce the *lower expectation value* by

$$\mathrm{E}_* f = \inf_{P \in \mathcal{C}} \mathrm{E}(f, P) \tag{5.76}$$

and the *upper expectation value* by

$$\mathrm{E}^* f = \sup_{P \in \mathcal{C}} \mathrm{E}(f, P). \tag{5.77}$$

More practicable is the equivalent representation via the derived measures

$$\begin{aligned} F^*(v) &= \mathrm{Pl}(\{x \in \mathcal{X} \mid f(x) \leq v\}), \\ F_*(v) &= \mathrm{Cr}(\{x \in \mathcal{X} \mid f(x) \leq v\}) \end{aligned} \tag{5.78}$$

by

$$\mathsf{E}^*(f) \ = \ \int_{-\infty}^{\infty} v \mathrm{d} F_*(v), \qquad \mathsf{E}_*(f) \ = \ \int_{-\infty}^{\infty} v \mathrm{d} F^*(v), \tag{5.79}$$

which show the character of expectation values clearly.

SMETS (1981) suggests introducing credibility and plausibility degree, respectively, for fuzzy sets A by

$$\mathrm{Cr}\,(A) = \mathsf{E}_*(\mu_A), \qquad \mathrm{Pl}\,(A) = \mathsf{E}^*(\mu_A) \tag{5.80}$$

and he shows that Cr and Pl satisfy the respective defining conditions. Unfortunately the different approaches yield *different* results. So we obtain, for $\lambda > 0$, using the generalisation according to SUGENO, a credibility degree $\mathrm{Cr}_{\mathrm{Sugeno}}(A) = Q_\lambda(A)$, which will, in general, differ from that one computed according to SMETS' suggestion.

The credibility approach is important especially for measure spaces with a *finite* σ-algebra $I\!B$. In analogy with conditional probabilities we can introduce conditional credibility and plausibility degrees. So, e.g., the credibility degree of $\mathcal{A} \in I\!B$ under the condition that $\mathcal{B} \in I\!B$ is "true", is given by

$$\mathrm{Cr}\,(\mathcal{A}|\mathcal{B}) = \big(\mathrm{Cr}\,(\mathcal{A} \cup \mathcal{B}^c) - \mathrm{Cr}\,(\mathcal{B}^c)\big)\big/\big(1 - \mathrm{Cr}\,(\mathcal{B}^c)\big) \tag{5.81}$$

(cf. SHAFER (1976)).

In analogy with (5.74) we can consider a set $\mathcal{D}$ of probability measures P over $[\mathcal{X}, I\!B]$, for which it holds

$$\forall \mathcal{A} \in I\!B : \ \mathrm{Nec}\,(\mathcal{A}) \le P(\mathcal{A}) \le \mathrm{Poss}\,(\mathcal{A}). \tag{5.82}$$

In this manner, we obtain, as in (5.79), upper and lower expectation values for possibility and for necessity measures, respectively,

$$\mathsf{E}^*(f) = \int_{-\infty}^{\infty} r \, \mathrm{d}\,\mathrm{Nec}\,\{x \in \mathcal{X} \mid f(x) \le r\} \tag{5.83}$$

and

$$\mathsf{E}_*(f) = \int_{-\infty}^{\infty} r \, \mathrm{d}\,\mathrm{Poss}\,\{x \in \mathcal{X} \mid f(x) \le r\}, \tag{5.84}$$

where supremum and infimum in (5.76) and (5.77) are to be extended over all $P \in \mathcal{D}$ (cf. DUBOIS/PRADE (1985)).

5.3   Fuzziness and Probability

In Section 5.1 probability theory was the starting point for an introduction of
fuzzy measures, where probability was recognised as a special fuzzy measure.
In Section 5.2 these measures, among them also probability, were extended to
fuzzy sets. However, these topics do not exhaust, by no means, the area of
interdependence of probability and fuzzy sets.

5.3.1   Probabilistic Sets

When specifying a membership function subjective factors sometimes play an
essential role. So, different experts will specify different membership functions
for the same value of some linguistic variable, perhaps even only with certain
regions of uncertainty. For taking into account this variability HIROTA (1981)
suggests that one considers for every $x \in \mathcal{X}$ the membership to the set A
as a random variable $\mu_A(x, .) : \Omega \to [0,1]$, i.e. $\mu_A : \mathcal{X} \times \Omega \to [0,1]$ defines
a random variable $\mathbf{M}(x)$ with respect to a probability space $[\Omega, \mathbb{B}, P]$. The
so randomised membership function $\mu_A(x, \omega)$ defines a so-called *probabilistic
(fuzzy) set* A.

Intersection, union, and complement of sets are performed by a *pointwise*
connecting of the membership functions of these sets. If the random variables
$\mathbf{M}_A(x), \mathbf{M}_B(x)$ of different probabilistic sets A and B are *independent*, then
they can be connected very easily (cf. YAGER (1984a), CZOGALA/HIROTA
(1986)). Let $F_A(z; x)$ and $F_B(z; x)$ be the corresponding distribution functions, then we have the well-known statements

$$
\begin{aligned}
C = A \cup B \quad &\Leftrightarrow \quad \mathbf{M}_C(x) = \max\{\mathbf{M}_A(x), \mathbf{M}_B(x)\} \\
&\Leftrightarrow \quad F_C(z; x) = F_A(z; x) F_B(z; x), \\
D = A \cap B \quad &\Leftrightarrow \quad \mathbf{M}_D(x) = \min\{\mathbf{M}_A(x), \mathbf{M}_B(x)\} \\
&\Leftrightarrow \quad F_D(z; x) = F_A(z; x) + F_B(z; x) - F_A(z; x) F_B(z; x).
\end{aligned}
$$

By these formulae the practical tractability is realised also for this type of
fuzzy sets.

5.3.2   Fuzzy Probability

Up to now probability was considered for fuzzy sets. However, even probability can become a fuzzy set, e.g. when stating "the reliability is high",
which can be expressed equivalently by "the *probability* of a failure in a time
interval of given length is *small*". Let the range of the random experiment
be *finite*, say $\Omega = \{\omega_1, \ldots, \omega_n\}$, then we have to specify only some vector
of fuzzy sets $(A(\omega_1), \ldots, A(\omega_n))$ over $[0,1]^n$. Although the probabilities are

fuzzy they must remain probabilities, i.e. the event that *any* out of the set of mutually excluding events ω_i occurs, must be the sure event. That means for the vector of variables $(p_1, \ldots, p_n)$, where p_i is the variable corresponding to $A(\omega_i)$, that the crisp condition $p_1 + \cdots + p_n = 1$ must be satisfied. Let $R(A(\omega_i))$ be the relation corresponding to $A(\omega_i)$, then we obtain the relation, which corresponds to the vector $(A(\omega_1), \ldots, A(\omega_n))$, by

$$R\big(A(\omega_1), \ldots, A(\omega_n)\big) = \Big(R\big(A(\omega_1)\big) \otimes \cdots \otimes R\big(A(\omega_n)\big) \Big) \cap Q \,,$$

where Q means the crisp relation

$$Q(p_1, \ldots, p_n) = 1 \quad \Leftrightarrow \quad p_1 + \cdots + p_n = 1. \tag{5.85}$$

Hence the variables are *interactive*. So $A(\omega_i)$ are also called linguisic probabilities (cf. Section 4.4).

The fuzzy probabilities for all the $\mathcal{B} \in \mathbb{B}$ are obtained by the *interactive sum* S, i.e. the sum computed keeping the condition of interactivity Q according to (5.85), using the extension principle, by

$$\mu_S(p; \mathcal{B}) = \sup_{\substack{p = \sum_{i \in \mathcal{I}(\mathcal{B})} p_i \leq 1}} \min_{i \in \mathcal{I}(\mathcal{B})} \mu_A(p_i, \omega_i) \tag{5.86}$$

with $\mathcal{I}(\mathcal{B}) = \big\{ i \in \{1, \ldots, n\} \mid \omega_i \in \mathcal{B} \big\}$. This can be the starting point for defining fuzzy expectation values, when a random variable $\mathbf{Y} \colon \Omega \to \mathbb{R}$ will be introduced (cf. DUBOIS/PRADE (1980)).

The problem becomes essentially more complicated, if the range of the probability space is no longer a finite set, but e.g. an interval. The generalisation can be performed in two different ways, which are not equivalent, in general. As is known from the theory of stochastic processes, on the one hand we can consider the set of *trajectories*, i.e. here a *fuzzy bundle* of probability distributions $\{P_a\}$, $a \in \mathcal{J}$; with a suitable index set $\mathcal{J}$ such that it holds

$$\int_{\Omega} dP_a(\omega) = 1 \quad \text{for all} \quad a \in \mathcal{J},$$

where the fuzzy set is specified over $\mathcal{J}$. This is *not* equivalent with the approach, which was chosen in the finite case described above. The disadvantage of the present point of view is caused by the possible ambiguity of the specified membership values for the fuzzy probability of a fuzzy event. Hence the fuzzy probability distribution is a fuzzy family of functions in the sense of Section 2.2.

As it is likewise known from the theory of stochastic processes, the stochastic process can be considered as a family of random variables, i.e. in a *pointwise* manner. This leads to fuzzy functions, if the fuzzy set is normalised for every point (cf.

Section 2.2), else to a respective generalisation, and corresponds with the approach via linguistic probabilities. For being sure that the result is a fuzzy probability we may demand (cf. DUBOIS/PRADE (1980)) that, for the kernel curve $\mu_A(p_1; \omega) = 1$ it holds

$$\int_\Omega p_1(\omega)d\omega = 1\,.$$

In the considerations on fuzzy probability, up to now, we assumed the random events as crisp sets. However, in some cases it seems to be scarcely comprehensible that fuzzy events are evaluated by crisp probabilities. So, in the case of the example on the ageing process of components we could, e.g., obtain the statement that the probability of the event "the component is worn out" is precisely 0.84 . This exact statement can be felt as an artificial one, whereas the statement "the probability is high" will be understood as an appropriate one with respect to the fuzziness of the specification of the problem. There are several suggestions on how to come to reasonable fuzzy probabilities for fuzzy events. However, all of them, for the sake of tractability, assume *finite* universes for the probability spaces.

Let B be a fuzzy set over Ω with the membership function $\mu_B(\omega_i), i = 1, \ldots, n$, and $\mu_A(p_i, \omega_i)$ be the membership functions of the components of the vector of the fuzzy probabilities $(A(\omega_1), \ldots, A(\omega_n))$. Then we obtain, as a generalisation of the expectation value

$$\sum_{i=1}^n \mu_B(\omega_i)p_i,$$

in analogy with (5.85), the fuzzy probability $\text{Prob}(B)$ defined by the membership function $\mu_{\text{Prob}(B)}(p)$ according to the extension principle as

$$\mu_{\text{Prob}(B)}(p) = \sup_{q \in \mathcal{Q}} \min_i \mu_A(p_i, \omega_i)\,, \tag{5.87}$$

where

$$\mathcal{Q} = \left\{ q = (p_1, \ldots, p_n) \,\middle|\, \sum_{i=1}^n \mu_B(\omega_i)p_i = p;\ \sum_{i=1}^n p_i = 1 \right\}\,.$$

The computation of $\mu_{\text{Prob}(B)}$ for $n > 2$ can be rather complicated. The computation is equivalent with solving the following optimising problem:

Maximise z under the conditions $\mu_A(p_i; \omega_i) \ge z$, $i = 1, \ldots, n$; $q \in \mathcal{Q}$.

In contrast YAGER (1984a) approaches the problem by considering the α-cuts $B^{\geq \alpha}$. Then the fuzzy probability is introduced as a fuzzy set over the probabilities $P(B^{\geq \alpha})$ of the α-cuts as

$$\text{Prob}(B) \quad \text{with} \quad \mu_{\text{Prob}(B)}(P(B^{\geq \alpha})) = \alpha. \tag{5.88}$$

YAGER remarks that this can be interpreted as "probability of an at least to a degree α existing satisfaction of the condition B". (Starting from a similar idea KLEMENT (1982) suggested to define the probability over all values from $[0, 1]$ by assigning, each time, the constant α-value from the left end of the interval to the values between.) The so defined probability is denoted by $\text{Prob}^*(B)$. With $\text{Prob}_*(B) = (\text{Prob}^*(B^c))^c$ YAGER (1984a) obtained finally

$$\text{Prob}(B) = \text{Prob}^*(B) \cap \text{Prob}_*(B) \tag{5.89}$$

as the desired fuzzy probability. With respect to the properties of this probability cf. YAGER (1984a).

5.3.3 Random Fuzzy Sets

Finally we can consider situations, where the fuzzy sets are even *random objects*, i.e. values of so-called *random fuzzy sets*.

For an evaluation of the randomly influenced degree of being worn out **Z** of components we may have, e.g., *several* values of a linguistic variable u over $[0, 100]$: $A_1 = $ **badly worn out**, $A_2 = $ **rather worn out**, ..., $A_m = $ **useful**. Let the probabilities

$$\text{Prob}(u = A_i) = p_i, \quad i = 1, \ldots, m, \tag{5.90}$$

be known. With respect to the number of possible values for **Z** the case is spoken of as the case of *discrete* random fuzzy sets, it is treated essentially by NAHMIAS (1979). So, e.g., the average degree of being worn out may be of interest, i.e. the expectation value

$$\text{E } \mathbf{Z} = p_1 A_1 \oplus \cdots \oplus p_m A_m , \tag{5.91}$$

which can be computed according to the extension principle (2.105):

$$\mu_{\text{E } \mathbf{Z}}(z) = \sup_{z} \min_{i} \mu_{A_i}(x_i)$$

with

$$\mathcal{Z} = \left\{ (x_1, \ldots, x_n) \in [0, 100]^n \mid z = \sum_{i=1}^{n} p_i x_i \right\} .$$

In the general case we will start with a probability space $[\Omega, \mathbb{B}, P]$ and define a random fuzzy set Z as a mapping of Ω into a subset $\mathbb{F}^*(\mathcal{X})$ of

$I\!F(\mathcal{X})$, since we have to demand measurability of Z with respect to a suitable σ-algebra of the domain. In this context, essentially, two approaches are considered.

In the approach due to PURI/RALESCU (1986) the concept of random sets on Euclidean spaces is fuzzified. Measurability of the mapping Z is obtained by demanding that every α-cut $Z^{\geq \alpha}$ of Z is a random set in a well-defined sense (cf. MATHERON (1975), STOYAN/KENDALL/MECKE (1987) for details). This is especially satisfied if normalised fuzzy sets B are considered as elements of the σ-algebra, the supports of which supp (B) are compact and for which μ_B is upper semi-continuous, such that the α-cuts for $\alpha \in (0,1]$ can be demanded to be compact random sets.

In papers inspired by PURI/RALESCU (1986) theoretical problems dominate the fore. We can find considerations on complete metric spaces of random fuzzy sets, notions of convergence and their application in limit theorems, and so on. An interesting topic for practical applications is the interpretation of fuzzy sets (fuzzy data in the sense of Chapter 6) as realisations of random fuzzy sets in the sense of PURI/RALESCU (1986), which opens possibilities of generalising methods of mathematical morphology (cf. SERRA (1982)), used for crisp sets in image processing, even to grey-tone pictures. With respect to erosion and dilation of grey-tone pictures with fuzzy structure elements cf. GOETCHERIAN (1980) and BANDEMER/KRAUT/NÄTHER (1989), with respect to a fuzzy analogon of the so-called Boolean models (random grains around Poisson distributed "germs") cf. ALBRECHT (1991).

Worth mentioning in this context is the fact that the membership function of a non-random set can be interpreted as the so-called *projection shadow* of a random crisp set (cf., e.g., WANG/SANCHEZ (1982)). More precisely formulated, this means that the membership degree $\mu_A(x)$ can be considered as the probability that a corresponding random set $\mathbf{S}$ covers the point x (one-point-coverage probability):

$$\mu_A(x) = P(x \in \mathbf{S}) = E\mu_{\mathbf{S}}(x)\,. \tag{5.92}$$

On the other hand every random set $\mathbf{S}$ is connected with a certain fuzzy set A (cf., e.g., GOODMAN/NGUYEN (1985)). This connection between fuzzy and random sets can be used in the case of modelling uncertainty, impreciseness, and vagueness in a concrete situation *by stages*.

Within a somewhat more detailed investigation in BANDEMER/NÄTHER (1992) the following possibilities are met:

a) Let all the fuzziness at the given information A (i.e. the datum in the sense of Chapter 6) and model this as a non-random (global) fuzzy set with a membership function μ_A.

b) Split off all the fuzziness from A and model it as a (total) random crisp set $\mathbf{S}$, the projection shadow of which is μ_A, the function mentioned already in a).

c) Recommendable will be a middle course, where fuzziness is partly split off from A and is then modelled by randomness, by which a (partly) random and (partly) fuzzy set in the sense of PURI/RALESCU is created (cf. NÄTHER (1990), BANDEMER/NÄTHER (1992)).

In the approach according to KWAKERNAAK (1978) the conditions with respect to measurability are directed towards the membership function in the domain. For all $\omega \in \Omega$ the function $\mu_{Z(\omega)}$ must be piecewise continuous and for all $\alpha \in (0,1)$ by

$$\inf[Z(\omega)]_\alpha =_{\text{def}} \inf\{x \in \mathcal{X} \mid \mu_{Z(\omega)}(x) \geq \alpha\} \tag{5.93}$$

and

$$\sup[Z(\omega)]_\alpha =_{\text{def}} \sup\{x \in \mathcal{X} \mid \mu_{Z(\omega)}(x) \geq \alpha\} \tag{5.94}$$

finite random variables on $(\Omega, \mathbb{B}, P)$ are to be defined, such that for every $\omega \in \Omega$ it holds

$$\inf[Z(\omega)]_\alpha \in [Z(\omega)]_\alpha, \quad \sup[Z(\omega)]_\alpha \in [Z(\omega)]_\alpha. \tag{5.95}$$

5.3.4 Statistics for Fuzzy Observations of Random Variables

This approach was applied successfully in the case that the realisation of a crisp random variable can be observed only fuzzily (cf. KRUSE/MEYER (1987)). Instead of some random variable, the original $\mathbf{Y}: \Omega \to \mathbb{R}$, only a fuzzy random variable, a *fuzzy coarsity*,

$$\mathbf{Z} : \Omega \to \mathbb{F}(\mathbb{R}) \tag{5.96}$$

is accessible. Let denote

$$\mathcal{Y} = \{\mathbf{Y} : \Omega \to \mathbb{R} \mid \mathbf{Y} \text{ is } (\mathbb{B}, \mathbb{B}^1)\text{-measurable}\} \tag{5.97}$$

the set of all possible originals $\mathbf{Y}$. Let $\mathbf{Z}$ now be a *given* fuzzy random variable, the original $\mathbf{Y}$ of which is unknown. The set of all originals for this $\mathbf{Z}$ is a fuzzy set over $\mathcal{Y}$. For every $\omega \in \Omega$ and every such original $\mathbf{Y}$ it must be valid

$$Y(\omega) \in Z(\omega) . \tag{5.98}$$

Since $Z(\omega)$ is a fuzzy set over $I\!\!R$ with the membership function $\mu_{Z(\omega)}$, the statement (5.98) is for every $\omega \in \Omega$ evaluated by $\mu_{Z(\omega)}(Y(\omega))$ and for all $\omega \in \Omega$ we obtain

$$\mu_Z(\mathbf{Y}) = \inf_\omega \mu_{Z(\omega)}(Y(\omega)) \tag{5.99}$$

as the membership value of $\mathbf{Y}$ over $I\!\!N$ with respect to the given $\mathbf{Z}$.

If the set of all possible originals can be parametrised, e.g. by assuming a certain type for the distribution, then (5.99) induces a fuzzy set over the parameter set. By means of the extension principle all the derivations usual in probability theory can be fuzzified. This can be performed best, if, as is usually assumed, the realisations are fuzzy numbers or intervals. For statistics with fuzzy observations Z_i of this kind, given by their membership functions μ_i, they are aggregated "in a suitable way" to form a fuzzy sample S with membership function μ_S. VIERTL (1990) suggests choosing the product or the minimum, where both of these possibilities can be motivated. With the so defined fuzzy sample S all the traditional principles for estimation and test can be extended to the corresponding fuzzy case by means of an extension principle. Let $I\!\!R^n$ be the usual crisp sample space and $\hat{\Theta} : I\!\!R^n \to \Theta$ a usual point estimator. Then a *fuzzy point estimator* $D \in I\!\!F(\Theta)$ can be obtained by the common extension principle as

$$\mu_D(\theta) = \sup_{\hat{\Theta}(x)=\theta} \mu_S(x)\,, \tag{5.100}$$

which includes the fuzziness of the observations and reflects it by the estimator. This approach can be performed even for confidence regions. Let $K(x) \subseteq \Theta$ be a confidence region with level $1 - \alpha$, then

$$\mu_{K_f}(\theta) = \sup_{\theta \in K(x)} \mu_S(x) \tag{5.101}$$

yields a *fuzzy confidence region*.

This concept can be extended to statistical tests, correlation and regression analysis, and the Bayesian approach to statistics, cf. VIERTL (1990, 1992).

In all these considerations, we must naturally keep the assumption that fuzziness is only generated by the process of observing realisations of the crisp random variable. The theory of fuzzy random variables of this type is already developed to the statement of limit theorems (cf. with respect to this topic MIYAKOSHI/SHIMBO (1984), KRUSE/MEYER (1987)).

5.4   Some Applications

The concepts of fuzzy measures and the connection of fuzziness and randomness are applied successfully in different fields. Moreover, some of these applications for their part are already further developed to concepts and theories. In the following we will present some of these settings.

5.4.1 Combining Fuzzy Knowledge

For *diagnosis*, e.g. in medicine, but not only there, we have to assign available information (the symptoms) $x \in \mathcal{X}$ to certain situations $d \in \mathcal{D}$ by a description (the diagnosis), which has to serve as a basis for decisions (the treatment). However, it is not possible to assign the given information to the situations uniquely. Using the framework of probability theory this problem is treated by specifying probabilities Prob $(x|d)$ for the event that a symptom x occurs in a situation d. If, additionally, a prior distribution with Prob (d), $d \in \mathcal{D}$, over the situations, is available, then we obtain posterior probabilities Prob $(d|x)$ for the event that we are in situation d when observing symptom x, by the Bayesian rule, e.g. in the finite case

$$\text{Prob}\,(d|x) = \frac{\text{Prob}\,(x|d)\,\text{Prob}\,(d)}{\sum\limits_{d' \in \mathcal{D}} \text{Prob}\,(x|d')\,\text{Prob}\,(d')}\,. \tag{5.102}$$

A *diagnosis* is a (verbal) description of the situation and hence can be described as a *fuzzy set* B over the universe $\mathcal{D}$ of situations, i.e. by a membership function μ_B. According to the definition (5.52) of probability for fuzzy sets we obtain the probability of the diagnosis B, if x is observed, from (5.102) as

$$\text{Prob}\,(B|x) = \sum_{d \in \mathcal{D}} \mu_B(d)\text{Prob}\,(d|x)\,. \tag{5.103}$$

In specifying such probabilities we sometimes meet certain difficulties: The union of all situations does not correspond to the sure event, which would be necessary for application of (5.52), the sum of the probabilities for certain complementary events cannot be 1, for factual considerations. The reason for this trouble consists in the fact that here the probabilities do not reflect some random mechanism but are evaluations on the basis of experts' knowledge.

Hence SMETS (1981a) suggested modelling the connections between situations and symptoms by specifying *credibility degrees*. Assuming the universes to be *finite*, the performance starts with specifying focal sets and basic probability assignments $p_{\mathcal{X}}(\cdot\,;d)$ and $p_{\mathcal{D}}(\cdot\,;x)$ in the sense of (5.36) and (5.37) in dependence on the elements of the respective other universe. So, according to (5.43),

$$\text{Cr}_{\mathcal{X}}(\mathcal{A};d) = \sum_{\mathcal{A}_h \subseteq \mathcal{A}} p_{\mathcal{X}}(\mathcal{A}_h;d) \tag{5.104}$$

is the credibility degree for $\mathcal{A} \in \mathbb{P}(\mathcal{X})$, if the situation $d \in \mathcal{D}$ is present. The sum is, as is known, to be taken only over all those focal sets $\mathcal{A}_h \in \text{supp}\, p_{\mathcal{X}}(\cdot\,;d)$

(i.e. with $p_{\mathcal{X}}(\mathcal{A}_h; d) > 0$), for which $\mathcal{A}_h \subseteq \mathcal{A}$ is valid. For simplicity let us assume that the prior credibility degree over the situations expresses total ignorance, i.e. $p_{\mathcal{D}}(\mathcal{D}) = 1$ and $p_{\mathcal{D}}(\mathcal{B}) = 0$ for all $\mathcal{B} \in \mathbb{P}(\mathcal{D})$ with $\mathcal{B} \neq \mathcal{D}$, then the posterior credibility degree for $\mathcal{B} \in \mathbb{P}(\mathcal{D})$, if an element x from $\mathcal{A} \in \mathbb{P}(\mathcal{X})$ was observed, cf. SMETS (1993), is

$$\mathrm{Cr}_{\mathcal{D}|\mathcal{X}:0}(\mathcal{B}; \mathcal{A}) = \Big(\sum_{d \in \mathcal{B}^c} \mathrm{Cr}_{\mathcal{X}}(\mathcal{A}^c; d) - a \Big) / (1 - a) \tag{5.105}$$

with

$$a = \prod_{d \in \mathcal{D}} \mathrm{Cr}_{\mathcal{X}}(\mathcal{A}^c; d), \tag{5.106}$$

where $\mathcal{X}:0$ within the index of Cr is a reminder that we have assumed total ignorance with respect to $\mathcal{D}$. SMETS (1981a) suggests in the case of an *informative* prior credibility degree $\mathrm{Cr}_{\mathcal{D}}$, i.e. different from total ignorance, connecting this degree with $\mathrm{Cr}_{\mathcal{D}|\mathcal{X}:0}$ from (5.105) by the Dempster rule of combination according to (5.109); cf. DEMPSTER (1967).

This connection, shortly $p_1 \cap p_2$, brings together two basic probability assignments over the same power set, where different direct or indirect assignments, called *conflicts*, for certain subsets are reconciled to a certain extent. Hence application of the Dempster rule is somewhat problematic, if these conflicts are very hard. For presentation of the rule an intermediate step seems useful. First we consider for all $\mathcal{A} \in \mathbb{P}(\mathcal{U})$

$$p_1 \cdot p_2(\mathcal{A}) = \sum_{\mathcal{B} \cap \mathcal{C} = \mathcal{A}} p_1(\mathcal{B}) \cdot p_2(\mathcal{C}). \tag{5.107}$$

This product is commutative and associative, the basic probability assignments for the product assume again values in [0,1], but the sum over all $\mathcal{A} \in \mathbb{P}(\mathcal{U})$ can be less than 1. The probability assignment to the empty set $\emptyset$ can be positive:

$$p_1 \cdot p_2(\emptyset) > 0. \tag{5.108}$$

This reflects the conflict between the two assignments p_1 and p_2. If we exclude the case of total conflict $p_1 \cdot p_2(\emptyset) = 1$, which seems to be reasonable, then we can renormalise $p_1 \cdot p_2$ and generate a conflict reconciling basic probability assignment for all $\mathcal{A} \neq \emptyset$:

$$p_1 \cap p_2(\mathcal{A}) = \frac{p_1 \cdot p_2(\mathcal{A})}{1 - p_1 \cdot p_2(\emptyset)}. \tag{5.109}$$

And this is the Dempster rule of combination (cf. DEMPSTER (1967), DUBOIS/PRADE (1985)).

Let $p_\mathcal{D}$ be the basic probability assignment for $\mathrm{Cr}_\mathcal{D}$ and $p_{\mathcal{D}|\mathcal{X}:0}$ the assignment for $\mathrm{Cr}_{\mathcal{D}|\mathcal{X}:0}$ according to (5.105), i.e. the posterior basic probability assignment belonging to the case of ignorance, then we obtain, by the Dempster rule, the posterior basic probability assignment for the informative case by

$$p_{\mathcal{D}|\mathcal{X}}(\mathcal{B};\mathcal{A}) = \sum_{\substack{\mathcal{G} \in \mathrm{supp}\, p_{\mathcal{D}|\mathcal{X}:0} \\ \mathcal{C} \in \mathrm{supp}\, p_\mathcal{D} \\ \mathcal{C} \cap \mathcal{G} = \mathcal{B}}} p_{\mathcal{D}|\mathcal{X}:0}(\mathcal{G};\mathcal{A}) p_\mathcal{D}(\mathcal{C})/k \qquad (5.110)$$

with

$$k = 1 - \sum_{\mathcal{G} \cap \mathcal{C} = \emptyset} p_{\mathcal{D}|\mathcal{X}:0}(\mathcal{G};\mathcal{A}) p_\mathcal{D}(\mathcal{C}) \qquad (5.111)$$

and $\mathcal{G}$ and $\mathcal{C}$ as in (5.110). Hence we can interpret $1 - k$ as an expression of the inconsistency between the prior and the "ignorant" posterior credibility degree.

For *infinite* universes SMETS (1981a) suggested using a connection rule due to SHAFER (1976) for the plausibility degree:

$$\mathrm{Pl}_\mathcal{D}(\mathcal{B};\mathcal{A}) = \sup_{d \in \mathcal{B}} \mathrm{Pl}_\mathcal{X}(\mathcal{A};d) / \sup_{d \in \mathcal{D}} \mathrm{Pl}_\mathcal{X}(\mathcal{A};d), \qquad (5.112)$$

from which we can deduce the credibility degree Cr according to (5.44). The formula, corresponding to (5.103), for the credibility of a *fuzzy* diagnosis B with the membership function μ_B over $\mathcal{D}$, if $x \in \mathcal{A}$ is observed, we obtain according to (5.80), so e.g.

$$\mathrm{Cr}_{\mathcal{D}|\mathcal{X}}(B|\mathcal{A}) = \mathrm{E}_*(\mu_B|\mathcal{A}), \qquad (5.113)$$

where the condition $|\mathcal{A}$ is to be introduced into the formula (5.74), which represents the basis for the expectation E_*. For more applications in knowledge based systems we refer to KRUSE/SCHWECKE/HEINSOHN (1991).

5.4.2 Fuzzy Decision Theory

With his theory of fuzzy measures and integrals SUGENO (1974) succeeded in developing a fuzzy analogon to statistical decision theory. The starting point is, like there, a given set of *states of nature* $z \in \mathcal{Z}$ and a set of *decisions* $a \in \mathcal{A}$. However, instead of giving some *loss function* $L : \mathcal{Z} \times \mathcal{A} \to \mathbb{R}^+$, now a membership function $l : \mathcal{Z} \times \mathcal{A} \to [0,1]$ is specified reflecting the *degree of loss*, if the decision a is used when the state of nature z is met. The place of the probability distribution with $\mathrm{Prob}\,(x|z)$ of the *observations* $x \in \mathcal{X}$, if the state z is met, is taken by the conditional fuzzy measure $S_{\mathcal{X}}(\cdot|z)$ whereas the prior distribution with $\mathrm{Prob}\,(z)$ is replaced by the fuzzy measure $Q_{\mathcal{Z}}(\cdot)$.

In the case that a decision must be chosen without any observation in $\mathcal{X}$ SUGENO considers the fuzzy expectation value with respect to a

$$\mathsf{E}_F l(a) = \fint_{\mathcal{Z}} l(z, a) \circ Q_{\mathcal{Z}}(\cdot)\,. \qquad (5.114)$$

Since the loss is introduced as a fuzzy set, SUGENO doubts whether a crisp decision, in analogy with the statistical approach, with

$$\mathsf{E}_F l(a^*) = \inf_{a \in \mathcal{A}} \mathsf{E}_F l(a) \qquad (5.115)$$

is reasonable. He suggested a *fuzzy* decision B with $\mu_B : \mathcal{A} \to [0, 1]$, which is a certain analogon with a randomised decision.

For an introduction of such a fuzzy decision he extended the "loss function" l to become a *set function* over $\mathbb{F}(\mathcal{A})$, that means that for all $B \in \mathbb{F}(\mathcal{A})$ it must be valid that

$$1 - l(z, B) = \max_{a \in \mathcal{A}} \min\{\mu_B(a), 1 - l(z, a)\}, \qquad (5.116)$$

and he suggested as fuzzy decision the fuzzy set A^* with the membership function

$$\mu_{A^*}(a) = \fint_{\mathcal{Z}} (1 - l(z, a)) \circ Q_{\mathcal{Z}}(\cdot). \qquad (5.117)$$

If we consider $1 - l$ as the "gain", then $\mu_{A^*}(a)$ represents the expectation of a gain when choosing decision a. The membership value is high, if this expectation is high, hence A^* is called *likely-good*. With definition (5.116) it can be shown, according to SUGENO (1974), that it holds

$$\fint_{\mathcal{Z}} \left(1 - l(z, A^*)\right) \circ Q_{\mathcal{Z}} = \max_{a \in \mathcal{A}} \fint_{\mathcal{Z}} \left(1 - l(z, a)\right) \circ Q_{\mathcal{Z}}\,, \qquad (5.118)$$

which is an analogon to a statement on optimal randomised decisions.

If observing is possible before deciding, then we have to choose a strategy $t : \mathcal{X} \to \mathcal{A}$. In analogy with the Bayesian risk we have the fuzzy expectation

$$\mathsf{E}_F l(t) = \fint_{\mathcal{Z}} \left[\fint_{\mathcal{X}} l(z, t(x)) \circ S_{\mathcal{X}}(\cdot|z) \right] \circ Q_{\mathcal{Z}}(\cdot)\,. \qquad (5.119)$$

A *fuzzy strategy* T is now given correspondingly by its membership function $\mu_T(x, a)$, from which we can obtain the fuzzy decision for a given x by the cut

$$\mu_{T(x)}(a) = \mu_T(x, a). \qquad (5.120)$$

Considerations as in the decision case without any observation lead us to a
likely-good strategy T^* with the membership function

$$\mu_{T^*}(x, a) = \int_{\mathcal{Z}} (1 - l(z, a)) \circ S_{\mathcal{Z}}(\cdot|x), \tag{5.121}$$

where $S_{\mathcal{Z}}(\cdot|x)$ now represents the conditional fuzzy measure over $\mathcal{Z}$ after observation of x. This measure is obtained by the corresponding analoga to the
Bayesian rule

$$\int_{\mathcal{F}} S_{\mathcal{X}}(\mathcal{E}|z) \circ Q_{\mathcal{Z}}(\cdot) = \int_{\mathcal{E}} S_{\mathcal{Z}}(\mathcal{F}|x) \circ Q_{\mathcal{X}}(\cdot) \tag{5.122}$$

(for all $\mathcal{F}$ and $\mathcal{E}$ in the respective σ-algebras $\mathbb{B}_{\mathcal{Z}}$ and $\mathbb{B}_{\mathcal{X}}$) and by the analogon
to the total probability rule

$$Q_{\mathcal{X}}(\cdot) = \int_{\mathcal{Z}} S_{\mathcal{X}}(\cdot|z) \circ Q_{\mathcal{Z}}(\cdot). \tag{5.123}$$

(With respect to the deduction of (5.122) and (5.123), cf. SUGENO (1974).)

Then the following statement, corresponding to (5.118), is valid

$$\int_{\mathcal{X}} \left[\int_{\mathcal{Z}} (1 - l(z, T^*(x))) \circ S_{\mathcal{Z}}(\cdot|x) \right] \circ Q_{\mathcal{X}}(\cdot)$$

$$= \int_{\mathcal{X}} \left[\max_{a \in \mathcal{A}} \int_{\mathcal{Z}} (1 - l(z, a)) \circ S_{\mathcal{Z}}(\cdot|x) \right] \circ Q_{\mathcal{X}}(\cdot), \tag{5.124}$$

which justifies the choice of $T^*(x)$ as an "optimal" strategy. Some applications
to practical situations, which cannot be treated by statistical methods, because they have to start from subjective evaluations, are presented by SUGENO
(1974).

Without any relation to decision theory SUGENO/TERANO (1977) use the
posterior concept of conditional fuzzy measures within a *learning model*. In
this context the set $\mathcal{Z}$ is interpreted as the set of causes for which a prior
measure $Q_{\mathcal{Z}}$ is available, which can be updated, given the observation x and
the conditional fuzzy measure $S_{\mathcal{X}}(\cdot|z)$, to the *posterior* conditional measure
$S_{\mathcal{Z}}(.|x)$. The latter can be used as a prior measure in the next step of observation. If the observations A over $\mathcal{X}$ are fuzzy the measures are to be extended
to fuzzy sets starting with (5.69).

5.4.3   Fuzzy Statistics

Finally we mention that with the fuzzy expectation value

$$E_F A = \oint_X \mu_A(x) \circ Q(\cdot) \tag{5.125}$$

we can develop a system of characteristic values for fuzzy observations A with respect to a given measure Q, which shows certain analogies with the system of characteristic values in descriptive statistics (mean, median, etc.) and is hence called "fuzzy statistics" by KANDEL (1986).

When applying the theory of differential equations to practical problems the importance of the results obtained is frequently reduced by the assumption, necessary for calculating the solution, that, e.g., the coefficients and boundary values must be known *precisely*. As a remedy a theory was developed assuming that the coefficients or boundary values are random variables obeying certain probability distributions. However, in the concrete cases of practical application frequently only rather imprecise "observations" of the present realisation of these random variables are available, e.g. only expert's estimations with evaluations of their impreciseness. Even in this case the estimation value of the solution can be *estimated crisply*, as becomes clear by the following example.

Let v be a parameter, which obeys the distribution P over $\mathcal{V}$, and given a differential equation with

$$dy/dx + q_1(v)y = q_2(v), \quad q_1(v) > 0 \text{ for all } v \in \mathcal{V}, \tag{5.126}$$

the coefficients q_1, q_2 of which are known functions of v. The general solution of (5.126) is

$$y(x, v) = c \exp\{-q_1(v)x\} + q_2(v)/q_1(v) \tag{5.127}$$

and for the (crisp) initial value $y(0) = 0$ we obtain the special solution

$$y(x, v) = \big(q_2(v)/q_1(v)\big)\big[1 - \exp\{-q_1(v)x\}\big] . \tag{5.128}$$

Let a fuzzy observation be given for v by the normalised fuzzy set V, then we can compute, according to (5.52), the solution as an expectation value with respect to the assumed probability distribution of the random parameter by

$$E_P y(x; V) = \int_{\mathcal{V}} \left(\frac{q_2(v)}{q_1(v)}\right)\big[1 - \exp\{-q_1(v)x\}\big]\mu_V(v)dP(v) . \tag{5.129}$$

Further examples are provided by KANDEL (1986). This approach is important, first of all, for problems of *fuzzy control* of processes if there is some differential equation in the background.

5.5   Fuzziness Measures

When having specified a fuzzy set A for every element x of the universe $\mathcal{X}$, the *local* fuzziness is given expressed by the membership function $\mu_A(x)$, interpreted as the degree for x of belonging to the set A. However, nothing is still stated on the *global* fuzziness of the set: namely the global evaluation of how fuzzy the set was specified as a whole. For a choice of set functions for evaluating this global fuzziness essentially *three* approaches are known differing in

   (a) which system of sets will serve as a *reference system* for the evaluation;
   (b) which sets are to be considered as *most fuzzy*;
   (c) how the sets are *comparable* with respect to their fuzziness.

Moreover, when specifying properties for such set functions and principles for their construction we have to distinguish the case of a *finite* universe from the case of an *infinite* one, since the mathematical tools and methods to be used may differ essentially.

5.5.1   Entropy Measures

Realised as a so-called *entropy measure* (in the sense of DELUCA/TERMINI (1979)) the fuzziness measure F will evaluate the *deviation from the type of crisp sets* (a). Hence all crisp sets will be evaluated by the same fixed value, without loss of generality, by zero:

$$\mu_A : \mathcal{X} \to \{0, 1\} \quad \Rightarrow \quad F(A) = 0 . \tag{5.130}$$

In this approach the *most fuzzy set* (b) is the set, in which for *every* element $x \in \mathcal{X}$ the membership and the non-membership is of the same degree:

$$U = X^{[1/2]} \quad \Rightarrow \quad F(U) = \max . \tag{5.131}$$

Finally a fuzzy set A will be considered *less fuzzy* (c) or *sharper than* a fuzzy set B, if the membership values of A are *nearer* to the values $\{0, 1\}$ of crisp membership than those corresponding for B. In this case, A is called a *sharpening* of B and we write $A \preceq B$ by defining

$$A \preceq B =_{\text{def}} \begin{cases} \mu_A(x) \leq \mu_B(x) & \text{if} \quad \mu_B(x) < 1/2 \\ \mu_A(x) \geq \mu_B(x) & \text{if} \quad \mu_B(x) > 1/2 \end{cases} \tag{5.132}$$

and thus having

$$A \preceq B \iff A \cap A^c \subseteq B \cap B^c. \tag{5.133}$$

In this way one is demanding

$$A \preceq B \quad \Rightarrow \quad F(A) \leq F(B) . \tag{5.134}$$

In his considerations for constructing functions satisfying (5.130) to (5.134), YAGER (1979/80) started from the fact that for *proper fuzzy* sets the intersection $C = A \cap A^c$ is different from the empty set $\emptyset$, whereas for crisp sets we know that $A \cap A^c = \emptyset$. Hence, e.g., card (C) is a suitable fuzziness measure for A. With

$$
\begin{aligned}
\mu_C(x) &= \min\{\mu_A(x), 1 - \mu_A(x)\} \\
&= \frac{1}{2}\Big(\mu_A(x) + \big(1 - \mu_A(x)\big) - \big|\mu_A(x) - \big(1 - \mu_A(x)\big)\big|\Big) \\
&= \frac{1}{2}\Big(1 - \big|\mu_A(x) - \big(1 - \mu_A(x)\big)\big|\Big)
\end{aligned}
\tag{5.135}
$$

we obtain for *finite* universes $\mathcal{X}$

$$
\operatorname{card}(C) = \frac{1}{2}\sum_{x \in \mathcal{X}}\Big(1 - \big|\mu_A(x) - \big(1 - \mu_A(x)\big)\big|\Big). \tag{5.136}
$$

After dividing by the constant $(1/2)\operatorname{card}\mathcal{X}$ this yields an entropy measure, normalised to the maximal value 1,

$$
F_{11}(A) = 1 - \sum_{x \in \mathcal{X}}\big|\mu_A(x) - \big(1 - \mu_A(x)\big)\big|\Big/\operatorname{card}\mathcal{X}, \tag{5.137}
$$

sometimes called *index of fuzziness*. The sum in (5.137) can be interpreted as a *distance* of the two sets A and A^c, called Hamming-distance $\varrho_1(A, A^c)$, with which we write

$$
F_{11} = 1 - \varrho_1(A, A^c)/\operatorname{card}\mathcal{X}. \tag{5.138}
$$

Alternatively we can use, e.g., the corresponding Euclidean distance

$$
\varrho_2(A, A^c) = \Big(\sum_{x \in \mathcal{X}}\big(\mu_A(x) - \big(1 - \mu_A(x)\big)\big)^2\Big)^{1/2} \tag{5.139}
$$

or, more generally, a distance ϱ_p, which contains a power p instead of 2.

Hence, on the other hand, we have for the $(1/2)$-level set $A^{\geq 1/2}$

$$
\min\{\mu_A(x), 1 - \mu_A(x)\} = |\mu_A(x) - \mu_{A^{\geq 1/2}}(x)|, \tag{5.140}
$$

so we can obtain, as an equivalent presentation of (5.138),

$$
F_{11} = 2 \cdot \varrho_1(A, A^{\geq 1/2})/\operatorname{card}\mathcal{X}. \tag{5.141}
$$

Moreover, we can use as a fuzziness measure an analogon to the Shannon entropy, adapted to fuzzy measures,

$$
\begin{aligned}
F_{12} = -c\sum_{x \in \mathcal{X}}\Big(&\mu_A(x)\ln\mu_A(x) + \\
&+ \big(1 - \mu_A(x)\big)\ln\big(1 - \mu_A(x)\big)\Big),
\end{aligned}
\tag{5.142}
$$

which leads DELUCA/TERMINI (1979) to the naming.

Finally, we will mention the simple fuzziness measure

$$F_{13} = \max_{x \in \mathcal{X}} \min\{\mu_A(x), 1 - \mu_A(x)\} = \text{hgt}\,(A \cap A^c). \tag{5.143}$$

Whereas the entropy measures F_{11} and F_{12} consider the pointwise fuzziness of A at all the points in $\mathcal{X}$, in F_{13} only the *most unfavourable* point is taken into account.

Obviously, for entropy measures it holds $F(A) = F(A^c)$.

By the relation in (5.134) a partial ordering is introduced into the set of fuzzy sets over $\mathcal{X}$, the minimal elements of which are the crisp sets and the maximal element of which is the set $U = X^{[1/2]}$ from (5.131). Sometimes it will be desirable to demand in (5.130), more strongly $\Leftrightarrow$ instead of $\Rightarrow$, but this does not always make sense in applications (cf. KNOPFMACHER (1975)).

Considerations by LOO (1977), DELUCA/TERMINI (1979) and GOTTWALD (1979) show that for *finite* $\mathcal{X}$ the set-up

$$F(A) = g\left(\sum_{x \in \mathcal{X}} f(\mu_A(x)) \right) \tag{5.144}$$

leads to a rich class of interesting fuzziness measures. The functions within the set-up have to satisfy some conditions, so $f : [0,1] \to I\!\!R^+$ is to be (strictly) monotonically increasing on the interval $[0, 1/2]$ and to be (strictly) monotonically decreasing on the interval $[1/2, 1]$ with boundary values $f(0) = f(1) = 0$; the function $g : I\!\!R^+ \to I\!\!R^+$ is to be a monotonically increasing function with $g(y) = 0 \Leftrightarrow y = 0$.

The function in (5.144) can be arranged according to the domain of μ_A, which leads, with

$$a_t = \text{card}\,\{x \in \mathcal{X} | \mu_A(x) = t\}, \quad t \in \mu_A(\mathcal{X}), \tag{5.145}$$

to the presentation

$$F(A) = g\left(\sum_{t \in \mu_A(\mathcal{X})} a_t f(t) \right). \tag{5.146}$$

This shows that $F(A)$, up to a transformation g, is a weighted sum over a_t, $t \in \mu_A(\mathcal{X})$, where a_t for t in the neighbourhood of $1/2$ receives the heighest weights.

The presentation (5.146) gives a hint to a possible performance in the case of an infinite universe. The counting measure in (5.145) is to be replaced by a suitable measure P over a measurable space $[\mathcal{X}, I\!\!B]$, and μ_A and f have to satisfy corresponding *conditions of measurability*. For making sure that F is finite $f(\mu_A(\cdot))$ over $\mathcal{X}$ is assumed to be P-integrable. Moreover, we must take into account that such fuzzy measures are not distinguished from each other, if they differ only on sets with measure zero with respect to P. Hence all statements always refer to corresponding *equivalence classes* of fuzzy sets with respect to the measure P. Provided these agreements, for the case of infinite universes the following set-up seems to make sense, in analogy with (5.144):

$$F(A) = g\left(\int_{\mathcal{X}} f(\mu_A(x)) \mathrm{d}P(x) \right).$$

(5.147)

If, especially, g is the identity and $f_1(u) = \min\{u, 1-u\}$, then we obtain an analogon to $F_{11}(A)$ according to (5.137), and with a corresponding f the analogy with the Shannon entropy (5.142).

Naturally, the fuzziness measures mentioned up to now rest on the assumption that the min-max-combination was chosen for the sets. For other systems of combination we have to modify the approach (cf., e.g., WEBER (1984)).

YAGER (1979/80) considered even fuzziness measures F, the values of which are no longer real numbers, but fuzzy subsets of [0,1]. Moreover, he extended his considerations even to fuzzy sets with generalised membership values in suitable lattices with negation.

5.5.2   Energy Measures

Called an *energy measure*, in the sense of DE LUCA/TERMINI (1979), the fuzziness measure F is to evaluate the *deviation from the empty set* (a):

$$F(\emptyset) = 0.$$

(5.148)

The *most fuzzy* set (b) is here the whole universe $\mathcal{X}$, more precisely: the universal set X over $\mathcal{X}$, which deviates the most from the empty set:

$$F(X) = \max.$$

(5.149)

Finally, two fuzzy sets A and B are comparable with respect to their energy measures (c), if one of them is contained in the other ($A \subseteq B$):

$$\forall x \in \mathcal{X} : \mu_A(x) \le \mu_B(x) \quad \Rightarrow \quad F(A) \le F(B).$$

(5.150)

The condition that $F(A) = 0$ holds if and only if $A = \emptyset$, is sometimes stipulated, but makes sense only seldom.

As energy measures we can offer

$$F_{21}(A) = \mathrm{card}\,(A)$$

(5.151)

and

$$F_{22}(A) = \sup_{x \in \mathcal{X}} \mu_A(x) = \mathrm{hgt}\,(A),$$

(5.152)

and sums (or integrals, respectively) over monotonically increasing functions on μ_A, e.g.

$$F_{23}(A) = \int_{\mathcal{X}} (\mu_A(x))^2 \mathrm{d}x,$$

(5.153)

if the integral exists.

By the relation (5.150) a partial ordering is introduced into the totality of fuzzy sets over $\mathcal{X}$. A maximal element is the universe itself. For infinite universes the statements given for entropy measures remain valid by analogy; minimal elements of the partial ordering are all sets from the equivalence class, which contains the empty set, hence e.g. all sets with a support, the measure P of which is zero. The corresponding statement holds for the equivalence class of the maximal elements. By analogous considerations, as for the entropy, we come to the recommendation to use a set-up of the structure (5.147) for specifying energy measures, though we have to modify the conditions on the functions within the set-up.

There is a useful connection between entropy and energy measures: If F_1 is an entropy measure, then, with $U = X^{[1/2]}$ for all $A \in \mathbb{F}(\mathcal{X})$

$$F_2(A) = F_1(A \cap U) \tag{5.154}$$

is an energy measure. If F_2 is an energy measure, then

$$F_1(A) = F_2(A \cap A^c) \tag{5.155}$$

is an entropy measure, where the indices here serve only to characterise the type of the measure. Naturally, the measures have to refer to the same universe, measurable space, and measure used for defining cardinality.

5.5.3 Other Suggestions

Finally HIGASHI/KLIR (1983) (cf. also KLIR (1987), DUBOIS/PRADE (1987)) suggested so-called *measures of nonspecificity*, which evaluate the *deviation from the type of a crisp point* (a), i.e. from a crisp one-point set $\{x_0\}$, more precisely: from the fuzzy 1-one-point set $\langle\!\langle x_0 \rangle\!\rangle_1$ for $x_0 \in \mathcal{X}$:

$$A = \langle\!\langle x_0 \rangle\!\rangle_1 \quad \Rightarrow \quad F(A) = 0 \,. \tag{5.156}$$

The *most fuzzy* set (b) is here again the whole universe $\mathcal{X}$, since it deviates the most from a one-point set (cf. (5.149)). The comparability (c) is given, as for energy measures, by the set inclusion (cf. (5.150)).

For a *normalised* set A over a *finite* universe HIGASHI/KLIR (1983) suggest

$$F_{31}(A) = \int\limits_0^1 \log_2(\operatorname{card} A^{\geq \alpha}) \, d\alpha \tag{5.157}$$

as the so-called *U-measure of uncertainty*. The same intention led YAGER (1981, 1983) to his proposal of a *measure of specificity* F_4, which is antiton to the partial ordering (5.150) $\subseteq$, such that the crisp one-point sets now obtain the *highest* evaluation. As an example for *finite* universes we mention

$$F_{41}(A) = \int_0^h (\operatorname{card} A^{\geq \alpha})^{-1} \mathrm{d}\alpha \tag{5.158}$$

with $h = \operatorname{hgt}(A)$.

A useful overview of fuzziness measures including entropy, energy, and specificity measures, is contained in KLIR/FOLGER (1988).

The measures F_{31} and F_{41} are used for evaluation of *crisp* decisions, deduced from fuzzily given results, e.g., by choosing the kernel element of some A, or for evaluation of fuzzy numbers.

CZOGALA/GOTTWALD/PEDRYCZ (1982) used both the energy measures F_{21} and F_{22} simultaneously for evaluation of fuzzy decision situations. They called a fuzzy decision D (α, β)-*acceptable*, if it is not too vague, i.e. $\operatorname{hgt}(D) \geq \alpha$, and not too fuzzy, i.e. $\operatorname{card}(D) \leq \beta$.

The fuzziness measures mentioned up to now are continuous with respect to the membership values of A. Sometimes it is reasonable to consider measures without this property, for instance, if we want to stress the case of "dead heat", i.e. the membership function has at least two maxima of equal height. Considering that specification of a membership function, as a rule, bases only on reflections on monotonicity, this case, when occurring, represents something *qualitatively* different from the case with *only one* maximum. Hence, in the case of a finite universe and $\operatorname{hgt}(A) = 1$, BANDEMER (1990) suggests the following measure of uncertainty

$$F_{32}(A) = \begin{cases} \operatorname{card}(A), & \text{if} \quad \operatorname{card}(A^{\geq 1}) \neq 1 \\ \operatorname{card}(A) - 1, & \text{if} \quad \operatorname{card}(A^{\geq 1}) = 1. \end{cases} \tag{5.159}$$

This measure signals the reaching of the membership value 1 for a second element of the universe by a jump of height 1. It can be generalised to the case of fuzzy decisions, as occurring, e.g., when adjusting control variables only fuzzily. Let $D(x_1)$, $x_1 \in \mathcal{X}$, be a class of normalised fuzzy decisions (i.e. with $\mu_D(x_1) = 1$), of which one has to be chosen based on a given fuzzy set A. For all x_2 from the kernel $A^{\geq 1}$ the difference $\Delta(x_2) = A - D(x_2)$ with

$$\begin{aligned} \mu_\Delta(x; x_2) &= \max\{\mu_A(x) - \mu_D(x; x_2), 0\} \\ &= [\mu_A(x) - \mu_D(x; x_2)]^+ \end{aligned} \tag{5.160}$$

is considered. Then

$$F_{33}(A) = \operatorname{card} \bigcup_{x_2 \in A^{\geq 1}} \Delta(x_2) \tag{5.161}$$

is a measure of uncertainty (cf. BANDEMER (1990)). The functional (5.161) will show small values, if the whole kernel of A for every "effective" $D(x_2)$ (i.e. such with $x_2 \in A^{\geq 1}$) will be contained in the region, where the membership is high; it will show large values, if the kernel of A disintegrates into subsets in a way that they cannot be covered by regions of high membership by all effective $D(x_2)$ simultaneously.

6 Fuzzy Data Analysis

6.1 Data and Their Analysis

The wording "datum" means, literally, "something actually given". It makes sense only in a certain context and expresses that "something" was found in a state characterised by just this datum. Obviously, such a *datum* contains information only if there are at least two different possibilities for the state of the "something" in question. Hence we can consider every datum as a *realisation* of a certain *variable* in a suitable set of values, usually called the universe, and reflecting these possibilities for the state in the given context.

The first problem in a mathematical modelling of such an affair consists in a *mathematical representation of the possible data* simultaneously specifying a suitable universe. For indicating the diversity of situations reached by the present approach it may suffice to consider some examples:

In the simplest case the datum only reflects whether a certain characteristic *property* (or an attribute) is *present* or *absent*, e.g. if a specimen of an industrial product is defective or not. The universe is a two-point-set and the values are chosen as $+, -$ or $1, 0$, or the like.

If the property can have some *grades*, shades or nuances, then the values usually are expressed by characters or natural numbers. The universe will be some finite set.

When considering *observations* or measurements the result in a concrete situation is usually given by a real *number* or by a vector. As universes Euclidean spaces are usually chosen.

If the observation or measurement is performed *continuously* in time or space (e.g. temperature records, spectrograms, geological profiles), then every result is presented by a trajectory or a (hyper-) surface, respectively. Then a suitable universe may be chosen as a space of functions, e.g. a Hilbert space, or as a finite dimensional approximation of it.

Moreover, *grey-tone pictures* can be used as data, e.g. when reflecting X-ray records, projections of transparent sections taken from cellular tissues, two-dimensional projections of three-dimensional particles registered by optical devices, or some scenes scanned by tv-equipment which can be recognised. The corresponding universe can be specified either by the set of all possible grey-tone pictures or only by the set of all possible pixel grids formed by using the finitely many distinct grey tones available on the screen. It remains a problem of further modelling and of the aim of the analysis, which of these two models serves better to tackle the concrete practical problem behind the modelling.

Finally, even *opinions of experts* or of panels of experts can be interpreted as data, when presented with respect to the state of a given "something". The opinions can be uttered as *statements, rules,* or *conclusions*. The appropriate formulation will then be taken from mathematical logic (cf. Chapter 4). The appropriate universe is then given by a suitable set of statements, rules, and conclusions as possible values for the "choice" of the opinions for the experts in question.

This may suffice for the moment to show the diversity of possible data. A given datum differs from the (potential) value of a variable in that it describes the state of a given "something" in a concrete case, so it contains information about this case. Hence frequently a datum is called a realisation of the variable, following the use in mathematical statistics.

Data analysis consists of an investigation and an evaluation of the given data, and of the drawing of conclusions from the data and of the evaluation of these conclusions. Data analysis is performed in *several stages* of increasing complexity.

In the *first* stage the data are investigated and evaluated with respect to some simple but important property. The very first arrangement is with respect to frequency. Frequency analysis deals with "usual" states of the "something" in question, e.g. with respect to its expected states in future. Frequency analysis is usually the starting point for the evaluation of each single datum with respect to its *reliability*. Data, which are suspected of being recorded under non-controlled conditions (e.g. *outliers*) or manipulated after observation are marked or even deleted. Moreover, data can be evaluated with respect to their *trustworthiness*, as reflecting the state truly, although recorded reliably. This is an interesting point with experts' opinions leading to competency weights and truth-values for their statements.

The *second* stage of data analysis consists of *pattern cognition*. The first method is a *grouping* after visual inspection or according to additional properties or background knowledge. Then the data are represented in or transformed into other structures using different techniques. The aim, in every case, is to find *structures* within the data to get ideas with respect to their arrangements or connections or to be inspired to specify mathematical models the data could obey.

These two first stages of data analysis form the body of *exploratory* data analysis, i.e. the data are investigated *without* any reference to a pre-chosen mathematical model, which would have to explain the occurrence and structure of the data.

The *third* stage of data analysis investigates the data with respect to a chosen mathematical *model* or to some competing such models. Models reflect assumptions about the mathematical structure of the data.

The analysis can be a *qualitative* one. Data are then grouped with respect to qualitatively expressed additional properties. A typical example is given by the expression of data *similarity*, and a typical method of data analysis is cluster analysis, usually applied to vector-valued data. We will tackle this problem in Section 6.2.

If the data are represented by quantities, then a *quantitative* analysis becomes possible. Such an analysis aims at a cognition and formulation of (functional) relationships among the data or among the different components of each datum. A typical example is the approximation of vector-valued data by functional relationships, e.g. by means of statistical regression methods.

The *last* and highest stage of data analysis is concerned with the conclusions drawn from the given data and the evaluation of these conclusions.

The most frequently demanded conclusion is the *prediction* of future or missing data if some assumptions concerning a mathematical model for the data are fixed. A typical case is here forecasting of time series.

A further kind of conclusion concerns the *assignment* of the whole body of data or of each single datum individually to one set of given standards. The situation occurs frequently with spectrograms and pictures.

Moreover, data are to be *combined*, in different manner, to form patterns or to make decisions, e.g. several blurred pictures of some original are to be "piled up" to restore them, or the statements of several experts are to be combined to obtain some objectivised opinion.

Finally, the conclusions drawn from the data can be *evaluated* within the framework of a mathematical theory developed for a class of models, e.g. decisions under certain model assumptions can be evaluated with respect to optimality. Such evaluation procedures can be used as necessary "feedback" rules with respect to the third stage, e.g. when the mathematical model is to be updated or changed.

When considering the data mentioned up to now more and more intensively we find them all burdened with *uncertainty* of different kinds. Hence also conclusions will inherit this uncertainty. Possibly the uncertainty is even increased by the methods of analysis applied, although apparently disappearing. Ignoring these circumstances the conclusions can become worthless or even misleading.

Naturally, there are approaches taking into account certain aspects of uncertainty in performing data analysis.

A first kind of uncertainty stems from the *variability* of the data: In equal or comparable situations the "something" in question does not show identical states. This kind of uncertainty is considered by *stochastics*, providing, within the framework of mathematical statistics, a whole "toolbox" of procedures for inference and evaluation. However, the problem with application of stochastics consists in the restriction that the conclusions are valid only with regard to a (hypothetical) population, from which the data are assumed to be generated.

Another kind of uncertainty is connected with the impossibility of observing or measuring *to an arbitrary level of precision*. In every case we must be content with a reasonable precision. This precision depends not only on the power of the sensors applied but also on the environment including the observer, e.g. when analysing spectrograms or grey-tone pictures. For simplest cases, for numbers and vectors as data, the field of *interval mathematics* was established. In this field a certain possible neighbourhood of each datum is specified, the elements of which are considered equivalent with the given datum in the given context. The problem with interval mathematics is the necessary specification of a precise border of the neighbourhood, e.g. the ends of the interval of equivalent values.

In the following sections data are taken as *fuzzy sets*. With this approach the case can even be considered that the given sensors can sometimes be so weak or the environment can be so complex or the knowledge of the observer with respect to the situation can be so minimal that he can give only his belief with respect to the present state of the "something". In this case we will use *fuzzy measures* in modelling uncertainty. Since probability is a fuzzy measure, too, even stochastic aspects in describing uncertainty can be taken into account.

The methods of (crisp) data analysis considered in the following are, as a rule, mathematically simple, hence they will be explained only shortly before being generalised to fuzzy data. This generalisation can then be applied to more complicated methods of crisp data analysis rather comprehensibly.

In the next section we will consider problems of qualitative data analysis, based on the notion of similarity. In Section 6.3 we will treat some problems of quantitative data analysis, whereas the last Section 6.4 contains some remarks with respect to an evaluation of the methods presented. With respect to the limited space within this textbook the explanations are rather short, hence we refer to the more detailed presentation including examples in BANDEMER/NÄTHER (1992).

6.2 Qualitative Data Analysis

In generalising known methods of data analysis to fuzzy data there are two approaches. The first approach consists of the choice of a suitable procedure for crisp data and its adapting to fuzzy data. The other approach considers the data and their structure as fuzzy sets and treats them according to the rules of fuzzy set theory.

Hence this section contains at first a presentation of methods from the first approach for handling cluster analysis, and then the treatment of a similar problem of set partition and classification of new elements using general methods from the theory of fuzzy sets.

6.2.1 Fuzzy Cluster Analysis of Crisp Data

In preparation of problems of diagnosis and therapy, of decision making and control (cf. e.g. STRAUBE (1986), SCHÜLER (1992)) the following problem occurs: A given set $\mathcal{O} = \{O_1, \ldots, O_N\}$ of distinguishable objects (or facts) is to be partitioned into subsets, so-called *clusters*, that the objects within each cluster are *very similar*, whereas objects from different clusters are *only a little similar*. One aim of the partition is that problems can be solved for each cluster separately.

The procedure for partitioning the set of objects into clusters must, as a rule, be highly context depending and heuristic. It consists usually of the following three stages (cf. e.g. ANDERBERG (1973), HARTIGAN (1975), BEZDEK (1981)):

1. Specification of those features of the objects, which are assumed to be essential: *feature selection*. For this task there are many recommendations (cf. the literature cited above). In the following we assume that the given features $M_1, \ldots, M_t$ already represent these essential features.

2. Choice of rules for aggregation and transformation of the values $x_{ij}, i = 1, \ldots, t; j = 1, \ldots, N$, given each for the i-th feature of the j-th object, their presentation as a set of comprehensible mathematical objects (points, functions, graphs, standard forms, etc.), and rules for the decisions: object O_j is allocated to cluster C_k: *cluster analysis*.

3. Finally, specifications are necessary, how future objects $O_{N+1}, \ldots, O_{N+r}$ are to be allocated to the clusters obtained: *classification*.

The heuristic of decision making is frequently supported or padded by model ideas, e.g. from mathematical statistics.

The formulation of the problem of cluster analysis, as given in the beginning of this section is a typical *fuzzy one* ("very similar", "only a little similar"). Even if the *feature values* are assumed *crisp*, which is assumed for the moment, there are two starting-points for the theory of fuzzy sets: specification of the similarity of the objects and the consideration of fuzzy partitions of the object set.

Frequently the similarity of two objects O_j, O_l can be expressed by a number $s_{jl} = s(O_j, O_l)$ obtained by a function $s : \mathcal{O} \times \mathcal{O} \to [0, 1]$, such that larger values of s mean higher similarity. Hence we can define by $\mu_{S_0}(O_j, O_l) = s(O_j, O_l)$, $j, l = 1, \ldots, N$, a *fuzzy relation* S_0 over $\mathcal{O} \times \mathcal{O}$ reflecting the similarity of the objects. Whereas with $s_{jj} = 1 \geq s_{jl}$ for $j \neq l$, i.e. each object is totally similar with itself, reflexivity of S_0 is obvious, symmetry $s_{jl} = s_{lj}$ is not always evident, but usually assumed valid. Hence every so specified fuzzy relation S_0 is a fuzzy neighbourhood relation. The usual transitivity, however, is lacking, as a rule, similarity can diminish in a chain of pairwise similar objects, as is well known. The specified relation S_0 is, in general, no sup-min-transitive similarity relation in the sense of Section 3.2. Sometimes the relation S_0 satisfies the criteria of some other transitivity; e.g. the condition $s_{jj} = 1 > s_{jl}$ for $j \neq l$, secures that the kernel of S_0 is a common equivalence relation and hence S_0 is sup-t_3-transitive with respect to the t-norm t_3 in $[0, 1]$; corresponding to the drastic product (2.100).

If transitivity of a special kind is desired, we can go over to the transitive hull of S_0, i.e. to that fuzzy relation R, which is the smallest one, in the sense of inclusion $\subseteq$, which contains S_0 and is transitive of the corresponding kind. This relation S, however, need not be in harmony with all the similarity ideas, which had been constitutive for S_0. Another way is the consideration of the family $(S_0^{\geq \alpha})_{\alpha \in [0,1]}$ whether it provides, for certain α, useful equivalence classes. A further way out would be the representation of S_0 as a graph, the nodes of which are the objects and the fuzzy edges of which are given by the similarity values s_{jl}. Then clustering is equivalent with the construction of partial graphs, either by connecting the nodes with the largest s_{jl}, or by breaking up the edges with the smallest s_{jl} until the graph falls apart into partial graphs. With respect to further details cf. e.g. BALAS/PADBERG (1976); GOWER/ROSS (1969).

If S_0 is obtained by a monotonic transformation from a metric d in analogy with (2.51), then it is already a similarity relation.

In the case that the objects O_j can be represented by their feature vectors $x_j = (x_{1j}, \ldots, x_{tj})^\top \in \mathbb{R}^t$ then for specifying of μ_{S_0} we can use the well-known L_p-norms

$$\mu_{S_0}(x_j, x_l; p) = (\sum_{i=1}^{t} \mid x_{ij} - x_{il} \mid^p)^{1/p}, \quad p \geq 0. \tag{6.1}$$

If a metric is given, then it suggests itself to interpret similarity as *vicinity* and an explicit specification of S_0 becomes superfluous in general. A witty proposal in this direction is due to GITMAN/LEVINE (1970), who interpreted the relative number of points in a ϑ-neighbourhood of an object O_j as a membership function of a fuzzy set A over $\mathcal{O}$:

$$\mu_A(x_j) = (1/N)\mathrm{card}\,\{O_l \in \mathcal{O} \mid d(x_j, x_l) \leq \vartheta\}. \tag{6.2}$$

The maxima of μ_A are chosen as the centers of the desired clusters, to which the objects are allocated.

All procedures mentioned up to now provide *crisp* clusters, i.e. for each object the membership is determined to one and only one of the subsets.

If a *fuzzy partition* of $\mathcal{O}$ is allowed, i.e. a partition of $\mathcal{O}$ into fuzzy subsets $Q_1, \ldots, Q_n$ on the condition that

$$\forall O_j \in \mathcal{O} : \sum_{k=1}^{n} \mu_{Q_k}(O_j) = 1, \tag{6.3}$$

then the sets Q_k can be considered as fuzzy clusters, which are to be determined. The standardisation according to (6.3) serves for an evaluation of the clusters with respect to their cardinality and to include the case of crisp clusters. The standardisation is always demanded in the literature cited in the following, although cluster analysis also seems to make sense without this condition. The problem of determination of clusters on the condition (6.3) is equivalent to the determination of a matrix $U = ((u_{jk}))$ with $u_{jk} = \mu_{Q_k}(O_j)$, for which according to (6.3) the following conditions

$$\sum_{k=1}^{n} u_{jk} = 1; \qquad 0 < \sum_{j=1}^{N} u_{jk} < N \tag{6.4}$$

must be valid for each j and k, respectively.

For the case that S_0 is symmetric, RUSPINI (1970, 1973) suggested computing the u_{jk} by minimising a suitable functional, e.g. choosing the following functional

$$G_1(U) = \sum_{j=1}^{N}\sum_{l=1}^{N}[w(u_{j1}, \ldots, u_{jn}; u_{l1}, \ldots, u_{ln}) - f(s_{jl})]^2, \tag{6.5}$$

where $w(.;.)$ is a function symmetric with respect to j and l and non-negative, which vanishes for $j = l$, and f is a non-negative, non-increasing, and non-identically vanishing function with $f(1) = 0$. In the case that these functions are given by corresponding norms in $\mathbb{R}^n$ and $\mathbb{R}^t$, respectively, then

$$G_{10}(U) = \sum_{j=1}^{N}\sum_{l=1}^{N}\left[c_0\|\boldsymbol{u}^{(j)} - \boldsymbol{u}^{(l)}\|^2 - \|\boldsymbol{x}_j - \boldsymbol{x}_l\|^2\right]^2 \tag{6.6}$$

with the abbreviation $u^{(j)} = (u_{j1}, \ldots, u_{jn})^{\mathsf{T}}$ and the positive constant c_0, is a special example of $G_1(U)$.

If the feature space is the Euclidean space $\mathbb{R}^t$ and the chosen metric is a norm $d^2(x, y) = \|x - y\|^2$, induced by an inner product, then it even makes sense to introduce hypothetical objects $v_1, \ldots, v_n \in \mathbb{R}^t$, so-called *prototypes* or cluster centres, and to choose the distance from these as a measure of non-similarity and as the starting-point for the construction of fuzzy clusters. DUNN (1975) and BEZDEK (1974, 1981) suggested minimising the functional

$$G_2(U, V) = \sum_{j=1}^{N} \sum_{k=1}^{n} (u_{jk})^p \|x_j - v_k\|^2 \tag{6.7}$$

with respect to the matrix $U = ((u_{jk}))$ with the elements $u_{jk}; j = 1. \ldots, N, k = 1, \ldots, n$, under the conditions (6.4) and $V = (v_1, \ldots, v_n)$, $p \in [1, \infty)$. The parameter p is an arbitrary weighting exponent, which can be used, theoretically motivated or by trying to adapt the clustering to subject-specific ideas with respect to the practical problem. The larger the chosen p *the more fuzzy* is the assignment of membership to the cluster; the smaller p is the more crisp (hard) is the clustering, hence: parameter of contrast p. For more details and with respect to the existence of a (global) minimum of G_2, cf. BEZDEK (1981).

For the solution of the so established optimisation problem an *iteration procedure* (ISODATA-FCM) is suggested:

Step 1: Choose the desired number of clusters n ($2 \leq n < N$), a norm $\|.\|$ in $\mathbb{R}^t$ induced by an inner product, and an exponent value $p \in (1, \infty)$. Choose a matrix $U^{(0)}$ satisfying the conditions (6.4) for initialising the procedure. Put $r = 0$.

Step 2: Calculate the n cluster centres $v_k^{(r)}$ according to

$$v_k^{(r)} = \sum_{j=1}^{N} (u_{jk}^{(r)})^p x_j \Big/ \sum_{j=1}^{N} (u_{jk}^{(r)})^p. \tag{6.8}$$

Step 3: Compute $U^{(r+1)}$ according to the following rule: Let

$$I_l = \{k \in \{1, \ldots, n\} \mid \|x_l - v_k^{(r)}\| = 0\}, \tag{6.9}$$

$$I_l^c = \{1, \ldots, n\} \setminus I_l. \tag{6.10}$$

If $I_l = \emptyset$, then choose

$$u_{jk}^{(r+1)} = \Big[\sum_{m=1}^{n} \Big(\frac{\|x_j - v_k^{(r)}\|}{\|x_j - v_m^{(r)}\|} \Big)^{2/(p-1)} \Big]^{-1}, \tag{6.11}$$

and if $I_l \neq \emptyset$, then choose

$$u_{jk}^{(r+1)} = 0 \text{ for each } k \in I_l^c \quad \text{and} \quad \sum_{k \in I_l} u_{jk}^{(r+1)} = 1. \tag{6.12}$$

Step 4: Choose a matrix norm appropriate to $\|.\|$ and an $\epsilon > 0$. If

$$\|U^{(r+1)} - U^{(r)}\| \leq \epsilon, \tag{6.13}$$

then stop the procedure with $U^{(r+1)}, V^{(r)}$, in any other case continue with Step 2.

With respect to the convergence of this procedure to a (local) minimum of G_2 cf. BEZDEK (1981).

We must stress the fact that *all* procedures for clustering are *proposals*, the usefulness of which depends on the given context. There is no procedure, by which in every situation a technically meaningful and best partition could be found. As a rule, especially if the procedure still contains arbitrary parameters, e.g. the number n of clusters or the exponent p, several partitions are provided. The final choice from this set can ideally be left to the specialist from the area of application. However, there are a lot of proposals to help in deciding, in which the partitions obtained are evaluated e.g. by functionals. Two of these evaluations are mentioned in the following (cf. BEZDEK (1981) for more proposals):

The *coefficient of partition* (BEZDEK (1974)) is

$$F(U;n) = \sum_{j=1}^{N} \sum_{k=1}^{n} (u_{jk})^2 / N \tag{6.14}$$

with $(1/n) \leq F(U;n) \leq 1$. The value 1 belongs to a crisp (hard) partition and the value $(1/n)$ to the most fuzzy one: $u_{jk} = (1/n)$.

The *entropy of partition* is

$$H(U;n) = -\sum_{j=1}^{N} \sum_{k=1}^{n} u_{jk} \log u_{jk} / N \tag{6.15}$$

with $0 \leq H(U;n) \leq \log n$. Here the value 0 is assumed for the crisp (hard) partition and $\log n$ for the most fuzzy one. Both are connected by the inequality

$$1 - F(U;n) \leq H(U;n)/\log e \tag{6.16}$$

where equality holds only in the crisp case. One will prefer partitions with a larger coefficient of partition and with a smaller entropy of partition. A strong optimisation with respect to the arbitrary parameters, however, can lead to technically senseless results. (BEZDEK (1981)).

For classification, i.e. for allocation of further objects into the clusters, a partition of the set of potential objects is required. This partition can be effected either, explicitly, by specifying of discriminance functions (so-called *classificators*), which are based on decision theoretic principles or ideas for modelling the set of all possible objects for classification, or can be effected, implicitly, by so-called *neighbourhood rules*, by which the nearest neighbours or the nearest cluster centres determine the cluster membership of the new objects. For this a distance function must be given.

These ideas can be adapted to the case of fuzzy clusters. For instance, for a *crisp* allocation of a new object that cluster could be chosen, in which its nearest neighbour has the largest membership value.

However, a *fuzzy* allocation of new objects into a fuzzy partition of the starting set $\mathcal{O} = \{O_1, \ldots, O_N\}$ is a totally new problem. A proposal for its solution is due to RUSPINI (1970):

Let $\mathcal{O}^q = \{O_{N+1}, \ldots, O_{N+q}\}$ be the set of new objects to be allocated into the cluster partition U. In $I\!\!R^n$ and $I\!\!R^t$ corresponding norms are given. Then it seems reasonable that the allocation vector $\boldsymbol{u}^{(N+p)}$ of the object O_{N+p} differs only slightly from $\boldsymbol{u}^{(j)}$ for O_j, if the corresponding feature vector $\boldsymbol{x}_{(N+p)}$ is in the vicinity of $\boldsymbol{x}_j$. This idea is realised by RUSPINI in adapting his functional $G_{10}(U)$ from (6.6):

$$ G_{11}(U, U^q) = \sum_{p=1}^{q} \sum_{j=1}^{N} \left[c_0 \| \boldsymbol{u}^{(N+p)} - \boldsymbol{u}^{(j)} \|^2 - \| \boldsymbol{x}_{N+p} - \boldsymbol{x}_j \|^2 \right]^2 . $$

In this expression the matrix $U = ((u_{jk}))$ with $j = 1, \ldots, N, k = 1, \ldots, n$ is fixed and minimisation is performed only with respect to the matrix $U^q = ((u_{(N+p)k}))$ with $p = 1, \ldots, q, k = 1, \ldots, n$. For a solution of this optimisation problem iteration procedures are used. Obviously $G_{11}(U, U^q)$ is a special case of more general possibilities, as $G_{10}(U)$ is for $G_1(U)$ according to (6.6), cf. RUSPINI (1970) for more details.

Procedures of fuzzy cluster analysis and of fuzzy classification based on this analysis are applied in different fields. An approach used for many application cases is described by BOCKLISCH (1987) in some detail and illustrated by examples of applications in engineering and in medical diagnostic.

6.2.2   Arrangements of Fuzzy Data
Using Their Similarity

Although the methods presented within the preceding section provide reasonable results in many practical facts, especially if controlled by useful knowledge of the applying scientists, there are a lot of objections against such a cluster analysis, particularly when an optimisation criterion is to be used. It is not only the arbitrariness in choosing such a criterion and its parameters and the difficulty of finding suitable starting values, but also the questionability of the optimality at all: stationary points of an objective function, as is well known, are not necessarily local minima. There is no assurance that even a global optimum of any objective function is a "good" clustering. Different choices of algorithmic parameters may yield different "optimum" partitions. There may be a different number n of clusters, which result in a "better" partitioning. In fact, there may be more than one value of n for which reasonable substructural interpretations exist. These objections superimpose the usual ones with respect to the necessity of specifications of a distance taking into account *all* the features simultaneously, which are usually of quite different character. Finally, we must point to the fact, that all the methods of cluster analysis mentioned so far can only be applied to *crisp* feature values.

Hence it seems worthwhile to consider the final aim of cluster analysis. Frequently searching for patterns is only a transient problem to specify classes, in which new objects can be allocated (e.g. typical situations in control or diagnosis in medicine), or to find dependencies among features. Moreover, when the set of features and objects become more and more extensive the problem with cluster analysis performance becomes more and more serious. For these reasons methods of local inference will be of interest, with which problems of classification of new objects and of feature dependence can be solved without the partitioning of the whole set of objects by some clustering procedure. Simultaneously we will allow that the obtained feature values can be *fuzzy data*. By this approach, especially, the problem of aggregation of fuzzy descriptions of situations and the determination of approximate control instructions (cf. Section 4.2) is examined and solved from another starting-point.

In the following we will allow that the representation of the i-th feature as found at the j-th object can be given as a *fuzzy* set over the universe $\mathcal{X}_i$ for the i-th feature. The totality of these sets for all features and all objects then forms the *data or knowledge base*

$$X = ((X_{ij})), \qquad \text{with} \quad i = 1, \dots, t; \ j = 1, \dots, N \qquad (6.17)$$

where we will not discuss here the different opinions with respect to the naming of this base.

As long as possible we will consider each feature separately. This is done not only with respect to the expected problems with their aggregation, but also to profit, as long as possible, from the background knowledge about the semantic contents of the special feature. Hence we denote, for the moment, by X_j the fuzzy feature value of the j-th object (for the i-th feature) and by $\mathcal{X}$ the corresponding universe. The problem consists in specifying a similarity relation over the set $\mathbb{F}(\mathcal{X})$.

The problems to be solved differ in that either there is already a similarity relation R for the crisp feature values introduced over $\mathcal{X}$, or a similarity relation should be or must be introduced ad hoc. For the moment we will consider the first case.

To simplify the notation we temporarily put $X_j = A$; $X_l = B$. Let a fuzzy similarity relation $R \in I\!F(\mathcal{X} \times \mathcal{X})$ be given on $\mathcal{X}$. Then it is possible, and sometimes more appropriate, to express the similarity of two fuzzy sets, say A and B, in the sense of R by a fuzzy set S, which can be explained as a value of a linguistic variable SIMILARITY on the similarity scale $[0, 1]$ as a universe. For computation of S, given A, B and R, an extension principle, with a suitable t-norm, can be chosen, i.e., we define, e.g., for all $A, B \in I\!F(\mathcal{X})$ and $R \in I\!F(\mathcal{X} \times \mathcal{X})$ the fuzzy set $S := S(A, B; R)$ by its membership function

$$\mu_S(z; A, B, R) = \sup_{(u,v):\mu_R(u,v)=z} \min\{\mu_A(u), \mu_B(v)\}. \tag{6.18}$$

This is a fuzzy set of type 2 in the sense of Section 2.1. We will call $S(A, B; R)$ *fuzzily expressed fuzzy similarity* of A and B in the sense of R. Here *fuzzy similarity* refers to the fact that $I\!F(\mathcal{X})$ is the universe, and *fuzzily expressed* means that this fuzzy similarity is expressed as a fuzzy set, i.e. e.g. as a value of some linguistic variable.

Although the procedure for computing μ_S seems rather complicated the notion is useful, on principle, to solve problems of classification. The working tool is the specification of neighbourhoods in the usual manner known from calculus.

Definition. *A crisp subset $J(A; c_0, m_0)$ of $I\!F(\mathcal{X})$ is called a (c_0, m_0)-neighbourhood of $A \in I\!F(\mathcal{X})$ with respect to R, iff*

$$J(A; c_0, m_0) = \{B \in I\!F(\mathcal{X}) \mid \sup_{z \geq c_0} \mu_S(z; A, B, R) \geq m_0\} \tag{6.19}$$

where $c_0, m_0 \in (0, 1]$ are the parameters of the neighbourhood.

The (c_0, m_0)-neighbourhood of A contains all those fuzzy sets $B \in I\!F(\mathcal{X})$, which are similar, in the sense of R, to A at least with a degree c_0 with a membership value of at least m_0. Moreover, it is even possible to introduce for every $c_0 \in (0, 1]$ a *fuzzy neighbourhood $J^f(c_0)$* of A in $I\!F(\mathcal{X})$. For this purpose for every $B \in I\!F(\mathcal{X})$ a membership value $\mu_J(B; A, c_0)$ is to be specified expressing the degree, to which B belongs to the neighbourhood $J^f(A; c_0)$ of A in the sense of R. A possible specification will be the following for every $B \in I\!F(\mathcal{X})$

$$\mu_J(B; A, c_0) = \sup_{z \leq c_0} \mu_S(z; A, B, R). \tag{6.20}$$

Since R and hence $S(A, B; R)$ are symmetric, the neighbourhood relation according to (6.20) is symmetric, too. If the similarity relation R is based on a distance d in $\mathcal{X} \times \mathcal{X}$, via a monotonically non-increasing function h : $\mathbb{R}^+ \cup \{0\} \to [0, 1]$, in analogy with (2.51)), as:

$$\forall u, v \in \mathcal{X} : \; \mu_R(u, v) = h(d(u, v)), \tag{6.21}$$

then the resulting fuzzily expressed fuzzy similarity does not depend on the order in which the extension principle is applied. Hence this order can be left to mathematical convenience.

In spite of this principal possibility one will prefer, in general, handling fuzzy similarity of fuzzy sets by *scalars*. However, one will maintain the requirement that similarity is considered *in the sense of a given similarity relation R*.

This problem is a particular case of the general question for the degree, to which a given relation R is satisfied by two sets. There are several approaches to answer this question.

One of these approaches starts with assigning a *degree of truth* to the statement "A and B are in relation R" for short ARB. KLAUA (1966, 1966a) considered three variants - the optimistic one with

$$ARB_{(opt)} \quad =_{\text{def}} \quad \exists u \exists v (u \varepsilon A \wedge v \varepsilon B \wedge (u, v) \varepsilon R) \tag{6.22}$$

the pessimistic one with:

$$ARB_{(pess)} \quad =_{\text{def}} \quad \forall u, \forall v (u \varepsilon A \wedge v \varepsilon B \to (u, v) \varepsilon R) \tag{6.23}$$

and the moderate one with:

$$ARB_{(mod)} \quad =_{\text{def}} \quad \forall u \exists v (u \varepsilon A \to v \varepsilon B \wedge (u, v) \varepsilon R)$$
$$\wedge \; \forall v \exists u (v \varepsilon B \to u \varepsilon A \wedge (u, v) \varepsilon R). \tag{6.24}$$

Here the logical symbols as $\exists, \forall$ and $\to$ are to be interpreted in the sense of appropriate quantifiers and connectives from many-valued logic, which are constitutive for the basic operations of fuzzy set theory (cf. Section 2.1). Usually $\exists$ is interpreted as sup and $\forall$ as inf. Other interpretations are possible, but almost never used.

As an example for the choice of $\wedge$ and $\to$ we mention here only

$$u \wedge v \doteq \min\{u, v\}; \qquad u \to v \doteq \max\{1 - u, v\}, \tag{6.25}$$

from which we could obtain the special *similarity degree* :

$$r_{(optmin)}(A, B, R) = \sup_{u,v} \min\{\mu_A(u), \mu_B(v), \mu_R(u, v)\}. \tag{6.26}$$

Further possibilities are listed in BANDEMER/NÄTHER (1992) or can be generated by inserting other variants for $\wedge$ and $\to$, as t-norm and corresponding φ-operator (cf. Sections 2.4 and 3.2 as well as GOTTWALD (1986, 1989, 1993)).

The similarity degrees so introduced use the membership functions of the two sets obviously involved only at some distinct and special points. This can be explained as a positive as well as a negative property. On the one hand it presents a certain robustness against the specification of the membership function as a whole, on the other hand the dependence on the specification at points essential for the determination of the similarity degree can be, possibly, considered as too hard. Hence it seems reasonable to look also for similarity degrees, which use the whole functions or essential parts of them for the determination of the similarity degrees. A principal possibility for constructing those similarity degrees is offered by the use of some cardinality card (cf. Section 2.1) instead of the height hgt expressed by sup in (6.26). Let $C = (A \otimes B) \cap R$, then

$$r_{\text{card}}\,(A, B, R) = \text{card}\,(C)/\text{card}\,(A \otimes B) \tag{6.27}$$

would be such a possibility, where $\cap$ may be explained as an intersection $\cap_t$ based on a suitable t-norm. Since with hgt and card measures of fuzziness are defined, a further generalisation is opened for the construction of similarity degrees via other suitable fuzziness measures.

In analogy with the performance of S according to (6.19), similarity degrees r of any descent can also be used to define neighbourhoods for every fuzzy set $A \in \mathbb{F}(\mathcal{X})$. For every crisp similarity degree r_0 a crisp subset $J_r(A; r_0)$ of $\mathbb{F}(\mathcal{X})$ can be determined containing all such fuzzy sets, which are at least with a degree r_0 are similar to A :

$$J_r(A; r_0) = \{B \in \mathbb{F}(\mathcal{X}) \mid r(A, B) \geq r_0\}, \tag{6.28}$$

where r is the chosen similarity degree according to any of the given principles and $r_0 \in (0, 1]$ is the parameter characterising the special neighbourhood.

Moreover, it is even possible to introduce a *fuzzy* neighbourhood J_r^f of A. For this purpose the value $r(A, B)$ is to be interpreted as the membership value of B to the fuzzy neighbourhood of A (and in reverse order):

$$\mu_{J_r^f}(B; A) = r(A, B). \tag{6.29}$$

Further similarity degrees for fuzzy sets of special structure are presented in the context of examples at the end of this section.

Now we return to the knowledge base (6.17). Having specified fuzzily expressed fuzzy similarities for all pairs O_j and O_l and all features M_i, then the hypermatrix

$$\boldsymbol{S} = ((S_{ijl})) \qquad \text{with} \quad i = 1, \ldots, t; \; j, l = 1, \ldots, N \tag{6.30}$$

represents the *similarity structure* of the feature value system for all given objects. This hypermatrix $\boldsymbol{S}$ can be used to tackle different problems.

For fixed $i = i_0$ the matrix of fuzzy sets

$$\boldsymbol{S}_{i_0} = ((S_{i_0jl})) \tag{6.31}$$

reflects the *fuzzily expressed similarity of all objects* with respect to the i_0-th features. This matrix can be used to introduce neighbourhoods of features (cf. BANDEMER/NÄTHER (1992)).

For fixed $j = j_0$ and $l = l_0$ the vector of fuzzy sets

$$\boldsymbol{S}(j_0, l_0) = (S_{1j_0l_0}, \ldots, S_{tj_0l_0}) \tag{6.32}$$

reflects the *fuzzily expressed fuzzy similarity of the two objects* O_{j_0} and O_{l_0} with respect to all features. In this case neighbourhoods of objects can also be introduced.

Obviously, the same considerations can be applied with respect to the similarity degrees r. Since these degrees define a relation S_i^f over $I\!\!F(\mathcal{X}_i \times \mathcal{X}_i)$ we take them as the membership values of the relation and put

$$\mu_i(j, l) = \mu_{S_i^f}(j, l) = r(X_{ij}, X_{il}). \tag{6.33}$$

As an additional argument of r the similarity relation R_i from the corresponding universe can occur. Then the hypermatrix

$$\boldsymbol{M} = ((\mu_i(j, l))) \qquad \text{with} \quad i = 1, \ldots, t; \; j, l = 1, \ldots, N \tag{6.34}$$

is the representation of the *similarity structure* of the knowledge base with respect to all objects and to all features.

For fixed $i = i_0$ the matrix

$$\boldsymbol{M}(i_0) = ((\mu_{i_0}(j, l))) \tag{6.35}$$

reflects the fuzzy similarity of all objects with respect to the i_0-th feature. A *neighbourhood* of the feature i_0 can now be specified, e.g., by

$$
\begin{aligned}
V_{r_0}(i_0, \epsilon) \;=\; & \{ i \in \{1, \ldots, t\} \mid \forall j, l \in \{1, \ldots, N\} : \\
& |\mu_{i_0}(j, l) - \mu_i(j, l)| \le \epsilon \},
\end{aligned} \tag{6.36}
$$

where $\epsilon > 0$ is a parameter characterising the neighbourhood. In (6.36), implicitly, the distance measure for matrices

$$d(\boldsymbol{E}, \boldsymbol{F}) = \max_{i,j} |e_{ij} - f_{ij}|$$

was used to define a neighbourhood of a given feature. Obviously, some other distance can also be used for this purpose, it reflects the opinion of the actual user with respect to the diversity of features in the context of the given data in the knowledge base. A small distance means that the two considered features behave quite similarly for the given set of objects and hence they bear only similar information with respect to the diversity of the objects. This can be used to decide whether one and which of the features can be omitted in the sequel. However, such similar features can also serve as a starting-point for interpolating missing values of one of them.

Moreover, the matrix M can be used to evaluate the *discriminability* of the i_0-th feature with respect to the given set of objects. If the elements $\mu_{i_0}(j, l)$ are all approximately equal then there is only little hope of finding any sub-structure by means of the i_0-th feature. If, on the contrary, $M(i_0)$ is the unit matrix, then the feature discriminates among the objects to the utmost, however, it does not yield any non-trivial sub-structure, either.

For fixed $j = j_0$ and $l = l_0$ the vector

$$M(j_0, l_0) = (\mu_1(j_0, l_0), \ldots, \mu_t(j_0, l_0)) \tag{6.37}$$

reflects the *fuzzy similarity* of the two objects O_{j_0} and O_{l_0} with respect to *all* features. A neighbourhood of an object O_{j_0} would then be

$$V_{r_{00}}(j_0; r_0) = \{l \in \{1, \ldots, N\} \mid \min_{1 \leq i \leq t} \mu_i(j_0, l) \geq r_0\}, \tag{6.38}$$

where r_0 is the parameter characterising the neighbourhoods. The so specified neighbourhood contains all objects of the knowledge base that are similar to O_{j_0} at least to a degree of r_0 in *all* features. Obviously, the neighbourhoods can be specified for only a part of the knowledge base and with different bounds for different features.

Finally, the similarity degrees $\mu_i(j, l)$ may be aggregated with respect to the features, e.g. by a functional V_{agg}^f

$$m_{jl} = V_{agg}^f(\mu_i(j, l)) \tag{6.39}$$

defining an overall degree of similarity between the objects O_j, O_l with respect to all features. Likewise $\mu_i(j, k)$ may be aggregated with respect to the objects, e.g. by a functional V_{agg}^O

$$m_{ih} = V_{agg}^O(\mu_i(j, l), \mu_h(j, l)) \tag{6.40}$$

defining an overall degree of similarity of the two features M_i, M_h with respect to all objects of the knowledge base. However, the choice and explanation of these functionals is perhaps controversial like the specification of a common distance involving all the features in the concept of usual cluster analysis.

The neighbourhoods can now be used to solve problems usually, i.e. when the feature values are all crisp, tackled by cluster analysis.

Neighbourhoods of features can suggest a reduction of the number of considered features by deleting or combining features allocated in the same narrow neighbourhood.

A partition of the set of objects into subsets of objects, which are very similar to each other, can be obtained using similarity degrees, e.g. when adapting clustering methods by means of representation by graphs. Moreover, if some objects are declared as typical representatives of different classes, as is usual in diagnosis, then the corresponding neighbourhoods of these objects represent the desired clusters.

The neighbourhood approach to inference is closely related to the *matching degree* approach presented by TURKSEN/ZHONG (1990) and used in fuzzy control. By computation of matching degrees, which are similarity degrees in the sense given above, between the condition feature values characterising the standard situations and the corresponding condition feature values of the new situation they specify an appropriate neighbourhood of this new situation with respect to the standard situations and the condition features. Within this neighbourhood the corresponding control rules are "fired" usually modified by the computed matching degree.

6.2.3   Some Practical Examples Using Similarity

Let us now consider some examples for the determination of similarity degrees in concrete situations.

In the following a problem from chemistry is tackled, where an obtained mass spectrogram is to be compared with a given reference spectrogram. There are a lot of different influences to the observation and recording, only a small part of which can considered as of stochastic character. For instance there is no possibility of repeating the observation under fixed conditions. Hence we will consider the sample spectrum as well as the reference spectrum as fuzzy sets. Since the peaks of the spectrogram are the most interesting for the chemist, BLAFFERT (1984) suggested specifying only these peaks as fuzzy sets. For embedding of each point-shaped peak of the reference spectrogram in NAGEL/FEILER/BANDEMER (1985) two-dimensional sets B_j of bean-type (cf. (2.53)) with membership function μ_j were chosen, i.e. for each $j = 1, \ldots, k$:

$$\mu_j(x, y; x_j, y_j) = \\ [1 - c_1(x - x_j)^2 - c_2(y - y_j)^2 - c_{12}(x - x_j)(y - y_j)]^+,$$

where (x_j, y_j) are the coordinates of the peaks in the reference spectrogram and the coefficients c_1, c_2, c_{12} were fixed after extensive preliminary investigation in an existing data base and after consultations with experts. Then the reference spectrum was replaced by the union of all its "beans":

$$B = \bigcup_{j=1}^{k} B_j \tag{6.41}$$

and the *crisp* sample spectrum was replaced by the vector of its pseudo-exact peak points :

$$\mathcal{A} = \{(x_{A_1}, y_{A_1}), \ldots, (x_{A_n}, y_{A_n})\}. \tag{6.42}$$

For eliminating systematic influences with respect to *all* peaks on the retention time (x-axis) and on the intensity (y-axis) of the sample spectrum, the spectrogram was shifted "continuously" within given small intervals Δx and Δy in both directions. Then the value of the similarity degree was computed by

$$\mu_S(\mathcal{A}, B) = \sup_{\Delta x, \Delta y} \text{ card}\,(\mathcal{A} \cap B)/\text{card}\,\mathcal{A}, \tag{6.43}$$

or written in full

$$\mu_S(\mathcal{A}, B) = \sup_{\substack{|\epsilon_x| \le \Delta x; \\ |\epsilon_y| \le \Delta y}} \sum_{i=1}^{n} \max_j \mu_j(x_{A_i} + \epsilon_x, y_{A_i} + \epsilon_y; x_j, y_j)/n. \tag{6.44}$$

Here we even have an example for the similarity of a fuzzy set B and a crisp set $\mathcal{A}$. In application an upper bound m_0 will be specified and spectra with lower values will be classified as "far from the reference spectrogram". An automatic ecological supervision device being sensible to some given pollutant spectra, stored in its memory, will sound the alarm, only if this critical bound m_0 is exceeded, in order to initialise more precise investigations. The bound m_0 will be chosen after some test runs to avoid too many false alarms as well as to exclude overlooking of any dangerous situation.

This method can be adapted to the case that the standard spectrogram is a fuzzy function F with the membership function $\mu_F(y; x)$ and the sample spectrum is a (pseudo-exact) crisp function $f(x)$. Let $\mathcal{X}$ be the domain of the argument x and $\mathcal{Y}$ the universe for the ordinate. Then

$$\mu_C(x) = \mu_F(f(x); x) \tag{6.45}$$

is a fuzzy set over $\mathcal{X}$ and the similarity of F and f over $\mathcal{X}$ can be expressed by the similarity degree

$$\mu_S(F, f; \mathcal{X}) = \text{card}\,(C)/\text{card}\,\mathcal{X}. \tag{6.46}$$

An application of this approach was used in OTTO/BANDEMER (1986a) and BANDEMER/OTTO (1988) (cf. also BANDEMER/NÄTHER (1992)) for a problem of quality control of pain relieving tablets by ultraviolet spectroscopy.

In the preceding example the deviation of the two considered functions from each other at every point was evaluated only by the membership value, i.e. only indirectly. If also the amount of the deviation on the ordinate scale is important, then we will start at the difference of crisp functions and transfer this difference by an extension principle to fuzzy functions. Hence let $d(x) = f_1(x) - f_2(x)$ be the difference of the two crisp functions and $\mu_1(y; x)$ and $\mu_2(y; x)$ be the membership functions of the corresponding fuzzy functions $F_1(x)$ and $F_2(x)$, respectively. The usual extension principle yields for the fuzzy difference $D(x)$:

$$\mu_{D(x)}(y; F_1, F_2) = \sup_{(u,v):y=u-v} \min\{\mu_1(u; x), \mu_2(v; x)\}. \tag{6.47}$$

As a similarity degree we can choose, e.g., the average amount of the difference over $\mathcal{X}$:

$$d(F_1, F_2) = \int\limits_{-\infty}^{\infty} |y| \int\limits_{\mathcal{X}} \mu_{D(x)}(y; F_1, F_2) \mathrm{d}x \, \mathrm{d}y \Big/ \int\limits_{\mathcal{X}} \mathrm{d}x. \tag{6.48}$$

A suitable standardisation can simplify the interpretation within a practical context. For instance, we will divide by the corresponding average amount according to (6.48), i.e. by $d(F_1, 0)$, if one of the functions vanishes identically, and then normalise to the interval $[0, 1]$ by

$$\mu_S(F_1, F_2) = \big[1 - d(F_1, F_2)/d(F_1, 0)\big]^+. \tag{6.49}$$

Although this relation is only a weakly reflexive one, it fulfilled all the requirements of the considered problem from application in chemometrics; cf. OTTO/BANDEMER (1986c), BANDEMER/OTTO (1988), and also BANDEMER/ NÄTHER (1992).

A further field of application for the specification of similarity is *shape analysis* as used in mineral processing. Here the problem consists in an evaluation of natural or produced particles with respect to their approximate shape. The shape of the particles has, as a rule, high influence on further processing (as e.g. with cement and ground coal) or on the speed of reaction in chemical reactors or when used as granules in agriculture. When processing particles or grains in a technical environment the process is investigated theoretically only for some standard shape assumed for all the particles, perhaps differing in scale, e.g. a ball or a cube, and there is always some hope of getting an approximate theory by introducing suitable *shape factors* into the "standard" formulae. Hence this characteristic reflects the similarity of particle shape with the "ideal" theoretical shape in a parametric manner. The shape of the particle can always and need only be described in a fuzzy manner, usually it is effected, for reasons of technical feasibility, from two-dimensional representatives (cut or projection) of a single three-dimensional particle. For a subjective evaluation of natural two-dimensional shapes specialists from mineral processing (cf. BEDDOW/VETTER/SISSON (1976)) suggested a fuzzy comparator:

1. The base line of the comparator consists of a set of equidimensioned, regular figures of 3, 4, 5, 6, 7, 8 sides and (as the regular form with infinite many sides) the circle. These are the basic shapes.

2. The basic shapes are modified in one of three ways or in a combination of two ways:

   a) extension in the ratios of height to base of 2 to 1; 4 to 1; 8 to 1; or of 10 to 1;

   b) contraction in ratios of height to base 1/2; 1/4; 1/8; 1/10;

   c) skew at an angle of 30° and at an angle of 60°.

3. All shapes are normalised to the same perimeter.

Then the given shape is compared with each of these standard forms and for each of them a similarity degree is specified between 0 and 1. Obviously this procedure is only practicable in a research laboratory. For preparation of an *automatic "objectivised"* method using an image processing device some investigations were performed by KRAUT (cf. BANDEMER/KRAUT (1988)), which will be referred shortly in the following.

Again the starting-point is a two-dimensional picture of the particle as it can be seen on the screen of an image processing device. This picture is, as a rule, a grey-tone picture, in its greyness reflecting somehow the three-dimensionality of the particle and its shape. The grey-tone picture corresponds to a fuzzy region. Usually this picture is subjected to some sharpening transformation and transferred into a binary picture in black and white, frequently by choosing a certain grey-tone value as a threshold. The contour of this binarised picture is then investigated by means of Fourier transformation or of some other procedure for contour classification leading, as a rule, to a crisp shape factor. Since the greyness of the picture contains certain information on the *third* dimension of the particle, sharpening of the picture, a tried procedure in scene recognition, does not seem reasonable for the present problem. Sharpening of the *spatial* contour, even when assumed to be practicable by simple means, would provide information on the possibly very irregular surface being of only little interest in the given context. The grey-tone picture contains, in all its vagueness and fuzziness, information about the third dimension of that particle, information which may suffice for the given purpose to describe roughly its spatial shape. A systematic variant to take into consideration the spatial character of the particle by picture-fuzziness may be the following performance: The particle is presented to a camera, in different positions, say z_i, but with the centre of gravity fixed. The grey-tone pictures obtained are averaged and yield a grey-tone picture with the intensity function

$$g(x, y) = \sum_{i=1}^{n} g(x, y; z_i)/n.$$

For this purpose n must be small, because otherwise effects of spherification can occur, i.e. pictures obtained looking like targets, where a dark centre is surrounded by concentric circles of decreasing grey-tone intensity, and all information on the particle disappears.

In the following the intensity function g is assumed given, irrespective of the setting by which it was obtained. For mathematical convenience this function g is normalised in $[0, 1]$ and renamed by μ_G. Then μ_G is interpreted as the membership function of a fuzzy set G, where $\mu_G(x, y) = 1$ means that (x, y) lies in the kernel of the particle, and $\mu_G(x, y) = 0$, means that (x, y) lies outside of the particle. The intermediate values refer to points lying in the spatial contour zone of the particle, the zone which is used to characterise the spatial shape of the particle.

Although $\mu_G(x, y) \in (0, 1)$ means that (x, y) belongs to the fuzzy boundary ∂G of G, the membership of (x, y) to ∂G is not yet specified. A strict decision can be avoided by introducing a *fuzzy boundary of second type* defining for every value of membership, say $\gamma \in [0, 1]$, a fuzzy set $B_G(\gamma)$, the *fuzzy γ-boundary of G*, by

$$\mu_{B_G(\gamma)}(x, y) = \min\{\mu_G(x, y)/\gamma, (1 - \mu_G(x, y)/(1 - \gamma)\}. \tag{6.50}$$

To return to an ordinary fuzzy set, γ may be specified, crisply or fuzzily, to express prior knowledge or feeling, for which γ the boundary will make sense in the practical problem. In the context of particle shape description (cf. BANDEMER/KRAUT (1988)) the crisp value $\gamma = 0.5$ was chosen to define a *fuzzy contour C* of the fuzzy set G, in such manner specialising (6.50) to

$$\mu_C(x, y) = 2\min\{\mu_G(x, y), 1 - \mu_G(x, y)\}, \tag{6.51}$$

using the idea that the cross-line (or region) $\mu_C(x, y) = 0.5$ separates the region "still picture" from that with "already environment" in a fuzzy sense. Since no planar contour of the particle is specified this simple choice suffices in the given context. For technical application it is advisable to have the picture cleaned from artefacts and basing noise in the usual manner, e.g. by turning to

$$\mu_G^*(x, y) = \begin{cases} \mu_G(x, y), & \text{if } \mu_G \in (\epsilon_1, 1 - \epsilon_2) \\ 0 & \text{otherwise,} \end{cases}$$

with suitably chosen (small) $\epsilon_1, \epsilon_2 > 0$. This ad hoc choice suffices to get rid of the possibly shaded background and of reflections from small holes.

A more adequate and considered procedure is to use methods from fuzzy mathematical morphology (see NÄTHER/KRAUT (1993)).

Now, the idea of BEDDOW's fuzzy comparator (cf. above and in BEDDOW/VETTER/SISSON (1976)) is taken into consideration again. For coming to a small number of parameters as desired, an appropriate family of planar standard shapes is chosen, which has, in spite of this small number, a high flexibility for fitting.

This family can be specified, e.g. by considering typical spatial particles in preliminary investigation. The fuzzy contours of these are then approximated and embedded into a family of functions showing a sufficient richness. In this way even typical asymmetries can be taken into consideration. For an example with a quartz particle (cf. BANDEMER/KRAUT (1988)) the well-known family of p-ellipses

$$| x/c |^p + | y/d |^p = 1$$

was chosen, where the parameters c, d, p have obvious meanings. This choice requires some agreement with respect to the position of the contour within the coordinate system. In the present context the centre of gravity of $\operatorname{supp}(G)$ was taken as the origin and the x-axis as the direction of its largest diameter. Every triplet (c, d, p) belongs to a particular shape $\mathcal{B}(c, d, p)$ in the plane. As a *similarity degree* (sometimes called sympathy value) of the given fuzzy contour, the datum C, and the particular shape $\mathcal{B}(c, d, p)$ the relative cardinality of C along the graph of $\mathcal{B}$ was chosen

$$r(C, \mathcal{B}) = \int_{\mathcal{B}} \mu_C(x, y) \mathrm{d}s \Big/ \int_{\mathcal{B}} \mathrm{d}s. \tag{6.52}$$

with respect to the definition and to the properties cf. the following Section 6.3. For a figure and numerical results we refer to BANDEMER/KRAUT (1988) or BANDEMER/NÄTHER (1992).

For practical application the evaluation of the crisp contour according to a fuzzy comparator is still too laborious. Hence one is content with a shape parameter expressing numerically e.g. deviation of the given contour from a circle. Such a shape factor, called *roundness* s, compares the perimeter P of the contour $\mathcal{C}$ belonging to the crisp shape $\mathcal{G}$ with the perimeter of a circle covering the same area F as the contour:

$$s(\mathcal{G}) = P/[2(\pi F)^{1/2}], \tag{6.53}$$

where

$$F = \int_{\mathcal{G}} \mathrm{d}x \, \mathrm{d}y; \quad P = \int_{\mathcal{C}} \mathrm{d}s. \tag{6.54}$$

The shape factor equals 1, if $\mathcal{G}$ is a disk itself and is larger than 1 in any other case. Obviously, s is invariant with respect to motion and scale. The reciprocal function $s^{-1}(\mathcal{G})$, taking values in $[0, 1]$, can be interpreted as *degree of similarity* with a disk, a special meaning of *roundness*. For illustration, some values for crisp contours are computed:

$s^{-1}(\text{square}) = 0.886;$
$s^{-1}(\text{rectangle with ratio of sides } 1/2) = 0.835;$
$s^{-1}(\text{rectangle with ratio of sides } 1/4) = 0.709;$
$s^{-1}(\text{equilateral triangle}) = 0.777.$

To start with it is assumed that the fuzzy area F and the fuzzy perimeter P of the fuzzy shape G are given by their corresponding membership functions, say μ_F and μ_P, then the *fuzzy roundness* S^{-1} can be computed by an extension principle, e.g. by

$$\mu_{S^{-1}}(s) = \sup_{(f,p):s=2(\pi f)^{1/2}/p} \min\{\mu_F(f), \mu_P(p)\}. \tag{6.55}$$

However, with the determination of μ_F and μ_P some problems arise. The usual way starts with considering the level sets $G^{\geq \alpha}$ of G. The assumption that for every such set the corresponding perimeter $P(\alpha)$ and area $F(\alpha)$ are defined is little restrictive for practical application. When computing the area values $F(\alpha); \alpha \in (0, 1]$ it can happen that only few different values are met, e.g. if μ_G looks like a staircase pyramid. In such cases μ_F becomes multivalued, i.e. an area value can have several α's belonging to it. Hence μ_F is fuzzy itself and F is a special type-2-fuzzy set (cf. Section 2.1). Since such cases are unwieldy and puzzling in application we must look for some remedy. Because of the monotonicity of $G^{\geq \alpha}$ with respect to set inclusion, we can consider two including fuzzy sets F_{low} and F_{upp} having the membership functions

$$\mu_{F_{low}} = \sup\{\alpha : F(\alpha) \geq f\}, \tag{6.56}$$

interpreted as the degree to which "the area of G is at least f" and,

$$\mu_{F_{upp}} = \sup\{\alpha : F(\alpha) \leq f\}, \tag{6.57}$$

which means the degree that "the area of G is at most f". The intersection

$$F_* = F_{low} \cap F_{upp} \tag{6.58}$$

is a common fuzzy set, which can be used as fuzzy area value of G. The perimeter $P(\alpha)$ does not show monotonicity with respect to set inclusion. The assumption of *convexity* for G will suffice for justifying specifications with respect to P analogous to the performance for F.

A different approach for specifying a fuzzy value for the perimeter uses the fuzzy γ-boundary $B_G(\gamma)$ according to (6.50). Let Γ with $\mu_\Gamma(\gamma)$ be the fuzzy set expressing the feeling, for which γ the boundary will make sense in the given context, then

$$\mu_C(x, y) = \sup_{\gamma \in (0,1]} \min\{\mu_{B_G(\gamma)}(x, y), \mu_\Gamma(\gamma)\} \tag{6.59}$$

is a fuzzy boundary being an ordinary fuzzy set. If every α-level set $C^{\geq \alpha}$ for $\alpha \in (0, 1]$ of this fuzzy contour C consists of a simple connected set with rectifiable (inner and outer) boundaries, then the corresponding perimeter values P_{in} and $P_{out}(\alpha)$ can serve for specifying a *lower fuzzy perimeter* by

$$\mu_{P_{low}}(p) = \sup\{\alpha : \max\{P_{in}(\alpha), P_{out}(\alpha)\} \geq p\}, \tag{6.60}$$

and an *upper fuzzy perimeter* by

$$\mu_{P_{upp}}(p) = \sup\{\alpha : \min\{P_{in}(\alpha), P_{out}(\alpha)\} \leq p\}. \tag{6.61}$$

The intersection

$$P_* = P_{low} \cap P_{upp} \tag{6.62}$$

can be used as fuzzy perimeter value to be inserted in (6.55).

There is also a connection with the notion of a *twofold fuzzy set* S (cf. DUBOIS/PRADE (1983a)), defined as an ordered pair (I, C) of fuzzy sets I, C with the additional property that $\operatorname{supp}(I) \subseteq C^{\geq 1}$, where I is called the *interior* of S and C the *closure* of S. The boundary B of S is then defined by $B = C \cap I^c$. This approach can be generalised to a γ-boundary, where γ is now interpreted as the degree of feeling or prior knowledge that G is a *closed fuzzy set*. For more details cf. BANDEMER/KRAUT (1990b).

6.3 Quantitative Data Analysis

Whereas in the preceding section fuzzy data are compared and handled with respect to their similarity, they are now analysed in quantitative terms, i.e. via parametrised models. In this context problems are considered, which are, tackled with crisp data, usually with methods from mathematical statistics, using assumptions from probability theory with respect to data generation.

For *quantitative analysis of fuzzy data* there are two different approaches. On the one hand one can try to adapt methods from mathematical statistics, known for crisp data, to the case of fuzzy data, e.g. by means of an extension principle, as is put into practice by VIERTL (1990) (cf. also Section 5.3). On the other hand one can adapt the corresponding problem of mathematical statistics to the fuzzy case and try to solve it with general methods of fuzzy set theory (cf. BANDEMER/NÄTHER (1992)).

6.3.1 Preliminary Exploratory Analysis

Usually *crisp* data are given as points in a *t*-dimensional space. The *crisp* analysis starts with the arrangement of these points according to further properties, mostly with respect to their frequency in pre-assigned classes. This arrangement is connected with a search for "untypical" data (so-called *outliers*), located far away from the "bulk", the reliability and representativity of which is questioned, at least for the moment.

If the data are points in a Euclidean space, which is desired as a rule, then in a next step of analysis the "point cloud" is transformed, usually by linear transformations, to detect some structure in it. If the data space has a dimension higher than two or three, which occurs in all interesting cases, then these transformations must be *projections*, to allow a visual inspection at the screen. Now, a sequence of projections is defined by some given rule of generation, and the result, when applied to the given point cloud, is observed at the screen to find out those projections, for which a special structure in the data becomes obvious. This performance is called *projection pursuit*. Such structures may be e.g. a decomposition of the whole cloud into partial clouds or an arrangement of the bulk of the points along curves or surfaces. This technique was first used by FRIEDMAN/TUKEY (1974), and the survey paper by HUBER (1985) can be recommended for a pregnant and coherent overview. If the search is to be performed automatically, then the computer must have some *measure of interestingness* for every constellation, according to which structures of the desired type can be recorded, when occurring. This technique was generalised to fuzzy data of a generalised "bean-type" by BANDEMER/NÄTHER (1988a) (cf. also BANDEMER/NÄTHER (1992)). Most of the methods of classical multivariate analysis, e.g. principal component analysis, discriminant analysis, and some methods of factor analysis, turn out to be partial cases of the projection pursuit technique with some given measure of interestingness. An example, a special case widespread in application, is the so-called partial least squares technique, PLS for short. It goes back to WOLD (1985) and forms the essential element of his "soft modelling". This technique tries to evaluate (linear) functional relationships among non-observable (latent) variables from observable ones, assumed to be dependent on those. Also this PLS-technique was adapted to fuzzy data (cf. BANDEMER/NÄTHER (1988)).

A field of special importance in data analysis is the search for functional relationships among the components of each single datum. The knowledge of such dependencies allows substantial statements on the fact described by the data, e.g. with respect to prognosis of unknown values of data components.

A *functional relationship* is a (parametric) family of mappings of a basic space $\mathcal{X}$ of factors (influencing variables) into a space $\mathcal{Y}$ of response variables:

$$\{f(.,c)\}_{c \in \mathcal{C}} \qquad \text{with } f(.,c) : \mathcal{X} \to \mathcal{Y} \text{ for all } c \in \mathcal{C}. \tag{6.63}$$

Usually the case is considered that $\mathcal{X} \subseteq I\!\!R^k$; $\mathcal{Y} \subseteq I\!\!R^1$; $\mathcal{C} \subseteq I\!\!R^r$. Obviously, $\mathcal{Y} \subseteq I\!\!R^l$ is also possible, we will omit this case for the sake of simple presentation. A functional relationship shows some similarity to a regression set-up as used in mathematical statistics. However, in the present case response and factors can have the same (fuzzy) character.

For the following we start with the assumption that the observed data are *fuzzy sets* A_i over $\mathcal{X} \times \mathcal{Y}$ with membership functions $\mu_i(x,y)$; $i = 1, \ldots, N$.

A usual method of analysing common point-shaped data is their fitting by some functional expression. If there is no idea with respect to the type of functions suitable for such fitting, which happens frequently in preliminary investigation, the given points are connected strictly or approximately taking into consideration *only their respective neighbourhoods*. The result of this performance can be used for finding a functional relationship fitting the points within the *whole domain of interest* $\mathcal{X}$. The former problem is called a *local* setting whereas the latter is called a *global* one.

First let us consider the local setting. To avoid a proliferation of terms for this simple problem we will tackle only the two-dimensional case $(x,y) \in I\!\!R^2$.

Since the supports of the single data supp (A_i) can overlap for the local setting we must choose an aggregation principle to obtain a unique aggregated datum A. Usually the union is chosen as aggregation, mostly using the maximum.

Then a first and near at hand recommendation for a local approximation of the functional relationship of y on x is the *modal trace*

$$F_{MOD}(x) = \{y \mid y = \arg\sup_z \mu_A(x,z)\} \tag{6.64}$$

defined for all x with $\sup_z \mu_A(x,z) > 0$. Here for every x the set of all y is considered having maximum membership to A at x, naturally only within the set, where information is given by A at all. This criterion can be interpreted in the sense of possibility theory (cf. Section 5.1) as aiming at maximum possibility for the fitted values. In general the modal trace will contain more than one element of y for some x. The trace will be neither unique nor continuous, but will show the behaviour of a natural range of mountains as we may see in topographic maps. All these shortcomings will not be a disadvantage: for a first impression it suffices to recognise an occurring trend. Moreover, a premature smoothing and pressing to uniqueness and spreading into unobserved regions may alter the information inherent in the original data inadmissibly and can be misleading for the following. If the trace branches out into several clearly separated ranges with respect to y, then we should inspect the original data for outliers, reconsider their specification, or, remind the possibility that the functional relationship can have an *implicit* form.

In the case of an implicit functional relationship the principle of modal trace can be modified. Interpreting now the values of the membership function μ_A as values of height in a topographical map, then we may adopt a principle of *watersheds*, where only those ridges are chosen to support the approximation, which are watersheds of the fuzzy "mountains". Methods for calculating such watersheds can be found in BANDEMER/HULSCH/LEHMANN (1986).

With respect to further principles for determination of local approximations we refer to BANDEMER/NÄTHER (1992), where also further literature is cited.

6.3.2   Evaluating Functional Relationships

For the treatment of the *global* setting there are at least two different attitudes for a model understanding. First we will turn to the *explorative* attitude. Here the data are taken as they are. Statements on the functional relationship use only these data and refer only to those parts of $\mathcal{X} \times \mathcal{Y}$, which are covered by the support supp (A) of the unified datum A. When considering the problem in the sense of *approximation* according to the second attitude, which we will tackle later, assumptions are introduced, which allow inclusion of regions outside that support as well.

For the explorative case we start with the functional relationship (6.63) and try to transfer the obtained (fuzzy) information contained in the fuzzy data $A_1, \ldots, A_N$ into the parameter set $\mathcal{C}$ of the functional relationship. The corresponding mapping

$$V : \mathbb{F}((\mathcal{X} \times \mathcal{Y})^N) \to \mathbb{F}(\mathcal{C}) \qquad (6.65)$$

is called *transfer principle*. The evaluation of every function $f(., c)$ of the functional relationship (6.63) is a fuzzy evaluation of c, i.e. by the membership function $\mu_C(c)$ of a mapping $C(A_1, \ldots, A_N)$.

The mapping V consists of two operations: an *aggregating* one V_{AGG}, which removes the dependence on the individuality of the data (represented by the index i), and an *integrating* one V_{INT}, which removes the dependence on the diversity of the x-points in the domain.

For mathematical convenience, theoretically as well as numerically, the two operations were specified individually and applied one after another. The proposed transfer principles used differ from each other in the specification of the partial mappings and in the order of their application.

Let us start with the aggregation of the data, i.e. with

$$A = V_{AGG}(A_1, \ldots, A_N). \tag{6.66}$$

If we look for points which belong to at least one of the fuzzy data A_i, and hence will possibly be met as points of the functional relationship, then we have to *join* all the A_i's, e.g. by maximising

$$A = \bigcup_{i=1}^{N} A_i \ : \quad \mu_A(x, y) = \max_i \mu_i(x, y). \tag{6.67}$$

If we want to use each datum at every point with equal rights, perhaps with different degrees of trustworthiness $\beta_i \in [0, 1]$, then we can collect them by averaging, i.e. computing a datum A with the membership function

$$\mu_A(x, y) = \sum_{i=1}^{N} \beta_i \mu_i(x, y), \tag{6.68}$$

with suitable chosen β_i's, such that μ_A remains in $[0, 1]$.

If we take as useful only such information that is contained in each of the given data, then even intersection of the data, e.g. by

$$A = \bigcap_{i=1}^{N} A_i \ : \quad \mu_A(x, y) = \min_i \mu_i(x, y) \tag{6.69}$$

makes sense as an aggregation principle.

Finally, if we want to make the transfer principles more robust against "outliers", we can allow that only a subset of the data is to be taken into consideration in the aggregation. Let $\mathcal{N}(n)$ denote the set of all subsets consisting of exactly $n \leq N$ elements, then

$$A : \mu_A(x, y) = \max_{H \in \mathcal{N}(n)} \min_{i \in H} \mu_i(x, y) \tag{6.70}$$

is a generalisation of (6.69).

Now, we can apply an integrating operation V_{INT} to the *unified datum A*. In general,

$$\mu_{A(f(., c))}(x) = \mu_A(x, f(x, c)); \quad x \in \mathcal{X} \tag{6.71}$$

represents the degree to which the graph $\{(x, f(x, c))\}_{x \in \mathcal{X}}$ hits the unified datum A in x for a given parameter value c. Considered over $\mathcal{X}$ then $A(f(., c))$ is a fuzzy set, i.e.

$$A(f(., c)) \in \mathbb{F}(\mathcal{X}). \tag{6.72}$$

Now, every integrating operation V_{INT} is an evaluation principle for $A(f(.,c))$ and hence for c.

For specifying a quite simple integrating operation we choose some weight function $w : \mathcal{X} \to I\!\!R^+ \cup \{0\}$ with $\int_{\mathcal{X}} w(x)\mathrm{d}x = 1$, expressing some additional knowledge or desirable requirements. For example, with

$$w(x) = w_0 \cdot \sup_y \mu_A(x, y) \tag{6.73}$$

we weight every x by the modal trace value of the membership (6.65) and omit regions without any information by fuzzy data.

Then

$$C_1^* : \mu_{C_1^*}(c) = \int_{\mathcal{X}} \mu_A(x, f(x, c)) w(x)\,\mathrm{d}x \tag{6.74}$$

is a (quantitative) evaluation and together with the chosen V_{AGG} a useful transfer principle. If $w(x)$ was chosen as the density of a certain probability measure, then (6.74) has the character of an expectation value. This has tempted use of the misleading term "transfer principle of expected cardinality" in early papers (cf. BANDEMER (1985)). Obviously, probabilistic interpretations are possible, but not necessary (cf. BANDEMER/NÄTHER (1992)). Naturally, if it makes sense and can be computed simply, a Sugeno integral can be used instead of the usual one in (6.74) (cf. Section 5.2). Finally, the membership function of $A(f(.,c))$ can also be interpreted as a possibility distribution leading to

$$C_2^* : \quad \mu_{C_2^*}(c) = \sup_x \mu_A(x, f(x, c)). \tag{6.75}$$

The given examples may suffice. Obviously, each aggregating operation with $A = V_{AGG}(A_1, \ldots, A_N)$ can be combined with an integrating operation $C^* = V_{INT}(A)$, if this combination makes sense in the practical problem.

Now, we turn to the opposite order of applying the operations, i.e. $C_i = V_{INT}(A_i)$ and $C^* = V_{AGG}(C_1, \ldots, C_N)$.

A first suggestion for V_{INT} is motivated by the extension principle and leads to the membership function

$$\mu_{C_{i,1}}(c) = \sup_{(x,y):y=f(x,c)} \mu_i(x, y) = \sup_x \mu_i(x, f(x, c)). \tag{6.76}$$

The membership function for C_i can be interpreted as the uncertainty induced by the fuzzy datum A_i to the parameter set $\mathcal{C}$, possibly as a sort of possibility distribution. The same operation is obtained, if the usual statement on the validity of a relation in a given set is fuzzified (cf. BANDEMER/SCHMERLING

(1985) and BANDEMER/NÄTHER (1992)). Obviously, the integral (6.74) can be computed also for each i separately leading to

$$\mu_{C_{i,2}}(c) = \int\limits_{\mathcal{X}} \mu_i(x, f(x,c))w_i(x)\,\mathrm{d}x, \qquad (6.77)$$

where the weight function may vary from datum to datum according to the practical context.

Having mapped each single datum into $\mathbb{F}(\mathcal{C})$ we have to aggregate the pictures according to some chosen V_{AGG}. Now, we will consider some proposals for this performance.

An *intersection*, e.g. by minimum

$$\mu_{C_3^*}(c) = \min_i \mu_{C_i}(c), \qquad (6.78)$$

can be explained as the degree that each of the fuzzy data A_i contains a point of the functional relationship $f(., c)$. Hence C_3^* was at first called "joint grade of validity" of the functional relationship with respect to the given data, cf. BANDEMER/SCHMERLING (1985). Naturally, in analogy with (6.70), only the "best" selection of the n data can be taken into consideration for aggregation. Yet another possibility is aggregation by averaging. This is preferred, when the data are taken from frequency records.

With respect to further principles and, in general, to special properties of and differences between the principles we refer to BANDEMER/NÄTHER (1992).

For a practical example, the investigation of the relationship between the value of Vicker's hardness and the distance to a hardened surface of a micro specimen, cf. BANDEMER/KRAUT (1990a) and BANDEMER/NÄTHER (1992).

6.3.3   Approximation of or by Functional Relationships

Up to now fuzzy data are handled only from the exploratory attitude, outside the support of the data no information was expected or used. This led to the recommendation to consider only that part of $\mathcal{X}$, on which the unified datum was projected, and to the strange result that sometimes C_1^* can be the empty set, e.g., if there is no $f(., c)$, the graph of which hits all given data simultaneously, although a lot of those graphs runs *through* the data "cloud".

Hence there are some proposals to overcome this unwanted property, taking into account *neighbourhoods* of the functions or of the data or of both these sets. The crisp or fuzzy parameter of the functional relationship is then determined by an optimisation procedure. Such proposals form the bridge to modelling assumptions with respect to the origin of the data, e.g. as being realisations of random fuzzy variables. In the following we will present, shortly, three proposals for *approximation principles* of this kind.

In the so-called *transfer principle for belts* instead of the graph of some $f(.,c)$ of the functional relationship its whole belt

$$\{f(.,c)+\Delta\}_{\Delta\in I\!\!R^1} \tag{6.79}$$

is considered. For every specified $\Delta_0 > 0$ this determines a neighbourhood of $f(.,c)$. Introducing (6.79) into a transfer principle leads to a fuzzy set over $\mathcal{C} \times I\!\!R^1$. The membership function of this set or of a set derived from it is now maximised within $|\Delta| \leq \Delta_0$. For more details cf. BANDEMER/NÄTHER (1992).

An other approach for "broadening" of $f(.,c)$ can be managed by replacing it by a fuzzifying function $F(.,c)$, of which it forms the kernel-function (cf. Section 2.2). Then the *individual* distance of each fuzzy datum from this *fuzzy* functional relationship is considered, i.e.

$$d(A_i, F(.,c)), \tag{6.80}$$

where d is some given distance defined for fuzzy sets on $\mathcal{X} \times \mathcal{Y}$.

The general principle consists of aggregating the distances with respect to i and in finding a parameter value $c^* \in \mathcal{C}$, for which the aggregated distance is minimum. Examples for this approach are given in CELMINS (1987), DIAMOND (1988), ALBRECHT (1992), and more extended in DIAMOND/KLOEDEN (1994); a detailed review is contained in BANDEMER/NÄTHER (1992).

Finally an approach of TANAKA is to be mentioned (cf. TANAKA/UEJIMA/ASAI (1982), TANAKA/WATADA (1988)), in which fuzziness of the data is allowed only with respect to the y-direction and in form of fuzzy numbers and only for linear functional relationships (cf. BANDEMER/NÄTHER (1992) for a review). In the meantime also the case with fuzziness in x- and y-directions was treated. For results we refer to SAKAWA/YANO (1992).

Sometimes a purely local consideration of the unified datum A, e.g. using the modal trace, is not satisfactory, however, on the other hand, the assumption of a global functional relationship seems to be too strong. Such a situation can happen, when the modal trace is rather broad and busy and shows small gaps, into which the support of the datum does not reach, but is nevertheless of interest. In the case of crisp data this problem is handled by empirical regression. The intention of this method is a smooth local approximation of the functional relationship, to which the data are assumed to belong, besides some superimposed random errors. The idea of the method is quite simple. Within a certain window, i.e. a small interval or segment of the space of independent coordinates, usually endowed with an *internal weight function*, the functional relationship is approximated by some simple set-up, e.g. a constant or a linear or, at the utmost, a quadratic function. This approximation is used only in the centre of the window, in practice in a small subset around this centre. Then the window is shifted by a small element of the line or by a vector element of small size, respectively, and the performance is repeated, until the whole region of interest is filled with approximating pieces for the functional relationship. These pieces are connected to form a smooth approximation. The connection is no problem in practice, since it is usually performed by a computer according to some "reasonable" given principle.

This approach can be adapted easily to fuzzy data. Let $w(x; x_0)$ be the internal weight function, vanishing outside the window, where x_0 is the mid-point of the window. For an approximation we choose – in the case $\mathcal{Y} \subseteq I\!\!R^1$ – either $f_0(x, c) = c_0$, $f_1(x, c) = c_0 + c_1 x$, or $f_2(x, c) = c_0 + c_1 x + c_2 x^2$. For an evaluation of c within the window we take a suitable transfer principle, cf. (6.65). As an example we consider the principle

$$\mu_{C^*}(c; x_0) = \int_{\mathcal{X}} \mu(x, f(x, c)) w(x, x_0)\, \mathrm{d}x. \tag{6.81}$$

This evaluation can be used to calculate a fuzzy value of the chosen simple functional relation f at x_0 by the extension principle

$$\mu_f(y; x_0) = \sup_{c:y=f(x_0,c)} \mu_{C^*}(c; x_0). \tag{6.82}$$

In analogy with the usual performance in empirical regression we can also obtain values in the neighbourhood of x_0 by

$$\mu_f(y; x) = \sup_{c:y=f(x,c)} \mu_{C^*}(c; x_0). \tag{6.83}$$

The further performance is then totally analogous to that with crisp data with shifting of the window and smoothing connection of the obtained fuzzy values.

Further generalisations in this sense are *fuzzy spline approximation* and a partially fuzzy adaptation of *multiphase regression*. With respect to the latter case cf. BANDEMER/BELLMANN (1991) and BANDEMER/NÄTHER (1992)).

6.3.4   Other Problems of Fuzzy Inference

In mathematical regression the obtained estimates of the parameters in a regression set-up are used for different problems of inference, e.g. for predicting the response at further observation points or for discriminating among competing models.

In fuzzy data analysis for evaluation of a functional relationship, interpreted either as estimation or as approximation, a fuzzy parameter set C^* is obtained, e.g. via a transfer principle. By this set over $\mathcal{X}$ a parameter fuzzy functional relationship

$$y = f(x, C), \qquad C \in I\!\!F(\mathcal{C}) \tag{6.84}$$

can be specified, forming the basis of a corresponding inference. The star at C is omitted in the following, since the origin of the fuzzy parameter set is not essential for the inference. The set could also be specified by a panel of experts.

For inference from (6.84) the extension principle is usually used. For the fuzzy value Y *interpolated* at the crisp point x_0 we obtain the membership function

$$\mu_Y(y; x_0) = \sup_{c:y=f(x_0,c)} \mu_C(c) \tag{6.85}$$

and at the fuzzy point $X_0 \in \mathbb{F}(\mathcal{X})$

$$\mu_Y(y; X_0) = \sup_{(c,x):y=f(x,c)} \min\{\mu_C(c), \mu_{X_0}(x)\}. \tag{6.86}$$

The formulae can be used for *extrapolation* as well, but with due caution, since extrapolation includes the silent assumption that the functional relationship is valid also in the extrapolation point.

In contrast with the difficulties found in the statistical approach, the problem of *calibration* is now symmetrical to that of interpolation. For the given crisp value y_0 the fuzzy argument X is calibrated by

$$\mu_X(x; y_0) = \sup_{c:y_0=f(x,c)} \mu_C(c) \tag{6.87}$$

and for the fuzzy value $Y_0 \in \mathbb{F}(\mathbb{R}^1)$ the calibrated argument value X is given by the membership function

$$\mu_X(x; Y_0) = \sup_{(c,x):y=f(x,c)} \min\{\mu_C(c), \mu_{Y_0}(y)\}. \tag{6.88}$$

Applications of these formulae in problems of chemometrics can be found in OTTO/BANDEMER (1986, 1988a, 1988b).

A further interesting problem of inference consists in the combination of fuzzily expressed information on the parameter c, obtained from different sources. Let, e.g., $C_P \in \mathbb{F}(\mathcal{C})$ be a fuzzy set specifying prior knowledge on c and $C_E \in \mathbb{F}(\mathcal{C})$ be the result of an estimation of c according to an extension principle.

In a first step we can multiply the respective membership function with factors of relative trustworthiness evaluating the information contained in each of the parameter sets, from an objective or from a subjective point of view. Then, in a second step, we will choose a connective, usually a t-norm, to combine the two sets. Finally, in a third step, the obtained result can be renormalised in a certain sense. Particularly, if the two sets are to be used

with equal rights, combined by *intersection expressed by the minimum* of the
membership functions, and renormalised by the *supremum*, then the result is

$$\mu_C(c \mid A) = \frac{\min\{\mu_P(c), \mu_E(c)\}}{\sup_{b \in C} \min\{\mu_P(b), \mu_E(b)\}}, \qquad (6.89)$$

where $\mid A$ means that the data $A_1, \ldots, A_N$ are taken into consideration, via
C_E. This is a fuzzy analogue of the well-known Bayes formula: if we interpret
the membership functions as possibility density functions (cf. Section 5.1),
then by (6.89) a possibilistic prior distribution is coupled with an actual possibility distribution yielding an a-posteriori distribution.

An interesting application in geostatistics, combining the Bayesian approach for kriging with fuzzy prior knowledge and fuzzy observations was
suggested recently by BANDEMER/GEBHARDT (1995).

Let us now turn to the problem of *model discrimination*. This problem
occurs if there are several functional relationships, say

$$f_1(., c^{(1)}), \ldots, f_r(., c^{(r)})); \quad c^{(j)} \in C_j;\ j = 1, \ldots, r \qquad (6.90)$$

competing to be used, motivated each either by different ideas with regard
to their respective scientific interpretation, or, merely, by the demand for a
good approximation with a number of parameters as small as possible. The
choice must be made with respect to a set of given fuzzy data $A_1, \ldots, A_N$. A
near at hand procedure consists in an evaluation of the parameters in each
given functional relationship, according to the same transfer principle, and in
an evaluation of the respective fitting of the data by the so obtained fuzzy
parameter functional relationships. As a measure of good fitting a measure
of fuzziness could be useful, which reflects the idea of the user of the desired
kind of goodness. As an example we consider the transfer principle with
$V_{INT} = \sup_x, V_{AGG} = \min_i$, then

$$\text{hgt}\,(C_j) = \sup_{c \in C_j} \min_i \sup_x \mu_i(x, f_j(x, c)) \qquad (6.91)$$

yields a useful criterion for the selection of a model f_j. The value on the left
side of (6.91) expresses, for each j, the highest membership value that the
graph of the respective functional relationship can reach for all fuzzy data
simultaneously. If there is only one datum, which is not met by the graph,
the corresponding membership function will vanish. Hence this principle is
a good one for model discrimination. However, the decision using the height
is based on only one point, hence we may consider also the approach by
CZOGALA/GOTTWALD/PEDRYCZ (1982), using a combination of height and
cardinality, as a possible basis for a decision. The approach was already
presented in Section 5.5 (cf. also BANDEMER/NÄTHER (1992)).

6.3.5 Sequential Optimisation of Fuzzifying Functions

Another field of application for mathematical statistics is *sequential optimisation* of empirically given functions. The problem occurs mainly in controlling, where a response is to be optimised depending on a vector of adjustable control variable. In real world problems the relationship between the response variable and the control variables cannot usually be described precisely and strictly by mathematical terms and the relationship is influenced by additional factors, usually assumed to be of random character. Moreover, the control variables can be adjusted only approximately and the response value allows only a coarse description, e.g. owing to the coarseness of the given scale. Usually this vagueness and impreciseness is omitted and only random errors are taken into account, superimposed to the crisp value of a "true" functional relationship. Sequential procedures suitable to this case are available in sufficient diversity, cf. e.g. Box/WILSON (1951) and KIEFER/WOLFOWITZ (1952).

It is possible to take the opposite view in neglecting the random error in favour of fuzziness. This point of view seems appropriate, when possible random deviations are much smaller than impreciseness and vagueness, e.g. when the quantity to be optimised can only be described verbally, as the operational robustness of a machine or the washability of a dress, in spite of long but questionable check lists for evaluation of these properties. In such cases it seems more appropriate to specify a linguistic variable for the property expressing either the stage of the property itself or some (fuzzy) degree of satisfaction with respect to the property. Moreover, some of the conditions of production can be described verbally, too, e.g. some properties of the material used. Even if the control variables are adjusted by a control equipment, e.g., the temperature by a thermostat, the actual values are imprecise and not known exactly. Optimisation of the response variable in such cases is frequently of interest to improve some properties of the product by investigation or in the course of production.

An approach for solving such problems was given in BANDEMER (1991). The response is interpreted as a fuzzy mapping F with the membership function $\mu_F(x, .)$ defined on a (compact) part of the $\mathbb{R}^k$. Without loss of generality we assume that the function is to be minimised.

Introducing the α-minimum of F

$$y_{min}(\alpha; F) = \inf\{y \in \mathcal{Y} \mid \mu_F(x, y) \geq \alpha\} \tag{6.92}$$

the *fuzzy minimum* of F (cf. DUBOIS/PRADE (1980)) is defined by

$$F_{min} : \quad \mu_{F_{min}}(y) = \sup\{\alpha \mid y = y_{min}(\alpha; F)\}. \tag{6.93}$$

Special condition on F are omitted here (cf. BANDEMER (1991) or BANDEMER/NÄTHER (1992)).

It does not make much sense, under the above mentioned conditions of impreciseness and vagueness, to look for a crisp value $x \in \mathcal{X}$, where the function F assumes its minimum. Under these circumstances and for the given purpose it will suffice completely to find a region, where the response is *approximately* minimum. Let us tolerate a deviation of $\Delta > 0$ with Δ "small" in our practical context. Then we define a *target region* $Z(\Delta, \alpha; F)$ for the process of minimising by

$$
\begin{aligned}
Z(\Delta, \alpha; F) \;=\; \{x \in \mathcal{X} \mid \exists y \in I\!\!R^1 \,\big(y \leq y_{min}(\alpha; F) + \Delta \\
\wedge \, (x, y) \in \mathrm{supp}\,(F)\big)\}. \quad (6.94)
\end{aligned}
$$

This target region is to be estimated by means of fuzzy observations $A_i \in I\!\!F(\mathcal{X} \times \mathcal{Y})$.

For estimation of the minimum one prefers such observations in which the response shows very small values. Hence it is necessary to introduce a suitable ordering among fuzzy observations. For fuzzy numbers there are many proposals, cf. e.g. ZADEH (1978), DUBOIS/PRADE (1983b), ROMMELFANGER (1994). In BANDEMER (1991) (cf. also BANDEMER/NÄTHER (1992)) suggestions by KLAUA (1966, 1966a), which had been proved a sound basis for similarity relations among fuzzy sets, are used anew starting with the crisp order relation to specify an ordering of fuzzy numbers. An example of such an evaluation of the larger-than-or-equal relation for fuzzy sets is the following

$$
r_{(optmin)}(A, B, \leq) = \sup_{u \leq v} \min\{\mu_A(u), \mu_B(v)\}, \quad (6.95)
$$

which corresponds to some degree of dominance in the literature cited above (cf. also BANDEMER/NÄTHER (1992)).

With a vector of *degrees of oblivion* we can favour "small" response values obtained against "larger" ones in constructing estimations for the target region. It is even possible to establish a concept of *fuzzy experimental design*, i.e. for the allocation of the next fuzzy observation point, possibly including prior knowledge with respect to the approximate location of the target region, via a pseudo-Bayesian performance. For more details we refer to the literature cited above.

With the analogies and adaptations of methods of statistical data analysis and inference just presented, the possibilities for a fuzzy data analysis are by no means exhausted. The reader will easily find more problems which invite similar treatment.

6.4   Evaluation of Methods in Fuzzy Data Analysis

In the preceding sections the methods presented are considered from the point of view of exploratory data analysis. The methods are explained and some-times some of their properties are mentioned. For a further mathematical treatment of the problems these methods are to be *ordered*, i.e. *evaluated* under special assumptions. We look at the methods *from outside* and com-pare them with each other. A *normative* theory, as there is, e.g., for math-ematical statistics, is not yet established for fuzzy data analysis. Interesting and promising beginnings are due to W. NÄTHER (cf. BANDEMER/NÄTHER (1992), Chapter 7).

We consider the problem in the manner of speaking of an experimentor. The first question after an experiment is always: What has happened? This question focuses all attention only at the one, possibly aggregated, *realised* outcome. All other previously possible outcomes are out of consideration. To answer our question we only need procedures from exploratory analysis. Another version of the above question is: What is meant by the possibly ver-bally described result of the experiment? If the result is uncertain, imprecise or vague, then it will be specified by a fuzzy datum and analysed by one of the suggested methods. Also this is exploratory data analysis, analysing the *realised* outcome. Further use of statements from this analysis, e.g. for prediction of further experimental results, bases only on the general scientific hypothesis: In similar cases we expect similar results.

Consider now the question, also after experimentation: What result of the experiment *will happen* in future? For a mathematical treatment of this ques-tion one has to take into consideration all possible outcomes. Evaluation of *all possible outcomes* requires a *model* about the uncertainty of the outcomes and a *theory* within this model, resulting in a justification of the appropri-ate inference rules and in an evaluation of predictions. We will call such a theory *normative analysis*. In some sense, the one realised outcome loses its individuality and is embedded into an ensemble of potential outcomes. In this connection we will speak about a *modelling of the environment*, which is assumed to generate the uncertainty of the data. In such a situation a pro-babilistic model of the data is often used, but other models are also imaginable and reasonable (e.g. possibilistic models or general fuzzy-measure models). With respect to the context here displayed, fuzziness belongs mainly to ex-ploratory analysis, whereas probability leads to (a possible kind of) normative theory of data analysis. Real situations, however, require both, strictly. The outcomes are specified as fuzzy data, however, we are not only interested in an exploratory analysis of the given "sample" but also in theoretically justified prediction. This requires a *normative analysis of fuzzy data*. Such a theory is just at its beginning. Most of the results reached up to now are with respect to probabilistic environments, which leads to a *statistical analysis of fuzzy data*. A general aim of a normative analysis for fuzzy data could be a *decision theory for fuzzy data*.

For preparing the presentation of some ideas for a normative data analysis we will consider *evaluated fuzzy data*. An *evaluation* (of fuzzy data) is a function defined for the set of all fuzzy sets, the data, over the corresponding universe. i.e.

$$g : I\!\!F(\mathcal{X}) \rightarrow [0,1]. \tag{6.96}$$

Examples are
a) evaluation by a fuzzy measure Q

$$g(A) = Q(A); \tag{6.97}$$

b) especially by the probability measure P

$$g(A) = \mathrm{Prob}_P(A) = \int_{\mathcal{X}} \mu_A(x) \mathrm{d}P(x); \tag{6.98}$$

c) especially by a possibility measure with the distribution function π

$$g(A) = \mathrm{Poss}_\pi(A) = \sup_{x \in \mathcal{X}} \min\{\mu_A(x), \pi(x)\}; \tag{6.99}$$

d) evaluation by the truth of A with respect to some x_0, which is simply another interpretation of the membership value of A at x_0

$$g(A) = \mathrm{Truth}_{x_0}(A) = \mu_A(x_0); \tag{6.100}$$

e) finally, evaluation by the relative cardinality with respect to a given density $p(.)$ (of a normalised measure over $\mathcal{X}$), cf. (2.22),

$$g(A) = \mathrm{card}_{rel(p)}(A) = \int_{\mathcal{X}} \mu_A(x)p(x)\,\mathrm{d}x. \tag{6.101}$$

Note that the evaluation function g can be interpreted as membership function for the fuzzy sets A to a fuzzy set on $I\!\!F(\mathcal{X})$, e.g. $g(A) = \mathrm{Prob}_P(A)$ as the membership function of all probable data according to P from $I\!\!F(\mathcal{X})$.

A fuzzy datum A is called g-*evaluated* with the degree $t \in [0,1]$, iff

$$g(A) = t. \tag{6.102}$$

This can be generalised to *fuzzily g-evaluated data* by specifying linguistic degrees $T \in I\!\!F([0,1])$ and introducing statements of the form

$$g(A) \quad \text{is} \quad T \tag{6.103}$$

Examples for this approach are the following:

"The probability that the device has a high lifetime is rather low",

which reads in the language of Chapter 4

Prob(high_lifetime) is rather_low,

and

"Most of the devices have high lifetime",

written in the corresponding form

card $_{rel}$(high_lifetime) is high.

For a treatment of a crisply or fuzzily evaluated fuzzy datum A by data analysis the main question is: How can we translate such a datum into a common fuzzy datum C over an appropriate universe? Now, with $u = g$ the datum (6.103) is a linguistic statement (a linguistic datum) in the sense of Chapter 4. The fuzzy evaluation T is a fuzzy set from $I\!\!F([0,1])$, but the "elements" t of T are the possible evaluation degrees of the fuzzy datum A, i.e. $t = g(A)$, (cf. (6.102)). Hence we have some kind of chain-rule and define

$$\mu_C(g) := \mu_T(g(A)), \qquad (6.104)$$

which, for given A and T, can be regarded as a membership function on the universe $[0,1]^{F(\mathcal{X})}$ of all evaluation functions and hence defines there a fuzzy set, say C. Thus, the translation rule of a fuzzily evaluated fuzzy datum "$g(A)$ is T" into a common fuzzy datum C reads

$$g(A) \text{ is } T \Rightarrow C \qquad \text{with} \qquad \mu_C(g) = \mu_T(g(A)). \qquad (6.105)$$

This relatively complicated assignment becomes more applicable if we replace the whole universe $[0,1]^{F(\mathcal{X})}$ by a suitable class of evaluation functions, preferably by a parametric family, e.g. of probability measures. For some examples cf. BANDEMER/NÄTHER (1992).

In the following the evaluation is used for another purpose: For a given evaluation principle, given (common fuzzy) data, and a given data analysis problem a solution is to be determined, the evaluation degree of which is as good as possible. For a numerical performance we restrict ourselves to parametric problems. This is, however, no restriction for practical application, since practical problems are nearly always given in a parametric form, cf. the preceding sections of the present chapter.

For the following we assume that $c \in I\!\!R^r$. As a simple example we consider the fuzzy straight line

$$Y = C_1 + C_2 z; \quad z \in I\!\!R^1; \qquad (6.106)$$

where $C_i = < m_i; \delta_i, \delta_i >_{L/L} = [m_i, \delta_i]_L$ for $i = 1, 2$ are symmetric fuzzy numbers; cf. (2.189). Then the four-dimensional vector

$$c = (m_1, \delta_1, m_2, \delta_2)^{\mathsf{T}} \qquad\qquad (6.107)$$

represents the parameter of interest.

Given N fuzzy data $A_1, \ldots, A_N$, the result of parametric fuzzy data analysis will be an "estimate"

$$C^* = C^*(A_1, \ldots, A_N). \qquad\qquad (6.108)$$

Since the data-input is fuzzy it seems reasonable to require that the output is fuzzy, too, i.e. $C^* \in IF(IR^r)$. Sometimes, however, we are satisfied just with a crisp representative c^* of C^*.

Our aim is to *evaluate* C^* or c^* *by normative methods* which arise from a reasonable modelling of the data environment and choosing such sets or values being optimum with respect to this evaluation.

We will consider here only some examples, with respect to theoretical investigations and special results we have to refer to BANDEMER/NÄTHER (1992).

When *evaluating by truth* a fuzzy parameter set $M(c) \in F(\mathcal{X})$ is chosen, called a parametric *set-up*, specified by the corresponding membership function, e.g. for the example according to (6.106), by

$$\mu_{M(c)}(z, y) = L\left(\frac{|y - m_1 - m_2 z|}{\delta_1 + \delta_2|z|}\right). \qquad\qquad (6.109)$$

Here $M(c)$ appears as a set-up in $F(IR^2)$ for the fuzzifying straight line.

Coming back to general set-ups $M(c)$ with $c \in C \subset IR^r$ the evaluation of the datum A_i with respect to $M(c)$ focuses at the "size" of A_i along the t-level line of $M(c)$,

$$M^{=t}(c) \quad =_{\text{def}} \quad \{x \in \mathcal{X} \mid \mu_{M(c)}(x) = t\}. \qquad\qquad (6.110)$$

Denoting the restriction of A_i to $M^{=t}(c)$ by $A_i \mid M^{=t}(c)$ and having in mind that the "size" of fuzzy sets can be evaluated by energy measures F (cf. Section 5.5), for an evaluation of A_i with respect to $M(c)$ we suggest the fuzzy set $T_i(c)$ over $[0, 1]$ with

$$\mu_{T_i(c)}(t) := F(A_i \mid M^{=t}(c)), \qquad\qquad (6.111)$$

with the best known specifications

$$\mu_{T_i(c)}(t) = \text{hgt}\,(A_i \mid M^{=t}(c)) = \sup_{x:\mu_{M(c)}(x)=t} m_i(x) \qquad\qquad (6.112)$$

and

$$\mu_{T_i(c)}(t) = \mathrm{card}_p(A_i \mid M^{=t}(c)) = \int\limits_{M^{=t}(c)} m_i(x)p(x)\,\mathrm{d}x. \qquad (6.113)$$

Note that (6.112) coincides with the compatibility of A_i with respect to $M(c)$, sometimes called the truth of A_i with respect to $M(c)$ (cf. YAGER (1984a)). This motivates the general notion also for (6.111).

The problem now consists in finding such a set-up $M(c^*)$ which is as true as possible for *all* given data. For a solution we have to choose an aggregation principle with respect to i and then to optimise with respect to the specified evaluation criterion. With respect to details we have to refer to BANDEMER/NÄTHER (1992).

This special approach via an evaluation with respect to truth appears as a mixture of exploratory and normative attitude. On the one side, the set-up $M(c)$ is assumed to describe not only the actual data but also all other potential data. This is the normative component of the approach. On the other hand, nothing is assumed about the concrete mechanism of data generation. Thus, we evaluate estimators of c only with respect to a given set-up $M(c)$ and not with respect to some kind of risk, e.g. with respect to an "expected" truth.

When *evaluating with respect to possibility*, unlike in the preceding case, the membership function of $M(c)$ is interpreted as a possibility distribution function:

$$\mu_{M(c)}(x) =: \pi(x, c). \qquad (6.114)$$

Now, as a model for the mechanism of data generation we assume that the crisp kernels, say $x_1, x_2, \ldots, x_N$, of the fuzzy data are realisations of a possibilistic variable X.

A possibilistic variable can be defined as follows. Let $(\Omega, I\!\!B_\Omega), (U, I\!\!B_U)$ be two measurable spaces and Poss a possibility measure over Ω, cf. Section 5.1, which is σ-finite, i.e. for any sequence $\{\mathcal{B}_i\}$ with $\mathcal{B}_i \in I\!\!B_\Omega$ it holds

$$\mathrm{Poss}\left(\bigcup_i \mathcal{B}_i\right) = \sup_i \mathrm{Poss}\,(\mathcal{B}_i).$$

Then a $(I\!\!B_\Omega, I\!\!B_U)$-measurable mapping $X : \Omega \to U$ is called a possibilistic variable on Ω.

Assuming so, the given data A_i, in some sense, lose their individuality. We only take the crisp kernels and model a common possibility law behind them, the idea of which comes from an "aggregated view" on the data leading to $M(c)$. The crisp kernels lead to a crisp estimator c^*. As an advantage, this approach offers an evaluation of the estimator c^* with respect to all potential outcomes. From the possibility measure $Poss_c$ according to (6.114) the possibility measure $Poss_{c^*|c}$ of c^* for fixed c can be derived. An evaluation of c^* may consist in a calculation of the possibility that c^* belongs to a certain parameter region J of interest, e.g.

$$\text{Poss}_{c^*|c}(J) = \sup_{t \in R^r} \min\{\pi_{c^*|c}(t), \mu_J(t)\}. \tag{6.115}$$

Moreover, a possibilistic risk can be introduced, i.e. a possibilistically evaluated loss function, by which the loss is evaluated gradually, cf. Section 5.4.

Finally we can consider a *probability evaluation* , where the fuzzy data A_i are interpreted as realisations of a random variable $\mathbf{X} : \Omega \to I\!\!F(\mathcal{X})$ living on a probability space $(\Omega, I\!\!B_\Omega, P)$. Since the range of $\mathbf{X}$ consists in fuzzy sets on $\mathcal{X}$, the mapping $\mathbf{X}$ usually is called *fuzzy random variable* (cf. Section 5.3).

Assume this fuzzy random variable depends on the unknown parameter of interest, i.e.

$$\mathbf{X} = \mathbf{X}(c). \tag{6.116}$$

For example consider a fuzzy random number $X = [m, \delta]_L$ with random centre m and random spread δ. Denote $c_1 = Em, c_2 = E\delta$ and let $c = (c_1, c_2)^\top$ be the parameter of interest.

Then the determination of the parameter vector c is a *statistical* problem and an estimator $c^*(A_1, \ldots, A_N)$ will be evaluated e.g. by the probability that c^* belongs to a certain region J of interest, i.e. by $\text{Prob}_{c^*|c}(J)$, where $\text{Prob}_{c^*|c}$ is the probability distribution of $c^*(A_1, \ldots, A_N)$ generated by P for a given c.

Even if J is a fuzzy region, this probability writes (cf. Section 5.2)

$$\text{Prob}_{c^*|c}(J) = \int_{I\!\!R} \mu_J(x) \, dP_{c^*|c}(x). \tag{6.117}$$

Also in this case a risk can be specified and introduced.

If one is interested in an evaluation with a fuzzy (may be linguistic) degree T of the probability for c^* belonging to J, we only mention here the approach by YAGER (1984a) with its main idea $\mu_T(\text{Prob}_{c^*|c}(J^{\geq \alpha})) = \alpha$

$$\mu_T(t) = \sup_{\alpha \in [0,1]} \{\alpha \mid \text{Prob}_{c^*|c}(J^{\geq \alpha}) \geq t\}, \tag{6.118}$$

where $J^{\geq \alpha}$ denotes the (strong) α-cut of the fuzzy region J.

With these ideas and approaches a theory for estimation and decision can be developed, using analogous notions as for mathematical statistics. A lot of statements look quite similar to those known from mathematical statistics and statistical decision theory, some statements, however, are rather strange, e.g. in the possibilistic approach, where "independent" but *identical* fuzzy observations do not lead to an improvement of estimations when compared with that estimation using only one of the observations.

With respect to theoretical results and further details we refer to NÄTHER (1990), NÄTHER/ALBRECHT (1990), as well as BANDEMER/NÄTHER (1992), Chapter 7.

Bibliography

Adlassnig, K.-P. (1982): A survey on medical diagnosis and fuzzy subsets. In: *Approximate Reasoning in Decision Analysis* (M. M. GUPTA, E. SANCHEZ, eds.), North-Holland Publ. Comp., Amsterdam, 203-217.

– ; Kolarz, G. (1982): CADIAG-2: Computer-assisted medical diagnosis using fuzzy subsets. In: *Approximate Reasoning in Decision Analysis* (M. M. GUPTA, E. SANCHEZ, eds.), North-Holland Publ. Comp., Amsterdam, 219-247.

Albrecht, M. (1991): Explorative und statistische Auswertung unscharfer Daten. Ph.D. Thesis, Bergakademie Freiberg.

– (1992): Approximation of functional relationships to fuzzy observations. *Fuzzy Sets and Systems* **49**, 301-305.

Alefeld, G.; Herzberger, J. (1974): *Einführung in die Intervallrechnung.* Bibliograph. Institut, Mannheim. [Engl. translation: *Introduction to Interval Computations.* Academic Press, New York 1983.]

Alexeyev, A. V. (1985): Fuzzy algorithms execution software: the FAGOL system. In: *Management Decision Support Systems Using Fuzzy Sets and Possibility Theory* (J. KACPRZYK, R. R. YAGER, eds.), Verlag TÜV Rheinland, Köln, 289-300.

Altrock, C. von; Krause, P.; Zimmermann, H.-J. (1992): Advanced fuzzy logic control of a model car in extreme situations. *Fuzzy Sets and Systems* **48**, 41-52.

Anderberg, M. R. (1973): *Cluster Analysis for Applications.* Academic Press, New York.

Asai, K.; Tanaka, H.; Okuda, T. (1975): Decision-making and its goal in a fuzzy environment. In: *Fuzzy Sets and Their Applications to Cognitive and Decision Processes* (L. A. ZADEH et al., eds.), Academic Press, New York, 257-277.

Atanassov, K. T. (1986): Intuitionistic fuzzy sets. *Fuzzy Sets and Systems* **20**, 87-96.

Balas, E.; Padberg, M. W. (1976): Set partitioning: A survey. SIAM *Rev.* **18**, 710-760.

Baldwin, J. F. (1985): A knowledge engineering fuzzy inference language – FRIL. In: *Management Decision Support Systems Using Fuzzy Sets and Possibility Theory* (J. KACPRZYK, R. R. YAGER, eds.), Verlag TÜV Rheinland, Köln, 253-269.

– ; **Baldwin, P.; Brown, S.** (1985): A natural language interface for FRIL. In: *Management Decision Support Systems Using Fuzzy Sets and Possibility Theory* (J. KACPRZYK, R. R. YAGER, eds.), Verlag TÜV Rheinland, Köln, 270-279.

Bandemer, H. (1985): Evaluating explicit functional relationships from fuzzy observations. *Fuzzy Sets and Systems* **16**, 41-52.

– (1987): From fuzzy data to functional relationships. *Math. Modelling* **9**, 419-426.

– (1990): A special measure of uncertainty. *Fuzzy Sets and Systems* **38**, 281-287.

– (1990a): Quantifying similarity for handling information in knowledge bases. *J. of Chemometrics* **4**, 147-158.

– (1991): Some ideas to minimize an empirically given fuzzy function. *optimization* **22**, 139-151.

– (1992): Fuzzy local inference in fuzzy knowledge bases. In: *Fuzzy Approach to Reasoning and Decision Making* (V. NOVAK et al., eds.), Kluwer, Dordrecht, 39-49.

– (ed.)(1993): *Modelling Uncertain Data.* Akademie-Verlag, Berlin.

– ; **Bellmann, A.** (1991): Unscharfe Methoden der Mehrphasenregression. In: *Beiträge zur Mathematischen Geologie und Geoinformatik* (G. PESCHEL, ed.), Verlag Sven von Loga, Köln, 25-27.

– ; **Gebhardt, A.** (1995): Bayesian fuzzy kriging. *Math. Geology* (to appear)

– ; **Gerlach, W.** (1985): Evaluating implicit functional relationships from fuzzy observations. In: *Problems of Evaluation of Functional Relationships from Random-Noise or Fuzzy Data* (H. BANDEMER, ed.), Freiberger Forschungshefte, No. D170, Deutscher Verlag für Grundstoffindustrie, Leipzig, 101-118.

– ; **Hulsch, F.; Lehmann, A.** (1986): A watershed algorithm adapted to functions on grids. *Elektron. Informationsverarb. Kybernetik* **22**, 553-564.

– ; **Kraut, A.** (1988): On a fuzzy-theory-based computer-aided particle shape description, *Fuzzy Sets and Systems* **27**, 105-113.

– ; – (1990a): A case study on modelling impreciseness and vagueness of observations to evaluate a functional relationship. In: *Progress in Fuzzy Sets and Systems* (W. JANKO, M. ROUBENS, M., H.-J. ZIMMERMANN, eds.). Kluwer Academic Publ., Dordrecht, 7-21.

– ; – (1990b): On fuzzy shape factors for fuzzy shapes. In: *Some Applications of Fuzzy Set Theory in Data Analysis II* (H. BANDEMER, ed.), Freiberger Forschungshefte, No. D197, Deutscher Verlag für Grundstoffindustrie, Leipzig, 9-26.

– ; – ; Näther, W. (1989): On basic notions of fuzzy set theory and some ideas for their application in image processing. In: *Geometrical Problems of Image Processing* (HÜBLER et al., eds.), Akademie-Verlag, Berlin, 153-164.

– ; – ; Vogt, F. (1988): Evaluation of hardness curves at thin surface layers – A case study on using fuzzy observations. In: *Some Applications of Fuzzy Set Theory in Data Analysis* (H. BANDEMER, ed.), Freiberger Forschungshefte, No. D187, Deutscher Verlag für Grundstoffindustrie, Leipzig, 9-26.

– ; Näther, W. (1988): Fuzzy analogues for partial-least-squares techniques in multivariate data analysis. In: *Some Applications of Fuzzy Set Theory in Data Analysis* (H. BANDEMER, ed.), Freiberger Forschungshefte, No. D187, Deutscher Verlag für Grundstoffindustrie, Leipzig, 62-77.

– ; – (1988a): Fuzzy projection pursuits. *Fuzzy Sets and Systems* **27**, 141-147.

– ; – (1992): *Fuzzy Data Analysis.* Kluwer Academic Publ., Dordrecht.

– ; Otto, M. (1986): Fuzzy theory in analytical chemistry. *Mikrochim. Acta (Wien)* 1986 II, 93-124.

– ; – (1988): Methods to compare functions and some applications in analytical chemistry. In: *Some Applications of Fuzzy Set Theory in Data Analysis* (H. BANDEMER, ed.), Freiberger Forschungshefte, No. D187, Deutscher Verlag für Grundstoffindustrie, Leipzig, 27-38.

– ; Roth, K. (1987): A method of fuzzy-theory-based computer-aided exploratory data analysis. *Biometrical J.* **29**, 497-504.

– ; Schmerling, S. (1985): Evaluating explicit functional relationships by fuzzifying the statement of its satisfying. *Biometrical J.* **27**, 149-157.

Beddow, J. K.; Vetter, A. F.; Sisson, K. (1976): Powder metallurgy review 9, Part II: Particle shape analysis. *Powder Metallurgy Internat.* **8**, 107-109.

Bellman, R.; Giertz, M. (1973): On the analytic formalism of the theory of fuzzy sets. *Information Sci.* **5**, 149-156.

– ; Zadeh, L. A. (1970): Decision-making in a fuzzy environment. *Management Science* **17**, B141-B164. [cf. Zadeh (1987)]

– ; – (1977): Local and fuzzy logics. In: *Modern Uses of Multiple-Valued Logic* (J. M. DUNN, G. EPSTEIN, eds.), Reidel, Dordrecht, 105-165.

Berenji, H. R. (1992): A reinforcement learning-based architecture for fuzzy logic control. *Internat. J. Approx. Reason.* **6**, 267-292.

– ; Khedkar, P. (1992): Learning and tuning fuzzy logic controllers through reinforcements. *IEEE Trans. Neural Networks* **3**, 724-740.

Bezdek, J. C. (1974): Numerical taxonomy with fuzzy sets. *J. Math. Biol.* **1**, 57-71.

– (1981): *Pattern Recognition with Fuzzy Objective Function Algorithms.* Plenum Press, New York.

− ; **Pal, S. K.** (Eds.) (1992): *Fuzzy Models for Pattern Recognition*. IEEE Press, New York.

Blaffert, T. (1984): Computer-assisted multicomponent spectral analysis with fuzzy data sets. *Anal. Chim. Acta* **161**, 135-148.

Bocklisch, S. (1987): *Prozeßanalyse mit unscharfen Verfahren*. Verlag Technik, Berlin.

Boole, G. (1854): *An investigation of the laws of thought on which are founded the mathematical theories of logic and probabilities*. McMillan, Dover reprint 1958.

Box, G. E. P.; Wilson, K. B. (1951): On the experimental attainment of optimum conditions. *J. Roy. Statist. Soc.*, Ser. B, **13**, 1-45.

Carlsson, C. (1984): *Fuzzy Set Theory for Management Decisions*. Verlag TÜV Rheinland, Köln.

Celmins, A. (1987): Least squares model fitting to fuzzy vector data. *Fuzzy Sets and Systems* **22**, 245-269.

Cerutti, S.; Pieri, C. T. (1981): A method for the quantification of the decision-making process in a computer-oriented medical record. *Internat. J. Bio-Medical Computing* **12**, 29-57.

Chapin, E. W. (1974/75): Set-valued set theory. I, II. *Notre Dame J. Formal Logic* **15**, 614-634; **16**, 255-267.

Cheeseman, P. (1986): Probability versus fuzzy reasoning. In: *Uncertainty in Artificial Intelligence 1* (L. N. KANAL, J. F. LEMMER,, eds.), North-Holland Publ. Comp., Amsterdam, 85-102.

Cholewa, W. (1985): Aggregation of fuzzy opinions − an axiomatic approach. *Fuzzy Sets and Systems* **17**, 249-258.

Choquet, G. (1954): Theorie of capacities. *Ann. Inst. Fourier (Grenoble)* **5**, 131-295.

Civanlar, M. R.; Trussell, H. J. (1986): Constructive membership functions using statistical data. *Fuzzy Sets and Systems* **18**, 1-13.

Cournot, A. A. (1843): *Exposition de la théorie des chances et des probabilités*. Paris.

Czogala, E.; Gottwald, S.; Pedrycz, W. (1982): Aspects for the evaluation of decision situations. In: *Fuzzy Information and Decision Processes* (M. M. GUPTA, E. SANCHEZ, eds.), North-Holland Publ. Comp., Amsterdam, 41-49.

− ; **Hirota, K.** (1986): *Probabilistic Sets: Fuzzy and Stochastic Approach to Decision, Control and Recognition Processes*. Verlag TÜV Rheinland, Köln.

− ; **Pedrycz, W.** (1981): On identification in fuzzy systems and its application in control problems. *Fuzzy Sets and Systems* **6**, 73-83.

D'Ambrosio, B. (1989): *Qualitative Process Theory using Linguistic Variable*. Springer, Berlin.

deBessonet, C. G. (1991): *A Many–Valued Approach to Deduction and Reasoning for Artificial Intelligence.* Kluwer Academic Publ., Dordrecht.

deCooman, G.; Kerre, E. E.; Vanmassenhove, F. R. (1992): Possibility theory: An integral theoretic approach. *Fuzzy Sets and Systems* **46**, 287-299.

deLuca, A.; Termini, S. (1979): Entropy and energy measures of a fuzzy set. In: *Advances in Fuzzy Set Theory and Applications* (M. M. GUPTA, R. K. RAGADE, R. R. YAGER, eds.), North-Holland Publ. Comp., Amsterdam, 321-338.

Dempster, A. P. (1967): Upper and lower probabilties induced by a multivalued mapping. *Ann. Math. Stat.* **38**, 325-329.

Diamond, Ph. (1988): Fuzzy least squares. *Information Sci.* **46**, 141-157.

– ; **Kloeden, P.** (1994): *Metric Spaces of Fuzzy Sets.* Theory and Applications. World Scientific Publ. Comp., Singapore.

diNola, A. (1984): An algorithm of calculation of lower solutions of fuzzy relation equation. *Stochastica* **3**, 33-40.

– (1985): Relational equations in totally ordered lattices and their complete resolution. *J. Math. Anal. Appl.* **107**, 148-155.

– ; **Sessa, S.; Pedrycz, W.; Sanchez, E.** (1989): *Fuzzy Relation Equations and Their Applications to Knowledge Engineering.* Theory and Decision Libr., ser. D, Kluwer Academic Publ., Dordrecht.

Driankov, D.; Hellendoorn, H.; Reinfrank, M. (1993): *An Introduction to Fuzzy Control.* Springer, Berlin.

Dubois, D.; Prade, H. (1978): Operations on fuzzy numbers. *Internat. J. Systems Sci.* **9**, 613-626.

– ; – (1980): *Fuzzy Sets and Systems.* Theory and Applications. Academic Press, New York.

– ; – (1980a): Systems of linear fuzzy constraints. *Fuzzy Sets and Systems* **3**, 37-48.

– ; – (1982): On several representations of an uncertain body of evidence. In: *Fuzzy Information and Decision Processes* (M. M. GUPTA, E. SANCHEZ, eds.), North-Holland Publ. Comp., Amsterdam, 167-181.

– ; – (1983a): Twofold fuzzy sets - An approach to the representation of sets with fuzzy boundaries based on possibility and necessity measures. *Fuzzy Mathematics* **3**, 53-76.

– ; – (1983b): Ranking of fuzzy numbers in the setting of possibility theory. *Information Sci.* **30**, 183-224.

– ; – (1984): A note on measures of specificity for fuzzy sets. BUSEFAL **19**, 83-89.

– ; – (1985): *Théorie des Possibilités*: Applications à la Représentation des Connaissances en Informatique. Masson, Paris. [Engl. translation: *Possibility Theory.* An Approach to Computerized Processing of Uncertainty. Plenum Press, New York 1988.]

– ; – (1987): Properties of measures of information in evidence and possibility theories. *Fuzzy Sets and Systems* **24**, 161-182.

– ; – (1990): Modelling uncertain and vague knowledge in possibility and evidence theory. In: *Uncertainty in Artificial Intelligence 4* (R. D. SHACHTER et al., eds.), North-Holland Publ. Comp., Amsterdam, 303-318.

Dunn, J. C. (1974): A fuzzy relative of the ISODATA-process and its use in detecting compact, well separated clusters. *J. Cybern.* **3**, 32-57.

Friedman, J. H.; Tukey, J. W. (1974): A projection pursuit algorithm for exploratory data analysis. IEEE *Trans. Comput.* **23**, 881-889.

Gaines, B. (1976): Foundations of fuzzy reasoning. *Internat. J. Man-Machine Studies* **8**, 623-668.

Geyer-Schulz, A. (1986): Unscharfe Mengen im Operations Research. Ph.D. Thesis, Wirtschaftsuniversität Wien.

– (1994): *Fuzzy Rule-Based Expert Systems and Genetic Machine Learning.* Physica-Verlag, Heidelberg.

Giles, R. (1976): Lukasiewicz logic and fuzzy set theory. *Internat. J. Man-Machine Studies* **8**, 313-327.

– (1979): A formal system for fuzzy reasoning. *Fuzzy Sets and Systems* **2**, 233-257.

Gitman, I.; Levine, M. D. (1970): An algorithm for detecting unimodal fuzzy sets and its application as a clustering technique. IEEE *Trans. Comput.* **19**, 583-593.

Goetscherian, V. (1980): From binary to grey-tone image processing using fuzzy logic concepts. *Pattern Recognition* **12**, 7-15.

Goguen, J. A. (1968/69): The logic of inexact concepts. *Synthese* **19**, 325-373.

– (1974): Concept representation in natural and artificial languages: axioms, extensions and applications for fuzzy sets. *Internat. J. Man-Machine Studies* **6**, 513-561.

Goodman, I. R.; Nguyen, H. T. (1985): *Uncertainty Models for Knowledge – Based Systems.* North-Holland Publ. Comp., Amsterdam.

Gottwald, S. (1971): Zahlbereichskonstruktionen in einer mehrwertigen Mengenlehre. *Ztschr. math. Logik Grundlagen Math.* **17**, 145-188.

– (1979): A note on measures of fuzziness. *Elektron. Informationsverarb. Kybernetik* **15**, 221-223.

– (1979a): Mengentheoretische Eigenschaften unscharfer Begriffe. *Math. Nachrichten* **91**, 363-374.

– (1980): A note on fuzzy cardinals. *Kybernetika* **16**, 156-158.

– (1981): Fuzzy-Mengen und ihre Anwendungen. Ein Überblick. *Elektron. Informationsverarb. Kybernetik* **17**, 207-235.

– (1984): On the existence of solutions of systems of fuzzy equations. *Fuzzy Sets and Systems* **12**, 301-302.

– (1984a): Criteria for non-interactivity of fuzzy logic controller rules. In: *Large Scale Systems: Theory and Applications 1983* (A. STRACZAK, ed.), Pergamon Press, Oxford, 229-233.

– (1984b): Fuzzy set theory: some aspects of the early development. In: *Aspects of Vagueness* (H. J. SKALA, S. TERMINI, E. TRILLAS, eds.), Reidel, Dordrecht, 13-29.

– (1986): Fuzzy set theory with t-norms and phi-operators. In: *The Mathematics of Fuzzy Systems* (A. DINOLA, A. G. S. VENTRE, eds.), Interdisciplinary Systems Res., *88*, Verlag TÜV Rheinland, Köln, 143-195.

– (1986a): Characterizations of the solvability of fuzzy equations. *Elektron. Informationsverarb. Kybernetik* **22**, 67-91.

– (1989): *Mehrwertige Logik*. Eine Einführung in Theorie und Anwendungen. Akademie-Verlag, Berlin.

– (1991): Fuzzified fuzzy relations. In: *Proc. IFSA '91 Brussels* (R. LOWEN, M. ROUBENS, eds.), Vol.: Mathematics, Vrije Universiteit Brussels, Brussels, 82-86.

– (1993): *Fuzzy Sets and Fuzzy Logic*. Foundation of Application – from a Mathematical Point of View. Vieweg, Braunschweig/Wiesbaden and Teknea, Toulouse.

– ; Czogala, E.; Pedrycz, W. (1982): Measures of fuzziness and operations with fuzzy numbers. *Stochastica* **6**, 187-205.

– ; Pedrycz, W. (1985): Analysis and synthesis of fuzzy controller. *Problems Control Inform. Theory* **14**, 33-45.

– ; – (1986): On the suitability of fuzzy models: an evaluation through fuzzy integrals. *Internat. J. Man-Machine Studies* **24**, 141-151.

– ; – (1986a): Solvability of fuzzy relational equations and manipulation of fuzzy data. *Fuzzy Sets and Systems* **18**, 1-21.

– ; – (1988): On the methodology of solving fuzzy relational equations and its impact on fuzzy modelling. In: *Fuzzy Logic in Knowledge-Based Systems, Decision and Control* (M. M. GUPTA, T. YAMAKAWA, eds.), North-Holland Publ. Comp., Amsterdam, 197-210.

Gower, J.; Ross, G. (1969): Minimum spanning trees and single linkage cluster analysis. *Appl. Statist.* **18**, 54-64.

Hartigan, J. (1975): *Clustering Algorithms*. Wiley, New York.

Hamacher, H. (1978): *Über logische Aggregationen nicht – binär explizierter Entscheidungskriterien*. Rita G. Fischer Verlag, Frankfurt/Main.

Hayashi, I.; Nomura, H.; Yamasaki, H.; Wakami, N. (1992): Construction of fuzzy inference rules by neural network driven fuzzy reasoning and neural network driven fuzzy reasoning with learning functions. *Internat. J. Approx. Reason.* **6**, 241-266.

Higashi, M.; Klir, G. J. (1983): Measures of uncertainty and information based on possibility distributions. *Internat. J. General Systems* **9**, 43-58.

Hirota, K. (1981): Concepts of probabilistic sets. *Fuzzy Sets and Systems* **5**, 31-46.

– ; **Arai, Y.; Hachisu, S.** (1986): Moving mark recognition and moving object manipulation in fuzzy controlled robot. *Control Theory and Advanced Technol.* **2**, 399-418.

– ; **Yoshinori, A.; Pedrycz, W.** (1985): Robot control based on membership and vagueness. In: *Approximate Reasoning in Expert Systems* (M. M. GUPTA et al., eds.), North-Holland Publ. Comp., Amsterdam, 621-635.

Holmblad, L. P.; Østergaard, J. J. (1982): Control of a cement kiln by fuzzy logic. In: *Fuzzy Information and Decision Processes* (M. M. GUPTA, E. SANCHEZ, eds.), North-Holland Publ. Comp., Amsterdam, 389-399.

Hopf, J.; Klawonn, F. (1994): Learning the rule base of a fuzzy controller by a genetic algorithm. In: *Fuzzy Systems in Computer Science* (R. KRUSE, J. GEBHARDT, R. PALM, eds.), Vieweg, Braunschweig/Wiesbaden, 63-74.

Huber, P. (1985): Projection pursuits. *Ann. of Statist.* **13**, 425-525.

Jahn, K.-U. (1975): Intervall-wertige Mengen. *Math. Nachrichten* **68**, 115-132.

Kandel, A. (1979): On fuzzy statistics. In: *Advances in Fuzzy Set Theory and Applications* (M. M. GUPTA, R. K. RAGADE, R. R. YAGER, eds.), North-Holland Publ. Comp., Amsterdam, 181-199.

– (1982): *Fuzzy Techniques in Pattern Recognition.* Wiley, New York.

– (1986): *Fuzzy Mathematical Techniques with Applications.* Addison-Wesley, Reading (Mass.).

Kaufmann, A. (1973): *Introduction à la Théorie des Sous-Ensembles Flous*; t.1: Eléments théorique de base. Masson, Paris. [Engl. translation: *Introduction to the Theory of Fuzzy Subsets; vol. I.* Academic Press, New York 1975.]

– ; **Gupta, M. M.** (1985): *Introduction to Fuzzy Arithmetic: Theory and Applications.* Van Nostrand Reinhold, New York.

Khurgin, J. I.; Polyakov, V. V. (1986): Fuzzy analysis of the group concordance of expert preferences, defined by Saaty matrices. In: *Fuzzy Sets Applications, Methodological Approaches, and Results* (ST. BOCKLISCH et al., eds.); Mathematial Research, *30*, Akademie-Verlag, Berlin, 111-115.

Kickert, W. J. M. (1979): An example of linguistic modelling: the case of Mulder's theory of power. In: *Advances in Fuzzy Set Theory and Applications* (M. M. GUPTA, R. K. RAGADE, R. R. YAGER, eds.), North-Holland Publ. Comp., Amsterdam, 519-540.

– ; **van Nauta Lemke, M.** (1976): The application of fuzzy set theory to control a warm water process. *Automatica* **12**, 301-308.

Kiefer, J.; Wolfowitz, J. (1952): Stochastic estimation of the maximum of a regression function. *Ann. Math. Stat.* **23**, 462-466.

Kiszka, J. B.; Gupta, M. M.; Nikiforuk, P. N. (1985): Some properties of expert control systems. In: *Approximate Reasoning in Expert Systems* (M. M. GUPTA et al., eds.), North-Holland Publ. Comp., Amsterdam, 283-306.

Klaua, D. (1966): Über einen zweiten Ansatz zur mehrwertigen Mengenlehre. *Monatsber. Deut. Akad. Wiss. Berlin* **8**, 161-177.

– (1966a): Grundbegriffe einer mehrwertigen Mengenlehre. *Monatsber. Deut. Akad. Wiss. Berlin* **8**, 781-802.

Klement, E. P. (1982): Some remarks on a paper of R. R. Yager. *Information Sci.* **27**, 211-220.

Klir, G. J. (1987): Where do we stand on measures of uncertainty, ambiguity, fuzziness, and the like? *Fuzzy Sets and Systems* **24**, 141-160.

– ; **Folger, T. A.** (1988): *Fuzzy Sets, Uncertainty, and Information.* Prentice Hall, Englewood Cliffs, NJ.

– ; **Yuan, B.** (1994): Approximate solutions of systems of fuzzy relation equations. In: *Proc. 3rd IEEE Internat. Conf. Fuzzy Systems*, FUZZ-IEEE '94, Orlando/FL, IEEE Soc., 1452-1457.

Knopfmacher, J. (1975): On measures of fuzziness. *J. Math. Anal. Appl.* **49**, 529-534.

Köhler, K. (1994): Adaptive fuzzy modifiers. In: *Proc. Second Europ. Congress on Intelligent Techniques and Soft Computing*, EUFIT '94, Aachen (H.-J. ZIMMERMANN, ed.), Augustinus-Buchhandl., Aachen, **2**, 946-950.

Kohlas, J.; Monney, P.-A. (1994): Representation of evidence by hints. In: *Advances in the Dempster-Shafer Theory of Evidence* (YAGER, R. R. et al., eds.), Wiley, New York, 473-492.

Kolmogorov, A. N. (1933): *Grundbegriffe der Wahrscheinlichkeitsrechnung.* Springer, Berlin.

Kruse, R. (1984): Statistical estimation with linguistic data. *Information Sci.* **33**, 197-207.

– ; **Meyer, K. D.** (1987): *Statistics with Vague Data.* Reidel, Dordrecht.

– ; **Schwecke, E.; Heinsohn, J.** (1991): *Uncertainty and Vagueness in Knowledge Based Systems.* Springer, Berlin.

Krusinska, E.; Liebhart, J. (1986): A note on the usefulness of linguistic variables for differentiating between some respiratory diseases. *Fuzzy Sets and Systems* **18**, 131-142.

Kwakernaak, H. (1978/79): Fuzzy random variables. I, II. *Information Sci.* **15**, 1-15; **17**, 253-278.

Lakov, D. (1985): Adaptive robot under fuzzy control. *Fuzzy Sets and Systems* **17**, 1-8.

Larkin, L. I. (1985): A fuzzy logic controller for aircraft flight control. In: *Industrial Applications of Fuzzy Control* (M. SUGENO, ed.), North-Holland Publ. Comp., Amsterdam, 87-104.

Larsen, R. M. (1980): Industrial applications of fuzzy logic control. *Internat. J. Man-Machine Studies* **12**, 3-10.

Leibniz, G. W. (1703): Brief an Bernoulli vom 3. 12. 1703. In: *Mathematische Schriften* (GERHARDT, ed.), *III/*1, Halle 1855.

Lesmo, L.; Saitta, L.; Torasso, P. (1982): Learning of fuzzy production rules for medical diagnosis. In: *Approximate Reasoning in Decision Analysis* (M. M. GUPTA, E. SANCHEZ, eds.), North-Holland Publ. Comp., Amsterdam, 249-260.

Lipp, H.-P.; Guenther, R. (1986): An application of a fuzzy Petri net in complex industrial systems. In: *Fuzzy Sets Applications, Methodological Approaches, and Results* (ST. BOCKLISCH et al., eds.); Mathematical Research, *30*, Akademie-Verlag, Berlin, 188-196.

Liu, X. H.; Wang, P. Z.; Chen, Y. P. (1985): Approximate reasoning in earthquake engineering. In: *Approximate Reasoning in Expert Systems* (M. M. GUPTA et al., eds.), North-Holland Publ. Comp., Amsterdam, 519-528.

Loo, S. G. (1977): Measures of fuzziness. *Cybernetica* **20**, 201-210.

Lowen, R. (1978): On fuzzy complements. *Information Sci.* **14**, 107-113.

Lukasiewicz, J.; Tarski, A. (1930): Untersuchungen über den Aussagenkalkül. *Comptes Rendus Soc. Sci. et Lettr. Varsovie,* cl. III, **23**, 30-50.

Mamdani, E. H. (1976): Advances in the linguistic synthesis of fuzzy controllers. *Internat. J. Man-Machine Studies* **8**, 669-678.

– ; Assilian, S. (1975): An experiment in linguistic synthesis with a fuzzy logic controller. *Internat. J. Man-Machine Studies* **7**, 1-13.

– ; Gaines, B. R. (eds.) (1981): *Fuzzy Reasoning and Its Applications.* Academic Press, New York.

Matheron, G. (1975): *Random Sets and Integral Geometry.* Wiley, New York.

Mirkin, B. G. (1979): *Group Choice.* Wiley, New York.

Mises, R. v. (1919): Grundlagen der Wahrscheinlichkeitsrechnung. *Math. Zeitschr.* **5**, 52-99.

Miyakoshi, M; Shimbo, M. (1984): A strong law of large numbers for fuzzy random variables. *Fuzzy Sets and Systems* **12**, 133-142.

Miyamoto, S. (1990): *Fuzzy Sets in Information Retrieval and Cluster Analysis.* Kluwer Academic Publ., Dordrecht.

Mizumoto, M. (1982): Fuzzy inference using max-$\wedge$ composition in the compositional rule of inference. In: *Approximate Reasoning in Decision Analysis* (M. M. GUPTA, E. SANCHEZ, eds.), North-Holland Publ. Comp., Amsterdam, 67-76.

– ; Tanaka, K. (1981): Fuzzy sets and their operations. *Information and Control* **48**, 30-48.

– ; **Zimmermann, H.-J.** (1982): Comparison of fuzzy reasoning methods. *Fuzzy Sets and Systems* **8**, 253-283.

Moon, R. E.; Jordanov, S.; Perez, A.; Turksen, I. B. (1977): Medical diagnostic system with human-like reasoning capability. In: MEDINFO 77 (D. B. SHIRES, H. WOLF, eds.), North-Holland Publ. Comp., Amsterdam, 115-119.

Moore, R. E. (1966): *Interval Analysis.* Prentice-Hall, Englewood Cliffs/NJ.

– (1979): *Methods and Applications of Interval Analysis.* SIAM, Philadelphia.

Murayama, Y. et al. (1985): Optimizing control of a diesel engine. In: *Industrial Applications of Fuzzy Control* (M. SUGENO, ed.), North-Holland Publ. Comp., Amsterdam, 63-72.

Näther, W. (1990): On possibilistic inference. *Fuzzy Sets and Systems* **36**, 327-337.

– (1991): Sugeno's λ-fuzzy measures as hit-or-miss probabilities of Poisson point processes. *Fuzzy Sets and Systems* **43**, 251-254.

– ; **Albrecht, M.** (1990): Linear regression with random fuzzy observations. *statistics* **21**, 521-531.

– ; **Kraut, A.** (1993): Grey-tone image processing with fuzzy structural elements. *Systems Anal. Modelling Simulation*, **11**, 79-86.

Nagel, M.; Feiler, D.; Bandemer, H. (1985): Mathematische Statistik in der Umweltanalytik. In: *Mathematische Statistik in der Technik* (H. BANDEMER, ed.), Tagungsvorträge, Bergakademie Freiberg, No. 1, 61-66.

Nahmias, S. (1979): Fuzzy variables in a random environment. In: *Advances in Fuzzy Set Theory and Applications* (M. M. GUPTA, R. K. RAGADE, R. R. YAGER, eds.), North-Holland Publ. Comp., Amsterdam, 165-180.

Nauck, D. (1994): Fuzzy neuro systems: an overview. In: *Fuzzy Systems in Computer Science* (R. KRUSE, J. GEBHARDT, R. PALM eds.), Vieweg, Braunschweig/Wiesbaden, 91-107.

– ; **Klawonn, F.; Kruse, R.** (1993): Combining neural networks and fuzzy controllers. In: *Fuzzy Logic in Artificial Intelligence* (E. P. KLEMENT, W. SLANY eds.), Lecture Notes in Artificial Intelligence, *695*, Springer, Berlin, 35-46.

– ; – ; – (1994): *Neuronale Netze und Fuzzy-Systeme.* Vieweg, Braunschweig/ Wiesbaden.

Neitzel, A. L.; Hoffman, L. J. (1980): Fuzzy cost/benefit analysis. In: *Fuzzy Sets. Theory and Applications to Policy Analysis and Information Systems* (P. P. WANG, S. K. CHANG, eds.), Plenum Press, New York, 275-290.

Neumaier, A. (1990): *Interval Methods for Systems of Equations.* Encyclopedia of Math. and its Applic., Cambridge Univ. Press, Cambridge.

Nguyen, H. (1978): On conditional possibility distributions. *Fuzzy Sets and Systems* **1**, 299-310.

− (1979): Some mathematical tools for linguistic probabilities. *Fuzzy Sets and Systems* **2**, 53-65.

Novak, V. (1986): The origin and claims of fuzzy logic. In: *Fuzzy Sets Applications, Methodological Approaches, and Results* (ST. BOCKLISCH et al., eds.); Mathematical Research, *30*, Akademie-Verlag, Berlin, 21-26.

− (1989): *Fuzzy Sets and Their Applications.* Hilger, Bristol.

Ogawa, H.; Fu, K. S.; Yao, J. T. P. (1985): SPERIL-II: an expert system for damage assessment of existing structure. In: *Approximate Reasoning in Expert Systems* (M. M. GUPTA et al., eds.), North-Holland Publ. Comp., Amsterdam, 731-744.

O'Higgins Hall, L.; Kandel, A. (1986): *Designing Fuzzy Expert Systems.* Verlag TÜV Rheinland, Köln.

Orlovsky, S. A. (1977): On programming with fuzzy constraint sets. *Kybernetes* **6**, 197-201.

Otto, M.; Bandemer, H. (1986): Calibration with imprecise signals and concentrations based on fuzzy theory. *Chemometrics and Intelligent Laboratory Systems* **1**, 71-78.

− ; − (1986a): Pattern recognition based on fuzzy observations for spectroscopic quality control and chromographic fingerprinting. *Anal. Chim. Acta* **184**, 21-31.

− ; − (1986c): A fuzzy method for component identification and mixture analysis in the ultraviolet range. *Anal. Chim. Acta* **191**, 193-204.

− ; − (1988a): A fuzzy approach to predicting chemical data from incomplete, uncertain, and verbal compound features. In: *Physical Property Prediction in Organic Chemistry* (C. JOCHUM, M. G. HICKS, J. SUNKEL, eds.), Springer, Berlin, 171-189.

− ; − (1988b): Fuzzy inference structures for spectral library retrieval systems. In: *Proc. Internat. Workshop on Fuzzy Systems Applicat.*, Iizuka, Fukuoka, 28-29.

Pappis, C. P.; Mamdani, E. H. (1977): Fuzzy logic controller for traffic junction. IEEE *Trans. Systems, Man and Cybernet.* **SMC-7**, 707-712.

Pawlak, Z. (1984): Rough probabilities. *Bull. Polish Acad. Sci. Math.* **32**, 607-612.

Pedrycz, W. (1989): *Fuzzy Control and Fuzzy Systems.* Research Stud. Press, Taunton and Wiley, New York. [2nd edition 1993]

Peschel, M.; Straube, B.; Mende, W. (1986): Fuzzy inferences for the analysis of qualitative behaviour. In: *Fuzzy Sets Applications, Methodological Approaches, and Results* (ST. BOCKLISCH et al., eds.); Mathematical Research, *30*, Akademie-Verlag, Berlin, 157-164.

Prade, H.; Negoita, C. V. (eds.) (1986): *Fuzzy Logic in Knowledge Engineering.* Verlag TÜV Rheinland, Köln.

Puri, M. L.; Ralescu, D. (1982): A possibility measure is not a fuzzy measure. *Fuzzy Sets and Systems* **7**, 311-313.

− ; − (1986): Fuzzy random variables. *J. Math. Anal. Appl.* **114**, 409-422.

Ralescu, D. (1982): Towards a general theory of fuzzy variables. *J. Math. Anal. Appl.* **86**, 176-193.

Raman, B.; Kerre, E. E. (1985): Application of fuzzy programming to ship steering. In: *Approximate Reasoning in Expert Systems* (M. M. GUPTA et al., eds.), North-Holland Publ. Comp., Amsterdam, 719-730.

Ramik, J.; Rimanek, J. (1985): Inequality relation between fuzzy numbers and its use in fuzzy optimization. *Fuzzy Sets and Systems* **16**, 123-138.

Ratschek, H. (1971): Die Subdistributivität der Intervallarithmetik. *Z. Angew. Math. Mech.* **51**, 189-192.

Ray, K. S.; Dutta Majumder, D. (1985): Structure of an intelligent fuzzy logic controller and its behaviour. In: *Approximate Reasoning in Expert Systems* (M. M. GUPTA et al., eds.), North-Holland Publ. Comp., Amsterdam, 593-619.

Rodabaugh, S. E.; Klement, E. P.; Höhle, U. (eds.) (1992): *Applications of Category Theory to Fuzzy Subsets*. Kluwer Academic Publ., Dordrecht.

Rommelfanger, H. (1994): *Fuzzy Decision Support-Systeme*. Entscheiden bei Unschärfe. 2nd edition, Springer, Heidelberg.

Ruspini, E. H. (1970): Numerical methods for fuzzy clustering. *Information Sci.* **2**, 319-350.

− (1973): New experimental results in fuzzy clustering. *Information Sci.* **6**, 273-284.

Saitta, L.; Torasso, P. (1981): Fuzzy characterization of coronary disease. *Fuzzy Sets and Systems* **5**, 245-258.

Sakawa, M.; Yano, H. (1992): Multiobjective fuzzy linear regression analysis for fuzzy input-output data. *Fuzzy Sets and Systems* **47**, 173-181.

Sambuc, R. (1975): Fonctions Φ-floues. Application a l'aide au diagnostic en pathologie thyroidienne. Ph.D. Thesis, University of Marseille.

Sanchez, E. (1977): Solutions in composite fuzzy relation equations: application to medical diagnosis in Brouwerian logic. In: *Fuzzy Automata and Decision Processes* (M. M. GUPTA, G. N. SARIDIS, B. N. GAINES, eds.), North-Holland Publ. Comp., Amsterdam, 221-234.

− (1984): Solution of fuzzy equations with extended operations. *Fuzzy Sets and Systems* **12**, 237-248.

Savage, L. J. (1972): *The Foundations of Statistics*. 2nd edition, Dover Publications, New York.

Scharf, E. M.; Mandic, N. J. (1985): Application of a fuzzy controller to the control of a multi-degree-of-freedom robot arm. In: *Industrial Applications of Fuzzy Control* (M. SUGENO, ed.), North-Holland Publ. Comp., Amsterdam, 41-62.

Schmerling, S.; Bandemer, H. (1985): Methods to estimate parameters in explicit functional relationships. In: *Problems of Evaluation of Functional Relationships from Random-Noise or Fuzzy Data* (H. BANDEMER, ed.), Freiberger Forschungshefte, No. D170, Deutscher Verlag für Grundstoffindustrie, Leipzig, 69-90.

Schmucker, K. J. (1984): *Fuzzy Sets, Natural Language Computations, and Risk Analysis.* Computer Science Press, Rockville.

Schüler, W. (1992): Specification of medical data with fuzzy methods. In: *Modelling uncertain data* (H. BANDEMER, ed.), Akademie-Verlag, Berlin, 111-114.

Schweizer, B.; Sklar, A. (1960): Statistical metric spaces. *Pacific J. Math.* **10**, 313-334.

– ; – (1961): Associative functions and statistical triangle inequalities. *Publ. Math. Debrecen* **8**, 169-186.

– ; – (1983): *Probabilistic Metric Spaces.* North-Holland Publ. Comp., Amsterdam.

Serra, J. (1982): *Image Analysis and Mathematical Morphology; 1.* Academic Press, New York.

– (1988): *Image Analysis and Mathematical Morphology; 2.* Academic Press, New York.

Sessa, S. (1984): Some results in the setting of fuzzy relation equations theory. *Fuzzy Sets and Systems* **14**, 281-297.

Shafer, G. (1973): Allocation of probability. Ph.D. Thesis, Princeton University.

– (1976): *A Mathematical Theory of Evidence.* Princeton University Press, Princeton.

Smets, Ph. (1981): The degree of belief in a fuzzy event. *Information Sci.* **25**, 1-19.

– (1981a): Medical diagnosis: fuzzy sets and degrees of belief. *Fuzzy Sets and Systems* **5**, 259-266.

– (1982): Probability of a fuzzy event: an axiomatic approach. *Fuzzy Sets and Systems* **7**, 153-164.

– (1983): Information content of an evidence. *Internat. J. Man-Machine Studies* **19**, 33-43.

– (1993): Belief functions: the disjunctive rule of combination and the generalised Bayesian Theorem. *Internat. J. Approx. Reason.* **9**, 1-35.

Smithson, M. (1987): *Fuzzy Set Analysis for Behavioral and Social Sciences.* Springer, New York.

Sombé, Léa (1991): *Schließen bei unsicherem Wissen in der Künstlichen Intelligenz.* Vieweg, Braunschweig/Wiesbaden.

Stoyan, D.; Kendall, W. S.; Mecke, J. (1987): *Stochastic Geometry and Its Applications.* Wiley, New York.

Straube, B. (1986): Model building and fuzzy systems. In: *Fuzzy Sets Applications, Methodological Approaches, and Results* (ST. BOCKLISCH et al., eds.); Mathematical Research, *30*, Akademie-Verlag, Berlin, 133-146.

Sugeno, M. (1974): Theory of Fuzzy Integral and Its Applications. Ph.D. Thesis, Tokyo Inst. of Technology, Tokyo.

– (1977): Fuzzy measures and fuzzy integrals: a survey. In: *Fuzzy Automata and Decision Processes* (M. M. GUPTA, G. N. SARIDIS, B. N. GAINES, eds.), North-Holland Publ. Comp., Amsterdam, 89-102.

– (1985a): An introductory survey of fuzzy control. *Information Sci.* **36**, 59-83.

– (ed.) (1985b): *Industrial Applications of Fuzzy Control.* North-Holland Publ. Comp., Amsterdam.

– ; Nishida, M. (1985): Fuzzy control of a model car. *Fuzzy Sets and Systems* **16**, 103-113.

– ; Terano, T. (1977): A model of learning on fuzzy information. *Kybernetes* **6**, 157-166.

Takagi, H.; Hayashi, I. (1991): NN-driven fuzzy reasoning. *Internat. J. Approx. Reason.* **5**, 191-212.

Takagi, H.; Lee, M. (1993): Neural networks and genetic algorithm approaches to auto-design of fuzzy sytems. In: *Fuzzy Logic in Artificial Intelligence* (E. P. KLEMENT, W. SLANY, eds.), Lecture Notes in Artificial Intelligence, *695*, Springer, Berlin, 68-79.

Tanaka, H.; Uejima, S.; Asai, K. (1982): Linear regression analysis with fuzzy model. IEEE *Trans. Systems, Man and Cybernet.* **SMC-12**, 903-907.

– ; Watada, J. (1988): Possibilistic linear systems and their applicaton to the linear regression model. *Fuzzy Sets and Systems* **27**, 275-289.

Terano, T.; Asai, K.; Sugeno, M. (1991): *Fuzzy Systems Theory and Its Applications.* Academic Press, New York.

Turksen, I. B.; Zhong, Z. (1990): An approximate analogical reasoning schema based on similarity measures and interval-valued fuzzy sets. *Fuzzy Sets and Systems* **34**, 323-346.

Umano, M. (1985): Fuzzy-set-theoretic data structure system and its application. In: *Management Decision Support Systems Using Fuzzy Sets and Possibility Theory* (J. KACPRZYK, R. R. YAGER, eds.), Verlag TÜV Rheinland, Köln, 301-313.

Viertl, R. (1990): Statistical inference for fuzzy data in environmetrics. *Environmetrics* **1**, 37-42.

- (1992): On statistical inference based on non-precise data. In: *Modelling Uncertain Data* (H. BANDEMER, ed.), Akademie-Verlag, Berlin, 121-130.

Wagenknecht, M.; Hartmann, K. (1986): On the solution of direct and inverse problems for fuzzy equation systems with tolerances. In: *Fuzzy Sets Applications, Methodological Approaches, and Results* (ST. BOCKLISCH et al., eds.); Mathematical Research, *30*, Akademie-Verlag, Berlin, 37-44.

- ; – (1986a): Fuzzy modelling with tolerances. *Fuzzy Sets and Systems* **20**, 325-332.

Wang P.-Z.; Klir, G. J. (1992): *Fuzzy Measure Theory.* Plenum Press, New York.

Wang P.-Z.; Sanchez, E. (1982): Treating a fuzzy subset as a projectable random subset. In: *Fuzzy Information and Decision Processes* (M. M. GUPTA, E. SANCHEZ, eds.), North-Holland Publ. Comp., Amsterdam, 213-219.

Weber, S. (1983): A general concept of fuzzy connectives, negations, and implications based on t-norms and t-conorms. *Fuzzy Sets and Systems* **11**, 115-134.

- (1984): Measures of fuzzy sets and measures of fuzziness. *Fuzzy Sets and Systems* **13**, 247-271.

Weidner, A. J. (1981): Fuzzy sets and Boolean-valued universes. *Fuzzy Sets and Systems* **6**, 61-72.

Wenstøp, F. (1975): Deductive verbal models of organizations. *Internat. J. Man-Machine Studies* **8**, 301-357.

- (1980): Quantitative analysis with linguistic values. *Fuzzy Sets and Systems* **4**, 99-115.

Wold, H. (1982): Soft modeling: The basic designs and some extensions. In: *Systems under Indirect Observations* (K. G. JÖRESKOG, H. WOLD, eds.), North-Holland Publ. Comp., Amsterdam, *2*, 1-54.

- (1985): Systems analysis by partial least squares. In: *Measuring the Unmeasurable* (P. NIJKAMP, H. LEITNER, N. WRIGLEY, eds.), Martinus Nijhoff Publ., Dordrecht.

Wu, W.-M. (1986): Fuzzy reasoning and fuzzy relational equations. *Fuzzy Sets and Systems* **20**, 67-78.

Wygralak, M. (1986): Fuzzy cardinals based on the generalized equality of fuzzy subsets. *Fuzzy Sets and Systems* **18**, 143-158.

- (1993): Generalized cardinal numbers and operations on them. *Fuzzy Sets and Systems* **53**, 49-85.

Yager, R. R. (1979/80): On the measure of fuzziness and negation. Part I: Membership in the unit interval. *Internat. J. General Systems* **5**, 221-229; Part II: Lattices. *Information and Control* **44**, 236-260.

- (1980): On a general class of fuzzy connectives. *Fuzzy Sets and Systems* **4**, 235-242.

– (1981): Measurement of properties on fuzzy sets and possibility distribution. In: *Proc. 3rd Internat. Seminar on Fuzzy Set Theory* (E. P. KLEMENT, ed.), Johannes-Kepler-University Linz, 211-222.

– (1983): An introduction to application of possibility theory. *Human Systems Management* **3**, 246-253.

– (1984): Fuzzy subsets with uncertain membership grades. IEEE *Trans. Systems, Man and Cybernet.* **SMC-14**, 271-275.

– (1984a): A representation of the probability of a fuzzy subset. *Fuzzy Sets and Systems* **13**, 273 - 283.

Yagishita, O.; Itoh, O.; Sugeno, M. (1985): Application of fuzzy reasoning to the water purification process. In: *Industrial Applications of Fuzzy Control* (M. SUGENO, ed.), North-Holland Publ. Comp., Amsterdam, 19-40.

Yasunobu, S.; Hasegawa, T. (1986): Evaluation of an automatic container crane operation system based on predictive fuzzy control. *Control Theory and Advanced Technol.* **2**, 419-432.

Yasunobu, S.; Miyamoto, S. (1985): Automatic train operation system by predictive fuzzy control. In: *Industrial Applications of Fuzzy Control* (M. SUGENO, ed.), North-Holland Publ. Comp., Amsterdam, 1-18.

Zadeh, L. A. (1965): Fuzzy sets. *Information and Control* **8**, 338-353. [cf. (1987)]

– (1965a): Fuzzy sets and systems. In: *Systems Theory* (J. FOX, ed.), Polytechnic Press, Brooklyn, 29-37.

– (1968): Probability measures of fuzzy events. *J. Math. Anal. Appl.* **23**, 421-427. [cf. (1987)]

– (1969): The concepts of system, aggregate and state in system theory. In: *System Theory* (L. A. ZADEH, E. POLAK, eds.), McGraw Hill, New York, 3-42.

– (1971): Similarity relations and fuzzy orderings. *Information Sci.* **3**, 159-176. [cf. (1987)]

– (1971a): Toward a theory of fuzzy systems. In: *Aspects of Network and System Theory* (R. E. KALMAN, N. DE CLARIS, eds.), Holt, Rinehart and Winston, New York, 469-490.

– (1973): Outline of a new approach to the analysis of complex systems and decision processes. IEEE *Trans. Systems, Man and Cybernet.* **SMC-3**, 28-44. [cf. (1987)]

– (1975): The concept of a linguistic variable and its application to approximate reasoning. I–III. *Information Sci.* **8**, 199-250, 301-357; **9**, 43-80. [cf. (1987)]

– (1976): A fuzzy-algorithmic approach to the definition of complex or imprecise concepts. *Internat. J. Man-Machine Studies* **8**, 249-291. [cf. (1987)]

– (1978): Fuzzy sets as a basis for a theory of possibility. *Fuzzy Sets and Systems* **1**, 3-28. [cf. (1987)]

- (1978a): PRUF – a meaning representation language for natural languages. *Internat. J. Man-Machine Studies* **10**, 395-460. [cf. (1987)]
- (1979): A theory of approximate reasoning. In: *Machine Intelligence 9* (J. E. HAYES, D. MICHIE, L. I. MIKULICH, eds.), Wiley, New York, 149-194. [cf. (1987)]
- (1981): Test-score semantics for natural languages and meaning representation via PRUF. In: *Empirical Semantics I* (B. RIEGER, ed.), Brockmeyer, Bochum, 281-349.
- (1982): Possibility theory as a basis for representation of meaning. In: *Sprache und Ontologie, Akten 6. Internat. Wittgenstein Symp. 1981, Kirchberg/Wechsel*, Hölder-Pichler-Tempsky, Wien, 253-262.
- (1983): The role of fuzzy logic in the management of uncertainty in expert systems. *Fuzzy Sets and Systems* **11**, 199-227. [cf. (1987)]
- (1984): A theory of commonsense knowledge. In: *Aspects of Vagueness* (H. J. SKALA, S. TERMINI, E. TRILLAS, eds.), Reidel, Dordrecht, 257-295. [cf. (1987)]
- (1985): Syllogistic reasoning in fuzzy logic and its application to usuality and reasoning with dispositions. IEEE *Trans. Systems, Man and Cybernet.* **SMC-15**, 754-763. [cf. (1987)]
- (1987): *Fuzzy Sets and Applications. Selected Papers.* (R. R. YAGER et al., eds.), Wiley, New York.

Zemankova-Leech, M.; Kandel, A. (1984): *Fuzzy Relational Data Bases – a Key to Expert Systems.* Verlag TÜV Rheinland, Köln.
- ; – (1985): Uncertainty propagation to expert systems. In: *Approximate Reasoning in Expert Systems* (M. M. GUPTA et al., eds.), North-Holland Publ. Comp., Amsterdam, 529-548.

Zhang, J.-W. (1980): A unified treatment of fuzzy set theory and Boolean-valued set theory – fuzzy set structures and normal fuzzy set structures. *J. Math. Anal. Appl.* **76**, 297-301.

Zimmermann, H.-J. (1976): Description and optimization of fuzzy systems. *Internat. J. General Systems* **2**, 209-215.
- (1978): Fuzzy programming and linear programming with several objective functions. *Fuzzy Sets and Systems* **1**, 45-55.
- (1979): Theory and applications of fuzzy sets. In: *Operational Research '78, Proc. 8th IFORS Internat. Conf. Toronto* (K. B. HALEY, ed.), North-Holland Publ. Comp., Amsterdam, 1017-1033.
- (1985): *Fuzzy Set Theory and Its Applications.* Kluwer-Nijhoff, Dordrecht. [2nd edition 1991]
- (1987): *Fuzzy Sets, Decision Making and Expert Systems.* Kluwer-Nijhoff, Dordrecht.

Index